9-8-95

Don + Arlene,

Hope you like it!

God bless!

Fr. Ed

NOTES ABOUT
THE UNITED STATES

NOTES ABOUT THE UNITED STATES

Edward R. Ward

**Publisher's Cataloging in Publication
(Prepared by Quality Books, Inc.)**

Ward, Edward R., 1946-
   Notes about the United States / Edward R. Ward.
   p.cm.
   Includes bibliographical references.
   ISBN 0-9645578-0-0

   1. United States–History.   2. United States–Social life and customs.   I. Title.
E178.1.W37 1995   973
                                    QBI95-20037

Acknowledgements

The following have helped significantly in the writing of this book:

William Muha of Sacramento, California
Nickie Barbosa of Joliet, Illinois
William Orth of St. Paul, Minnesota
Mark Derringer of Lancaster, New York
John Eaton of Buffalo, New York
Mark and Clare Lindauer of Buffalo, New York
Daniel Carroll of Chicago, Illinois
Anne Doolin of Ashland, Illinois
Cecil Pickert of Scipio, Kansas
Gavin Quinn of Chicago, Illinois
Polly Rausch and Georgia Reilly of Darien, Illinois
Frank Catalano, Sr. and family of Kenmore, New York
James and Sharon Chmidling of Leavenworth, Kansas
Thomas and Adele Devine of Shorewood, Illinois
John Comerford of Mundelein, Illinois
Richard B. Heaney of Teaneck, New Jersey
Margaret Ward of Joliet, Illinois
Kevin Shanley and Aloysius Sieracki of Darien, Illinois
Donald Davis of Kansas City, Missouri
Daniel Ullrich of Chicago, Illinois
John Russell of South Orange, New Jersey
Nancy Bauman of Topeka, Kansas
Peter McGarry of Chicago, Illinois
Martha Burbulla of Johnstown, Pennsylvania
The late Leonard Kinzler of Washington, DC
The late Cassian Corcoran of Schenectady, New York
The late DeSales Snyder of Chicago, Illinois
The late Edward J. and Hazel Ward of Chicago, Illinois
Luis Soto-Ruiz of Milwaukee, Wisconsin
Jack and Dale Micek of Downers Grove, Illinois
Mary and Richard Price of Darien, Illinois

Myles Colgan of Niagara Falls, Ontario
Eamon Carroll of Chicago, Illinois
Paul Robinson of Boston, Massachusetts
The Memorial Library at Marquette University,
　　Milwaukee, Wisconsin
The Founders Memorial Library at Northern Illinois
　　University, DeKalb, Ilinois
The Teaneck Public Library, Teaneck, New Jersey
The New York Public Library, New York City
The Cullom-Davis Library at Bradley University,
　　Peoria, Illinois

　I extend many thanks to the people and to the institutions named above.

　　　　　　　　Edward R. Ward
　　　　　　　　Bogota, New Jersey
　　　　　　　　May 25, 1995

CONTENTS

Acknowledgments ix
Introduction 1

The East   Syracuse and Friends................................5
New York   Senecas and Mohawks 10
New Jersey   Void Where Prohibited 24
Pennsylvania   Not Quite a Rectangle 31
Delaware   Pocket-sized 38
Maryland   Much to Do 42
Washington, D.C.   Supply is Limited 46
Massachusetts   The Second Glorious Mystery 51
Connecticut   Nutmeg and Spice 57
Rhode Island   A Fly on the Windshield.........................62
Vermont   Bellows Falls and Friends 65
New Hampshire   Rates May Vary 70
Maine   Here Comes the Sun...............................74
Illinois   The Lands of Lincoln 80
Michigan   Macho, Cold, and Teetering 90
Wisconsin   Escape To or From?................................97
Indiana   Wander..105
Ohio   Big in the Shoulders 114

The South   Old Times There 121
Virginia   Residence of Presidents........................126
West Virginia   Some Assembly Required 132
North Carolina   Luv Those Heels! 137
Tennessee   Easy Does It 142
Kentucky   The Flag is Up!.....................................149
Georgia   On Everyone's Mind 154
Alabama   White Bathroom, Colored Bathroom ..160
South Carolina   Historical Treasure 165
Mississippi   A Forest of Chimneys 169
Arkansas   A Quiet Paradise...................................175
Louisiana   The Devil May Care 180
Florida   Minimum Purchase Required..............185

The Breadbasket	Play Ball!	193
Minnesota	Modern, Renewing, and Improving	198
North Dakota	Remote and Quiet	205
South Dakota	Thirty Days Same as Cash	209
Iowa	Really a State of Mind	215
Nebraska	While Supplies Last	221
Kansas	Former Desert, Current Oasis	226
Missouri	Bushwackers and Baseball	231
Oklahoma	Two o'clock, No Sooner	237
Texas	Urban Giant	242
The West	Lots of Hydrocarbons	254
Colorado	Cowboys, Water, and Broncos	259
Wyoming	High Altitude, Low Multitudes	266
Montana	No Indoor Sports	270
Idaho	Betwixt and Between	275
Utah	A Large Agenda	279
Nevada	A House Divided	285
New Mexico	Enchantment and Encampment	291
Arizona	Copper, Cotton, and Crooks	296
California	A Shining Colossus	302
Oregon	Ecostate and Enjoying It	324
Washington	Both Sides Now	329
Alaska	A Life Apart	334
Hawaii	Last Stop	339
References		344

Introduction

I was born in 1946. That year may mark the beginning of my desire to take some notes about the world swirling around me and past me.

As a youngster in school I found that taking notes in American History class was not fun. I enjoyed batting averages more. I did not enjoy history in school at all.

Over the years, however, I became enamored with trying to understand life in the United States, and I began to take some notes. The Dust Bowl, the 1927 New York Yankees, and the presidency of Grover Cleveland seemed interesting to me after all.

This book, therefore, represents hours and hours of trying to understand the values and priorities (and the history!) of the American people. Since 1983 I have taken notes in and about such "faraway" places as Franklinville, New York and Las Cruces, New Mexico.

The year 1946 itself is a good start for some note-taking. People flocked then to see "The Best Years of Our Lives" with Frederic March. Wrestler Gorgeous George (Wagner) was a fixture on television (radio with pictures?). Ted Williams played in the World Series, but did not hit .300. Cigarettes were about $1.40 a carton, and $5,600 bought a nice home. Alabama beat Southern California in the Rose Bowl. Comedians Bob (Elliott) and Ray (Goulding) were combining their talents on radio in Boston. A loaf of bread was 10¢. The *Chicago Defender* was describing how two black baseball players were going to Canada in order to be accepted, thereby avoiding the dangers of living in the United States. One night at the Hindman Hotel in McLean, Texas along Route 66 cost $2.00 for a double room. Those were the days.

I grew to enjoy imagining how people lived their lives years ago. Events surrounding Babe Ruth, Teddy Roosevelt, and those old Burma-Shave ads seemed fascinating.

I found that life in the United States is definitely, absolutely, and positively a regional thing. Columbus Day as a paid holiday is not observed uniformly across the country. Bilingual education and military schools "go over" better in certain parts of the country than in others. I wanted to pursue an understanding of the regional nature of life in the United States.

In my travels I found places over the years to be bland (Rochester, New York), cute (Dime Box, Texas), matter-of-fact (Kansas City, Missouri), foreign (Ruidoso, New Mexico), and unpronounceable (Pyuallup, Washington).

In what category does this book belong? On what shelf? I

Introduction

am not skilled enough in this to know. History? Culture? American Studies? Travel? Oral History? Social History? Read the book for your own purposes, remembering that Edward Hallett Carr has said that sociology and history should stand closer together.

The book goes best, I hope, if the human spirit is engaged a little, not just the mind. See what I mean after "drinking in" the history along Acorn Street on Beacon Hill in Boston.

Naturally the book is a little uneven, due to the vast nature of it. Treating a variety of places and a number of people in a totally "even" way is, of course, impossible. Utopian communities and Coney Island do not receive much mention. Hagerstown, Maryland is neglected entirely. Philip Abrams was correct when he said that it is not easy to explain "the elegant patterning of connections seen from a distance."

The book, I said earlier, should be fun. Fun should be part of most recipes, or at least that is what Al McGuire used to say about maintaining one's sanity when coaching basketball. The wise McGuire took no chances, of course, winning 87 percent of his games at Marquette University from 1964 to 1977.

I must pay tribute to author Joel Garreau, too. His *Nine Nations of North America*, published in 1981, is an excellent book to read before reading this one. As corny as it sounds, my life was changed a little on Sunday, April 22, 1979 when I first read about Garreau's *Nine Nations*.

Enjoy the people mentioned in this book, not just the places. Imagine the joy in meeting Edward Livingston "Phonograph" Jones in Cody, Wyoming around 1902 or Baltazar Zaph in Cattaraugus County, New York in 1880. Write your own book about one of those fellows.

I have written about some things that should require lengthy study, like the case labeled Plessy v. Ferguson (1896). That case said, "If the civil and political rights of both races be equal, one cannot be inferior to the other civilly or politically. If one race be inferior to the other socially, the Constitution of the United States cannot put them on the same plane." Homer Adolph Plessy, an octoroon, should play a role in our notes about American life.

Baseball provides a glimpse or two about life in the United States, of course. The 1890 Brooklyn Bridegrooms, the 1944 St. Louis Browns, and the number of homers hit by Babe Ruth at night (not one) make me want to read more and more from the pens of Jerome Holtzman and Thomas Boswell. It has been said that baseball is "a grain of sand that reveals the universe." How could a person not be enamored with the history of Sportsman's Park (1909-1966) in St. Louis?

I have tried to mix the linear (i.e. the history, which happens over time) with the lateral (i.e. the geography, which happens over space). We remember that Wounded Knee took place in 1890 in the West, but we forget that at the same time in the South James B. Duke was selling cigarettes in record numbers. Try to remember the linear/lateral distinction.

In some chapters I have mentioned a few heroes and a few villains, too.

This book attempts to mention a few things that are not well known, with the hope that some "loose ends" might be tied together. Many realize that slavery was thought by some to be very Christian years ago, but few realize that illiteracy was thought by some to be very un-Christian. The difference may spur some readers to do some intelligent research on the subject.

In the words of Professor Howard Zinn I have tried to select, simplify, and emphasize.

In the words of author Marc Simmons I have attempted to interpret a bit, too.

Grab an atlas and an underliner.

Let us get moving.

The East

Syracuse and Friends

This chapter will provide one "slant" concerning the East.

That is, some will go to their graves believing that Ashtabula, Ohio is in the Midwest, while others will say with authority that Cedar Rapids and Altoona are similar.

Both positions are mistaken.

First, you are in the East when you notice that manufacturing is more important in the lives of people than farming, more important than computer chips, and more important than digging up chromium. Watching the rodeo and fishing for salmon do not come close, either.

Second, the East contains blacks, Mexicans, Puerto Ricans,

Italians, Irish, Jews, Slovaks and others all jumbled together. (Tally all those people and you have bigger numbers by far than you do in the entire Mountain Time Zone.)

Third, decaying buildings, railroad tracks, old parabolic bridges, high-pressure sodium lights, and nodular iron dot Eastern landscapes.

Fourth, the East is filled with shot-and-a-beer, macho types who scratch their heads in January wondering why their NFL team must play the Super Bowl in a climate 50 degrees warmer than their own.

The East, then, is perhaps best understood when the term is translated "Foundry," the area where things like ethnic peoples, steel, large populations, cold winters, and aging factories come together.

The magic words there are "understood" and "translated." A person from Northern Indiana, reared on plastics and sheet metal, is easily understood by someone from Newark.

A person from Eau Claire, Wisconsin, however, will not be understood if she mentions polled herefords or moisture content to people from Allentown.

Harrisburg, Pittsburgh, Newark, Albany, and Ashtabula are in the East.

Boston? It is in New England, never to be confused with Wheeling, Toledo, and the American Foundry.

Omaha? It is in the Midwest.

St. Louis? The city has both a Midwest(ern) and a Southern feel to it. The wide streets (Market, Pine) seem to be trademarks of the Midwest, although local church bulletins advertise quilt socials with "a whole hog sausage dinner," which some would equate with the South.

Ft. Wayne? It appears to some to be in the Midwest, but it is not. Ft. Wayne walks, talks, works, and smells like cities in the East. People at Harrison and Main streets believe that cows and soybeans are not more important than gas pumps, light bulbs, and refrigerators.

Toledo? People in Toledo at North Summit and Jefferson cut deals concerning glass and plastics, not udder butter, at the drop of a hat, so that separates Toledoans from Iowans and Nebraskans. Toledo people drink Labatt's and Molson's, a sign that Canada (and the East) are close at hand. The sign downtown that reads "Ft. Industry, 1805" tells a tale, too.

Chicago? The city seems to have a Midwest address, but the presence of steel plants, sheet and tube factories, railroads, and ethnics enables Chicagoans to relate easily to folks from Erie, Syracuse, and Saginaw. A similar kinship does not exist with people from Des Moines, Kansas City or Sioux Falls, a part of the American Breadbasket.

Many Easterners have come to and settled in Chicago, however. Architect Daniel Burnham was born in Jefferson County, New York. George Cardinal Mundelein was born in New York City. Anton Cermak was born in Kladno, Czechoslovakia. Marshall Field was born in Conway, Massachusetts. (Some who became Chicagoans came from the South, of course. There was Archibald Clybourn, the city's first commercial butcher, who came from Virginia, and there was Jack Leroy Cooper, the father of black-appeal radio. He came from Memphis.)

Even superficial research about Chicago's railroads (see the history of the Michigan Central) and Chicago's use of Lake Michigan (see *Hunt's Merchants' Magazine*) reveals how Easterners have moved to Chicago over the decades. One historian speaks of "blood relationship, culture, sentiment, and interest" involved in this scene. (Is it any wonder that many Chicagoans today have little or no understanding about life down the road in Peoria, Champaign, Bloomington, Springfield, Galesburg, or Moline?)

Railroad people know that the Gandy Tool Company of Chicago produced picks and hammers for railroads in the East. There were gandy dancers from Hartford to Chicago.

Dayton and Cincinnati? They seem to be in the same situation as Chicago, since they are thought to be in the Midwest, but relate more easily to loading docks and thermostats, not so much to silos, dent corn, and bovine affairs.

Factory people understand perfectly that many businesses in the East have been losing workers to other parts of the country for some time now. There's another characteristic of the East.

The East is where one sees old buildings, too, and that is not news, either. Chicago's new sports buildings hide the fact that the four buildings used there until recently for hockey, baseball, basketball, and football did not change from 1929 until 1991.

Notice the old places that once hummed in Cleveland as you head these days for the theater district there.

Look for old Crosley Field in Cincinnati.

Visit (real soon!) the Mt. Vernon Hotel in Easton, Pennsylvania.

Read the history of Newark.

Ask for the Hotel Roanoke in Buffalo.

A landmark for decades in the East was the ethnic parish. Such things have been seen from Hartford (St. Ann's, French) to Lemont, Illinois (St. Matthew, German). Several have been closed recently for lack of a purpose.

The East and steel are synonymous for some people. Steel seems to bring with it the feeling that life never changes. Those who have been "through the mill" seem to see life that way.

People from Buffalo find great purpose in steel, and it hurts some to admit that recycling aluminum is so popular today.

The three "r words" in the East are rehabilitation, reuse, and renovation.

In the world of sports one can see in the East a love of football still, although the rest of the country seems to be humming a different tune. The coaches at Moeller High in Cincinnati and at Cathedral Prep in Erie, Pennsylvania will talk about glorious football traditions, but in St. Louis a talk about soccer gets a good hearing. In St. Paul just try to get into the Civic Center for the hockey tournament played by high schoolers.

But all is not lost in the East.

The East does have a precious commodity in abundance that the likes of Telluride, Colorado and Los Angeles do not. It is called water. Those who leave Flint and Toledo are well advised to know about water problems in Salt Lake City, Spokane, and Amarillo.

The multitudes who live east of the Wabash and north of the Ohio can brag about big numbers. Steubenville (22,000 folks) has more people than Trinidad, Colorado does. Syracuse (163,000 souls) has almost twice the population of Provo, Utah.

The heavy in the East is, of course, New York City, which likes to determine who is important, what makes the news, and so forth.

Take good notes about the East because the millions and millions who live there are an active bunch.

Dove Creek, Colorado and Phenix City, Alabama cannot say the same thing.

New York

Senecas and Mohawks

New York, unlike all Gaul, is divided into six parts: Long Island, metropolitan New York, Eastern New York, Northern New York, Central New York, and Western New York.

Long Island is divided into simply Nassau and Suffolk. That is pretty easy to keep in mind.

Metropolitan New York is the Bronx, Manhattan, Queens, Brooklyn, and Staten Island, too.

Eastern New York contains the following counties: Westchester, Rockland, Putnam, Orange, Dutchess, Ulster, Sullivan, Delaware, Greene, Columbia, Albany, Rensselaer, Saratoga, Schentectady, and Washington. If you can think of a mnemonic device with those counties, you get preferred seating at the Saratoga Performing Arts Center.

Northern New York contains these counties: Fulton, Hamilton, Warren, Essex, Lewis, Oswego, Jefferson, St. Lawrence, Franklin, and Clinton. Those who like snow should head for Watertown, a part of Jefferson County.

Central New York includes counties by the name of Schoharie, Montgomery, Otsego, Herkimer, Oneida, Madison, Chenango, Broome, Tioga, Chemung, Stueben, Livingston, Yates, Ontario, Seneca, Schuyler, Tompkins, Cortland, Onondaga, and Wayne. The most beautiful part of Central New York is downtown Norwich. The most bland may be the corner of Court and Hawley in Binghamton.

Lastly, but not leastly, there is Western New York, which includes counties with names like Allegany, Wyoming, Monroe, Genesee, Orleans, Niagara, Erie, Chautauqua, and Cattaraugus.

Did we forget New York County? No matter. Let us go on. To Long Island.

There is much to talk about when considering the two counties on the Island, Nassau and Suffolk, but we will restrict ourselves to a brief mention of some things in Suffolk.

That is, the residents in Southampton get worked up about whether their phones start with a 283 or 324. The numbers indicate wealth. So do the numbers 287 and 329. The need to recycle and a taste for wines, well chronicled in the area's good newspapers, also fit the Suffolk mind pretty well. Suffolk people scowl at visitors in bathing suits. Suffolk County is not supposed to look like Coney Island. Those in Suffolk and Nassau like it there. Only 62 percent of those on the Island leave it for work. One must approach New York City (population 7.3 million) with caution and with a sense of humor. Think of Milton Berle ("I believe in Jewish foreplay: three hours of begging") or Steven Wright ("I saw a sign along the highway that said 'breakfast served any time,' so I ordered French toast at the time of the Renaissance."). Such humor is necessary for reasons to be explained in a moment.

New York City and environs have everything from "a" to "z": the "A" train, Broadway, Colombians, Dominicans, entertainment, Fordham University, Greeks, Hungarians, Italians, Jews, Knickerbockers basketball, Lincoln Center, Madison Square Garden, Nuyoricans, operas, panhandlers, Queens, Rangers hockey, subway vigilantes, Times Square, the United Nations, vagabond shoes, the Westchester Kennel Club, Xerox (in Stamford, Connecticut!), the Yankees, and the zoo (aka the International Wildlife Conservation Park) in the Bronx.

Whether dining in a fancy restaurant or riding the subway, one quickly gets the impression that New York City is something else.

New York's tremendous population (18 million people in metro area?) makes for fantastic people-watching and interesting social interaction. Every night at the Rainbow Room (ask for Rockefeller Plaza) one can see friends and lovers dreaming about having a nicer life, while a few feet away one can see the homeless, too. The contrast can be a shock along the sidewalks of New York.

The sidewalks are often filthy, too. Styrofoam cups, yesterday's *Times*, and today's discarded cigarette pack swirl freely. The dirt of Gotham is always either a shock to the system or part and parcel of living in America's most populated city. (Colonel George E. Waring, Jr. was New York's best-ever Commissioner of Street Cleaning, by the way. He reigned from 1895 to 1897. He was a hero.)

Garbage does not prevent New Yorkers from being proud of their place. New Yorkers think that what happens in New York (with a flair!) cannot be found in Chicago, the country's "Third City," nor in Los Angeles, the smog-infested bruiser quite a distance west of the Hudson.

New York is loud, too. Neighborhood noise from 80 to 85 decibels is not uncommon. A sense of humor can distract a person from all the commotion.

New York City provides ample material for the music studio. Billy Joel has said that the Drifters were correct in 1962 when they sang of seeing life in New York from "up on the roof." Indeed, from certain roofs in New York the world can appear to be one's oyster. In May the average high/low is 68/53.

The pride of New Yorkers makes it easy to say who the next superstar is going to be in any number of areas. People in New York are always being named "the next Barbra Streisand," "the next Luciano Pavarotti," and so forth, although frequently an opposite phenomenon takes place. Was not Roger Repoz supposed to be "the next Mickey Mantle"? Or was that Bobby Murcer?

Mentioning Mantle brings up another point, which is that some New Yorkers believe that certain times in American history will never again be duplicated. Ever. By anyone. People who were teenagers in the 1960's will recall listening to the likes of Murray the K, Cousin Brucie Morrow, and Jazzbo Collins on the radio. Remember WABC and WINS back then? Mantle was in center field for the Yanks. The Beatles visited Shea Stadium. Those were the days.

Yankee Stadium is in the Bronx, of course, and here are some notes to ponder on the subway to the game. First, Yankee Stadium is the house that (Babe) Ruth built, but it is also the house that beer mogul Jacob Ruppert built. Second, the number (3) worn by Babe Ruth has been retired. Only a few players wore it before Ruth, and they are Cliff Mapes, Allie Clark, Bud Metheny, and "Twinkletoes" Selkirk.

Basketball is played with vigor in New York City, too. Writer Jeff Greenfield has spoken of the difference between "black basketball" (the use of skill to adapt to the limits of space) and "white" (the pulverization of that space by sheer intensity). Two different styles.

A more difficult situation to ponder is the slow but steady decline of New York in the minds and hearts of millions of Americans, and that is not news, either.

A bitter pill to swallow for some is that certain American cities other than New York have balanced their money, their power, and their politics so that regional problems can be solved regionally. The days of expecting "an expert from New York" to solve UAW problems in Detroit or coal production problems in Lander, Wyoming are long over.

Declining Bedford-Stuyvesant in Brooklyn needs a few new angles, too, since dozens of young blacks are buried from the S. McMillan Funeral Home every year. Some "have beef" with others violently. Those who do not recognize the name of Yusuf Hawkins might skip a tour of Fulton Street.

Living in New York can be dangerous. In 1993 a total of 32 cabbies were killed between January 1 and October 31 only.

Wall Street is known to practically everyone. It is mind-boggling to walk through the area wondering who is cutting a deal with whom, or how the little guy can at all compete with the corporate giants. For the record there have been two Great Depressions, but more than half a dozen Panics. Some people head to Trinity Church to ponder their financial losses.

Economics and metaphysics dance a neat dance with each other in New York. Somehow what costs a lot has to be good, the logic goes. Be aware, too, that "Prices may vary in Manhattan."

On Christmas Day, 1994 the *Times* explained that the gap between rich and poor was widening in the city and the region. Six subway stops (and three miles) separate the rich in Carnegie Hill from the poor in Bradhurst.

Prices were high in 1900 along Allen Street on the Lower East Side. Girls there worked in the first "red light district." Whites came by in their cars and honked their horns. Hence the term "honkeys."

Everyone has heard of Harlem (pop. 475,000), and most whites associate the place with blacks. However, there is more to Harlem than the Apollo Theater and, believe it or not, some white people were born in Harlem. The late Walter Winchell was one.

Take the "A" train to Harlem, and look for a sale on kente cloth and dashikis. Musicians, artists, and writers can be seen in abundance. Strivers Row and Sugar Hill should be noted.

Life in Haitian Harlem, as a matter of fact, could be someone's next book. Compare and contrast Little Haiti in Miami with Haitian Harlem.

Some good research can always be done about Ellis Island (born 1892). Into the Great Hall flocked 560,971 people in 1921. American life was never the same after that time.

Virtually no one remembers the forerunner to Ellis Island, Castle Garden (1855-1892).

The old Grand Central Depot could be a good study, too.

Let's return to Brooklyn beyond Bedford-Stuyvesant for a moment. Try now to locate areas once known as Pigtown, Goatville, Tin Can Alley, and Crow Hill. The hayseed image of Brooklyn, compared to chic Manhattan, will be better understood thereby. Second, make a bet that no one can name the "big name" involved in the 1950's with studying the possibility of a new ballpark for the Dodgers (answer: Buckminster Fuller).

Willard Mullin's image of a bum is still vivid and significant to many Brooklynites. So is the last game played by the (trolley) Dodgers at Ebbets Field on September 24, 1957.

A Brooklynite of considerable merit on the diamond was Sanford Braun, who pitched for the Dodgers both in Brooklyn and on the West Coast. We now know this man as Sandy Koufax.

Going past the old location of Ebbets Field today will not produce much. Some will recall the work of songwriter Joe Raposo who penned "There Used to Be a Ballpark." He had Ebbets in mind.

Few remember that the Dodgers were not the only "death" in Brooklyn in the 1950's. Those who follow journalism know that the *Brooklyn Eagle* newspaper ceased operations in 1955 after 114 years in the community.

A big deal involves the Downtown Athletic Club in New York every year. The University of Chicago's Jay Berwanger won the first Downtown Athletic Club Trophy in 1935. Now the prize is called the Heisman Trophy.

To little ones at Coney Island years ago the Heisman Trophy looked pretty small next to a kewpie doll won along Surf Avenue.

Let us leave the city and head north.

Eastern New York

One native son of Columbia County is none other than Martin Van Buren, whose greatest contribution (the revival of the two party system) is often overlooked for a smaller one, and that is he used the initials "O.K." to mean okay. Van Buren was known to have two nicknames: "the little magician" and "Old Kinderhook." Kinderhook does appear on the map. The year 1790 marks the beginning of "O.K.," although some Choctaws dispute the origin, saying that "oke" means "it is so." These details are about as tedious as life itself gets in Columbia County.

The origins and the history of the Hudson River are significant. The Hudson is a wild setting for the backpacker, a livelihood for a fisherman, a barrier for commuters, and a respite for the city dweller. The river is a cause to an environmentalist, too.

Details are important in Eastern New York, especially if you are Jewish and can remember vacations in Ulster County ("where the Catskills meet the Hudson"). This "Borscht Belt" was a summer refuge for thousands of New Yorkers who enjoyed Milton Berle, Danny Kaye, and other tummlers. Roslyn Siegel once described the place as "an area of 250 square miles of Yiddish culture and Yankee ambition north of New York City." Memorizing that quote may be more difficult than naming the seven kinds of herring served in the area.

The Catskills were once labeled "the Sour Cream Sierras" as well as "the Lower East Side with its hair down."

Journey over to Rockland County and ask for Letchworth Village if you need to "come down" from the comedy found in Ulster County. At Letchworth anyone can give directions to the graveyard for the mentally retarded. There one will see numbers, not names, marking the burial sites of many who rest nameless for fear of "embarrassing" their families. Saying a prayer for Number 440 may be difficult.

It may be difficult, too, to remember that Isabella Van Wagner (aka Sojouner Truth) was born in Ulster County. It is easier in these parts to think about the 1969 Woodstock Festival (pop. 400,000 then). Peace and love were in abundance at the intersection of Groovy Way and Gentle Path. No one over 30 was trusted.

Some of those who did drugs at Woodstock I can be found having breakfast these days at the track in Saratoga. Wagering began in 1863. The late Red Smith said it best when he advised his readers, "From New York City, drive north 175 miles, get off at exit 14, head west on Union Avenue and go back 100 years."

To stand at Eagle and State Streets in Albany (pop. 100,000) is to ponder a noteworthy history. The city is "the other city on the Hudson." Read about long-reigning politicians, inadequate snow removal, and urban decay (e.g. Arbor Hill).

Albany people may not relate to the western end of the state very much. Albany to Montreal by car is faster than Albany to Buffalo. Albany to Boston is easy, too.

Realize that a vacation in New England starts only a short drive east of Albany, where the Foundry gives way to New England. Two different cultures.

Students who study Albany in 1650 will know that the Dutch preferred to "navigate the land," as opposed to the English who wanted to "occupy the land." One group's trade location was another's crop yield.

Schenectady (67,970 people and murder to spell) is similar to other cities in the Foundry. Generous Electric is a factor in the area. Going from Schenectady to Poughkeepsie is done on the Electric City Express. Little else needs to be said about Schenectady.

Troy, a part of Rensselaer County, gave the world Uncle Sam Wilson. He provided meat to people during the War of 1812. On the packages of meat one could read U.S. which means "Uncle Sam". Now you know the rest of the story.

NORTHERN NEW YORK

Northern New York's place in history may center around Lake Placid where the USA scored four goals to the Soviet Union's three on February 22, 1980 in a friendly game of hockey. Some observers, both in the Adirondacks and out, feel that the game was the ultimate.

The ultimate for Civil War students may be found at the farm of John Brown. Begin your study of Brown with the year 1849 and end with 1859, the year he died.

In Watertown, a part of Jefferson County, be sure it is not snowing as you read this. If it is, you may be in for a long stay. Watertown at times makes Syracuse look mild. Perhaps tough winters make it easy to invent things like the railroad sleeping car, the fountain pen, the safety pin, the bed spring, chloroform, and the cast iron plow. All of those things got their start in Watertown.

Artist Winslow Homer came to the Adirondacks in 1870. Choose either oils or watercolors yourself.

The most significant thing that can be said about this section of New York is that the area is very nice and should be left alone. Do not tell anyone how nice Northern New York is.

CENTRAL NEW YORK

Utica (population 91,000 in 1970, but only 68,000 in 1990) is not to be confused with Attica. The former is a city in the Mohawk Valley (east of Syracuse, to keep it simple), and the latter is in Western New York, a short distance east of Buffalo.

A Utica success story, and the city today needs a few, is the F. X. Matt Brewing Company. Started in 1888 as the West End Brewing Company, the Matt folks gave the world Utica Club beer. Matt claims that it was the first beermaker to attain a permit in order to renew sales when Prohibition was repealed – 90 minutes after FDR signed the repeal measure into law.

Not far from Utica is Cooperstown and the baseball Hall of Fame, where many opinions are offered about the greats of baseball. Tell friends that Joe DiMaggio struck out only 369 times in his entire career. Second, mention softly that Shoeless Joe Jackson never won a batting title, although his career batting average was .356.

The old Negro Leagues had a few people who are seldom mentioned with the great white players. Clifford (Connie) Johnson, Buck O'Neil, and Satchel Paige are three examples.

A note, too, should be made about Dolgeville, a place which fan(atic)s will equate with Adirondack bats that say "Northern White Ash." That is music to the ears of some people.

Only a few people know about the Women's Hall of Fame in Seneca Falls, a part of Seneca County. Ask about Annie Oakley or Wilma Mankiller.

Even fewer people remember signs in Herkimer County that said "Hebrew Patronage Not Solicited" between 1900 and 1920.

In Madison County it is worth one's while to stop in Canastota. The place does not alter the world's events these days, but years ago an important name once picked onions there – Carmen Basilio. His name alone symbolized aggressiveness in the boxing ring and long hours of rigorous training. His bouts with Sugar Ray Robinson were legendary.

In these parts behind the scenes in the boxing world of the 1950's there were some interesting characters: Frankie Carbo, Gabriel Genovese, and "Blinky" Palermo. That's right. The Mob. (One is advised to know that the Mafia was not always and forever thought of as it is today. The word itself meant "a place of refuge" or "protection against the arrogance of the powerful, remedy to any damage, and sturdiness of body." Mafia, then, is a state of mind, a way of life, not a secret criminal organization. Contrast this idea with the Chinese word "tong." The similarities are striking.)

How about Syracuse? The city (pop. 163,800) plods along, steering people to its Carrier Dome for sporting events and to nearby lakes for water sports.

Note the narrow streets (Fayette, Washington, Water) in Syracuse. They are reminders that certain cities were constructed years ago for walking, not for cars.

The cool air that visits Syracuse can remind a person of Willis Haviland Carrier, the man who cooled America. His "Apparatus for Treating Air" was patented, appropriately, in January 1906.

People in air-conditioned cars now go south along Interstate 81 to get an education at Cornell in Ithaca. A Cornell President, Andrew D. White, once made a famous remark about football. He did not want his boys to play against the University of Michigan in Cleveland. He remarked, "I will not permit 30 men to travel 400 miles merely to agitate a bag of wind." Academic life beats football at Cornell.

Western New York

Rochester (230,000 people) was once called "the first boom town" when the New York State Barge Canal arrived in 1823. As this country was moving westward, Rochester was thought to be so remote from the East Coast that a Buffalo priest quipped, "there is no sabbath west of the Genessee River."

As that river winds through the city today, inhabitants realize that the population is dropping, despite the presence of powerful Eastman Kodak, Xerox, and Bausch & Lomb.

Bragging that Rochester is recession-proof may not outweigh 197 cloudy days a year.

Please do not compare Rochester with Syracuse or Buffalo.

Syracuse gets about 110 inches of snow a year. Buffalo gets 92, while Rochester gets 89.6. The Rochester figure is a little less than Bangor, Maine, which is enough to frighten off a few people.

History students will enjoy Rochester. At one time buggy whips were said to be a better investment than cameras. George Eastman was given lodging in the city by some people who thought the whips would outlast cameras. Whips in Rochester now play an entirely different role.

A cute tidbit about Rochester is that the city has an area called the South Wedge, which is never to be confused with Chicago's South Side, Pittsburgh's South Hills, Philadelphia's South Street, or Louisville's South End. Those from San Francisco could enter the West Portal and the Western Addition in a contest some day featuring such things.

Kodak people in Rochester will tell you that image is everything, although that image was tarnished a bit in August 1992 when people learned that 38 percent of the city's children were living in poverty.

Smart kids in Rochester test their computer literacy at the Cornell Theory Center nearby in Ithaca. Transparent access is a major issue there.

Quiet Batavia may be the quintessential Western New York town. There is the *Daily News* building (born 1890), minor league baseball (Dwyer Field), and Nest 493 of the Polish Falcons. Italian names are about as plentiful as Polish ones.

Buffalo (pop. 328,000) is the land of chicken wings, lawn fetes, beef on weck, and ethnic politics. Topics include the days O.J. Simpson ran crazy and the day Bethlehem Steel ran out.

Buffalo has good restaurants and hospitals, not to mention access to two Great Lakes and lovely Septembers.

The bad news, however, is the image problem created by a sagging economy, snowy Januarys, and a departing populace. One look at the channel 7 news at night will show you that a fire has destroyed another building in the "Queen City."

Buffalo, believe it or not, was the ninth largest city in population back in 1900. Busy hands then worked with wheat carted on the Lake that became flour hauled along the Canal.

Spoken of in reverential tones in this area is baseball great Warren Spahn. He won 23 games in the 1963 season. That's pretty good, especially because he was born in 1921.

On the way to Memorial Auditorium a person will notice the hand of architect Daniel H. Burnham at Ellicott Square. The note is made for the benefit of Chicagoans who believe that their city was the only stage on which Burnham performed.

Those who believe that global warming is a problem did not live in Buffalo in July 1992. Only twice did the thermometer get above 80 Fahrenheit the entire month.

Heroes and villains in Buffalo?

Decide for yourself which label belongs to Millard Fillmore. He had more ups and downs than most people. One of his defeats he attributed to voters of foreign birth. There was no easy walk through the park for Millard Fillmore.

Lastly, Buffalo can be confusing. Some people think the American bison is the basis for the city's name. Not true. The name comes from the French ("beau flueve"), indicating the "pretty waters" which now touch the Erie Basin Marina.

Niagara Falls, a short distance from Buffalo, is "a favorite resort of lately married pairs," and an expensive one, too. Let us hope that those who honeymoon in the Falls grow closer to one another than the American and Canadian dollars. Tightwalker Jean Francois Gravelet ("Blondin"), a sensation in 1859, would lose his balance thinking of how high Canadian prices can get these days.

Some people lose their balance and their lives when they jump in the water at Niagara Falls. Notice the telephones at Prospect Point on the American side for those who wish to talk.

To the south of Buffalo there are two rural gems, counties

by the name of Cattaraugus and Chautauqua. On the menu are grapes, scenic hills and valleys, good winter skiing, and quiet nights at the Castle Lodge in Olean, a part of Cattaraugus County.

Welcome to New York, one and all.

New Jersey

Void Where Prohibited

Where do we begin in this state, known for large populations, the Pine Barrens, a certain toughness, Victorian homes in Cape May, and an attractive shore?

We begin by sharing a joke about New Jersey. Some jokes have already appeared over the years in the state's monthly magazine of history.

Some humor is not out of order.

David Letterman once said not long ago, "they are trying to write a song for the state of New Jersey, but no one can find a word which rhymes with dioxin."

Now all those who wanted a chuckle about New Jersey have had one.

Let us go on.

On first glance one sees in New Jersey many people per square mile, a large number of people who do not speak English as a first language, and many elderly.

On second glance one notices brown skies, cogeneration plants, a Gold Coast, many petrochemical tanks, 127 miles of coastline, and declining fertility.

That densely packed mix is spread over the Metro area, the Shore, the Raritan Valley, South Jersey, and the Delaware Valley.

South Jersey and North are divided by either the Turnpike's Exit 8 (Hightstown-Freehold) or by Interstate I95, depending on one's point of view.

West is the "left" side of either the Keith Line (born 1687) or the Lawrence Line (born 1743). The lines start in Little Egg Harbor and proceed to the northwest, the former to Hunterdon County, the latter to the middle of Sussex County.

Opening remarks must mention, too, that densely packed New Jersey has not one micropolitan area.

Much of the state is old, of course. The narrow intersection of Main and Bergen Streets in Hackensack suggests an era gone by. So does the 200 block of West State Street in Trenton. So do certain parts of Hughes Street in Cape May.

Those with a sense of history take pride in telling everyone about the Princeton-Rutgers in November 1869. Those without a sense of history will think that only South Bend and Tallahassee have ever played the game.

These days New Jersey (pop. 7.7 million) is filled with so many things to do and so many places to go that the state is one of many prohibitions. "No Turn on Red," "Eating in Cars Prohibited," and "Don't Honk – Except as Warning" are noticed from Mahwah to Egg Harbor.

Certain things must be prohibited in New Jersey lest one person get a leg up on someone else. In the Garden State being able to compete is essential. Arrive with skills in hand.

The not so busy side of New Jersey enjoys itself in Springfield at Baltusrol Golf Club, named after Baltus Roll. He was murdered in 1831 by robbers, but his name lives on for those who love the United States Golf Association. Some golfers at Baltusrol talk to the ball as it moves along. The thing never seems to respond.

Let us visit some cities now.

Be ready to zig and zag around signs that say "Road Construction Ahead."

Newark, the city into which some fly and from which many flee, is the state's largest in population (275,000 souls). Its past is storied. Its present is "under construction." Its future is "under discussion."

The city of Newark glories in its Foundry past, when things like chemicals, leather, and Ballantine beer were in the headlines. Harnesses were important at the 1872 Industrial Exposition.

The jewel of Newark today may be McGovern's Tavern (born 1936). Regulars converse about the evils of gentrification. Visitors express surprise that there is no television. McGovern's is to Newark as McCuddy's was to Chicago (at

245 W. 35th Street). Those labeled "Foundry Irish" will understand once a Guinness or two are consumed.

Some Newark folks still remember the (black) Newark Eagles playing at Ruppert Stadium in the 1940's.

From Newark years ago came a Jewish baseball player named Moe Berg, a graduate of Princeton. He had a good year with the 1929 Chicago White Sox. Baseball and scholarship were two of his loves, but espionage in the 1940's was another. The great line about him is, "he could speak a dozen languages, but could not get a base hit in any one of them." Maybe a more significant line about Berg was written by columnist Harold Kaese from the *Boston Globe* after Berg's wake in 1972. Kaese wrote, "Goodbye, Moe Berg, in any language."

Many in Newark today say good-bye to women between the ages of 25 and 44 due to AIDS. The disease was outrunning heart disease and cancer not long ago.

Students at Shabazz High in Newark are taught about those dangers. Some wish to flee from them, but cannot afford to.

Some people wish to flee from troubled Camden. An awful 61 percent of Camden's children were living in poverty in the early 1990's. Once known for "soil fitted for gardening," Camden now counts the buildings that have been burned recently.

A Camden landmark, Campbell Soup, announced in 1990 that the company's oldest manufacturing plant would be closing. In 1869 icebox maker Abram Anderson and fruit merchant Joseph Campbell began canning vegetables, jellies, and mincemeat, and the rest is American history.

Ask about Walt Whitman in Camden in 1873 to get a nicer picture of the city's history.

New Jersey cities like Camden and Newark exist in sharp contrast to places like Allendale, Saddle River, Ridgewood, and Tenafly. The contrast can be shocking, he said economically.

Smaller than Camden are the cities and boroughs of densely populated Bergen County, a place that contains 825,380 people.

Take Englewood, for example. Englewood (pop. 24,800) now houses a mix of Irish, Italians, blacks, Colombians, and Salvadorans, among others. The city gave the world the great Leroy ("Slam") Stewart in September 1914. Jazz enthusiasts are familiar with Stewart's "Flat Foot Floogie with the Floy Floy." If that item seems trivial, be certain that the history of St. Cecilia's High School in Englewood is not. The school shut down its football program a few years before the school closed. Many predicted that the closing would follow the loss of football. The late Vince Lombardi once coached there. At one point (1942? 1943?) he taught four subjects and coached three sports for $22 a week.

At the "opposite end" of the state, in more ways than one, is Trenton, about which only a few notes are necessary. First, the city wanted to be the seat of the federal government in 1790, but the deal fell through. Second, the great Willie Mays toiled in Trenton in 1950, but that didn't last long, either. Third, Academy Street had a history of being a really tough place not long ago. The history and the toughness are both important in Trenton today.

Tough and durable Union City, a part of Hudson County, was once as Italian as New York's Little Italy or Boston's North End, but has many Cubans now. Some along Bergenline Avenue watch Havana more closely than Trenton. There is the complaint that Cubans with darker skin and newly-acquired passports are a pain to live with.

Atlantic City is another matter. The city modeled for Monopoly. It used to be "three months of hurry and nine months of worry." Now life involves "three months of tears and nine months in arrears." Busloads come and go, seldom staying the night. The casino businesses have been labeled "an urban tire patch," fun at the Steel Pier notwithstanding.

Optimists were as popular as saltwater taffy before the advent of gaming in Atlantic City.

After gaming some psychics ply their trade with abandon.

Those who gamble do their thing with the belief that a "hot hand" will bail them out. (Is there really any such thing as a "hot hand"?)

Ask a psychic if Atlantic City is making progress. Then get back on the bus. (Board games have come a long way, of course. About a century ago players were made aware of their virtue or lack of it when they played a board game. Now the aim is more materialistic. Interestingly, Parker Brothers initially passed on Monopoly decades ago, but then changed their minds. The game was called The Landlord Game around 1903. Long live capitalism.)

Baseball is a natural in talking of New Jersey since Hoboken says it is the real birthplace of baseball, never to be confused with a cow pasture in Cooperstown, New York. Baseball historians use June 19, 1846 as a starting point.

For many years both beer and baseball were big deals in densely packed Hoboken (pop. 33,400 and decreasing). The city was at one time labeled "the stronghold of lager beer."

Those who follow American life will point out that Hoboken really hit the skids in 1968. In that year the Tootsie Roll company moved to Chicago to be closer to where corn syrup could be acquired. Tootsie Roll executives will not confirm or deny that it takes 1,634 licks to finish the tasty job.

A success story takes place in Passaic (pop. 58,000), too. There years ago three black girls escaped adverse surroundings and became very successful. The reference is to the Shirelles, the group which gave the world "Soldier Boy" and "Will You Still Love Me Tomorrow." The Shirelles have seen Los Angeles, Paris, London, and New York. Some Passaic people have not yet visited the last city mentioned in that list.

Jersey City, synonymous with railyards, is the home address of the Statue of Liberty. The Lady's address is 1 Communipaw Avenue, Jersey City, 07305.

Baseball again must be mentioned because of Roosevelt

Stadium in Jersey City. That is where Jackie Robinson came calling years ago as a second baseman with the Montreal Royals.

The legendary Frank "I am the Law" Hague, a native of an area called the Horseshoe, ruled Jersey City from 1917 to 1947. Some knew him as the "Hudson County Hitler," but others knew him as a man who put some rabbis on the payroll as "special inspectors."

Foundry workers in Jersey City have their Colgate clock (born 1924), just as Green Bay, Wisconsin factory people had their Hurlbut clock. Clocks, factories, and a love of Vince Lombardi are found in both places.

New Jersey baseball fans report that it is easier to steal someone's car than it is second base. Newark, Irvington, Camden, East Orange, Elizabeth, Trenton, Jersey City, and Passaic were all in the top thirty for car thefts per 100,000 people in 1990.

Stealing a car in Paterson (pop. 140,800) near the old Silk Machinery Exchange on Spruce Street is not difficult. Grandchildren of warpers, reelers, and winders in the silk industry are left behind to worry about such things today.

New Jersey has given the world an impressive list of people through the years. Grover Cleveland, Frank Sinatra, Frankie Valli, Jon Bon Jovi, Alexander Hamilton, John Travolta, Rick Nelson, Clara Barton, Aaron Burr, and Bruce Springsteen are a few big names.

New Jersey has exported Ring Dings, Devil Dogs, and Yankee Doodles, too. The things lined the stomachs of countless people who grew up in the Northeast. The treats came from Drake Bakeries in Wayne. What could be better than a Ring Ding (born 1961)?

Some would argue that the best New Jersey has to offer can be seen easily along the 142 miles of the New Jersey Turnpike (opened November 1951). Writer Karen Heller once cutely described the Turnpike as "the vernacular on steroids."

Away from the Turnpike is quiet and lovely Warren County. Notice the hills. Memorize the word "hydrography." Do not think of staying. Notice that the people there do not wish to relate to New York, Philadelphia, or Newark.

A curious twist to the heroes and villains theme took place at Glassboro State/Rowan College not long ago. A change of name took place when monies changed hands. Someone asked what would happen if the monies were "tainted." One administrator remarked, "t'aint never enough money in higher education."

Plan a visit to New Jersey some day.

See if the state is not what Governor Belcher called it in 1745 ..." the best country for midling fortunes, and for people who have to live by the sweat of their brows."

That says it.

Pennsylvania
Not Quite a Rectangle

Large Pennsylvania is a factor. The state contains many people, 45,308 square miles, much to do, some big cities, and numerous hills and valleys which house some simple and honest people.

From Punxsutawney to Upper Darby, and from Harrisburg to East Stroudsburg, the state receives high marks for trying to balance its advancing age with a need to work hard in order to help the kids.

Notice the age of the folks eating stromboli at the Fairgrounds in Allentown every summer.

Look at the condition of the roads in Pennsylvania.

Old bridges (Howe, Pratt, and lenticular) are easily spotted, too.

We all know the condition of the steel business, and it is old news that young, bronze bodies are found in the South and in the West, not along Twelfth Street in Erie.

Regardless, Pennsylvania plods along, emphasizing the importance of iron both in the blood and in the workplace.

Pennsylvania was the second state admitted to the Union (1787), and some interesting place names have developed. There is Slippery Rock, Sinking Spring, Paint, Scalp Level, and Kegg. Did we forget Venus, Frogtown, and Lickingville? The list is long.

So is the list of larger places to be covered. Another pen (purchased at J. J. Newberry Company?) may be a must.

Why not begin the tour of the cities with Scranton (81,800 folks)? Notice the flashy Steamtown Mall, but for straight answers about life's problems visit the place that every Foundry town used to have – a Coney Island restaurant. Scranton's version (515 Lackawanna Street) has been doing its thing since 1923. Scranton has indeed "been there."

So has Allentown (pop. 105,300), a city that may end up

being a sociologist's dream. The age of the people plus the rapidly advancing average age of the priests in the Catholic Diocese there will doubtless result in some massive social and religious changes. The holy water may hit the fan when people are told that no one will replace an aging pastor.

Allentown has changed since the days when the Liberty Bell was stored there in 1777. These days the homeless as well as some newly-arrived Puerto Ricans walk past the steps of the church (Zion's Reformed) where the bell was hidden from the British.

Approximately 12 percent of changing Allentown speaks Spanish. An English-only law raised a few hairs recently.

Billy Joel was right about Allentown when he sang, "it's getting very hard to stay." Those along Hamilton Street downtown will grudgingly agree.

Another city in the orbit of New York and Philadelphia is Easton, one of the tri-cities with Allentown and Bethlehem. Easton is not Valhalla, but the city does provide treasures like Crayola crayons and Silly Putty. The flesh tone crayons a while back caused a furor among those with varying flesh tones.

Not changing much under a cerulean sky is the gem along the Schuykill River, Reading, where two people once published *A Beer Drinker's Guide to the Bars of Reading*. A certain bar on the northwest side was mentioned for its decor ("dark Afro"), clientele ("black on black") and overall rating ("rough"). Another bar had a decor that was "Northern New Jersey," the clientele "horney," and the overall rating was "time will tell." Outlet shopping does better than the bars today.

Downtown Reading is an easy study. A five and dime (in art deco!), a vacant Kinney shoe store, and dirty bus stops are noticed easily. The old Anthracite Cafe (what else in Reading?) is long gone. It at one time was frequented by the spraggers and door boys who worked the mines nearby.

Where better than in Reading to study the importance of the railroads? The iron rails promised and delivered prosperous times, and did so amid a flurry of metaphors. One learns that "the iron bands were bonds" and that "iron streams" connected all Americans on "railroad time." Those were the days.

Where better than in Reading to contemplate the demise of the railroads in the hearts of millions and millions of Americans?

Reading in Reading can be done at the good-looking library at Fifth and Franklin downtown.

Not far from Reading is Harrisburg (pop. 52,300), the capital, where there are some hard feelings. It seems that some Midstaters feel that "Pennsylvania German" is a forgotten category when it comes to affirmative action assistance. Certain "Pennsylvania Deutsch" (not Dutch) feel that their voices are not heard by government officials in Harrisburg. People of color who walk along Front and Market don't pay much attention.

Erie (pop. 119,000) is a good distance from Harrisburg culturally as well as geographically. Sometimes called "dreary" and always called a haven for the Mafia, Erie has an international airport (chuckle, chuckle), a tiny zoo, and some private schools that are pretty good (Gannon University, Mercyhurst College).

Erieites boast that a total of 85 million people live within a 500-mile radius of the city.

High school football is big in Erie.

Visit Erie in September, not January. It snows a little in the "Gem City" (83 inches per year).

Misery Bay near the Perry Monument in Erie is not miserable. Many Erie people, tired after a day at the mill, have dreamed of a better life along Misery Bay.

A walk in Erie can be nice in good weather, but a mention of the history of nitroglycerin in Titusville can bring a person down to earth rapidly. A simple, hard-working folk live and toil in Titusville. "Intelligent oil" can be discussed there.

The heart of western Pennsylvania is Pittsburgh (2.3 million in the metro area), of course.

The city has pretty much seen it all, from Henry John Heinz cultivating horseradish in 1869 to a visit by Nikita Khruschev in 1959, to the ecstasy of the 1970's, courtesy of the football Steelers. Sunday baseball was started in April 1934. All is well.

To get a feel for Pittsburgh get a can of Iron City beer and discuss the Depression. After the chat you may be glad you were raised elsewhere.

Pittsburgh may be the quintessential "shot-and-a-beer" town. Ask for an "Imp and Iron."

Of all the characters who have graced the "Smoky City," there is one who gave the place many years of amusement without equal – Cy Hungerford of the *Post-Gazette*. His editorial cartoons began in 1927 and lasted until his retirement in 1977. Fun was poked at Queen Elizabeth, at presidents from Coolidge to Carter, and at hundreds of others. Cy Hungerford passed away in 1983 at the age of 94. His ready smile and bow tie are still missed.

The announcement of the closing of a Pittsburgh landmark took place on September 30, 1977. The headline that day was "West View Park, Age 71, Will Close." Similar to Chicago's Riverview (1904-1967), West View Park featured exciting rides (the Dips, the Roto-Plane) and romantic opportunities (the Cuddle Up). For years a sign greeted those who rode the Dips. It said, "do not get in or out of cars while they are in motion. Buckle your straps." Many a young man brought his girl to West View for a Coke and later in the evening tried to squeeze it out of her.

No mention of liquids in the Pittsburgh area is complete without a tip of the hat to Olde Frothingslosh of the Pittsburgh Brewing Company. There is Rolling Rock from Latrobe, too. Quite a legacy.

Baseball in Pittsburgh has had a long and storied past, and a great line once came from Honus Wagner. He was told that John Henry Lloyd was "a black Honus Wagner." The Pirate star responded, "I am a white John Henry Lloyd." More streets should go two ways in Pittsburgh. Directions are easy in these parts. Just go across the river, down the boulevard, and up over the hill. Those should suffice.

A final note about Pittsburgh is that English is most definitely the official language in town, although there are times when one has doubts. A person's shirt once in a while "needs washed" and people are "laid out" at the local funeral parlor. Be aware of these things, or you may be "laid out without a flower" in Pittsburgh.

About two hours by car from Pittsburgh is New Baltimore, a borough that is quiet, peaceful, and typical of rural Pennsylvania life. "New Balymer" is suspicious of visitors, especially if their last names are not Hillegass or Bittlebrun. For decades a Catholic religious order operated its novitiate in New Baltimore, but withdrew operations in 1970. Many of the young trainees (New Jerseyites, Bostonians, Chicagoans) fell in love with western Pennsylvania during their stay of one year.

The big city to which New Baltimore relates is Johnstown, the home of the flood of May 1889. The legendary flood (500 feet wide, 20 feet deep for 14 miles) is well known. It killed 2,209 people, nearly three times the toll of the San Francisco earthquake in 1906. A 1977 flood shook up Johnstown ("new, rough and busy" in its day), too.

South of Pittsburgh on Route 51 is Uniontown, full of funeral homes, fast food restaurants, and closed department stores. Ask about the old White Swan Hotel. Locals remember a study done which claimed that getting cancer and living in Fayette County were practically synonymous.

In Connellsville one finds old coke ovens. Pennsylvania life cannot be understood without a reference to them.

East Chocolate Avenue and Cocoa Avenue are located in Hershey, of course, and the first recorded sale of Hershey's chocolate took place on April 17, 1895.

In 1995 Hershey Bears hockey is a big deal at folksy Hersheypark Arena.

In Luzerne County (see Wilkes-Barre area) life is quiet and the people elderly. In the late 1980's 19 percent of Luzerne County was 65 years old or older.

In Lackawanna County (see Scranton again) the figure was 18 percent. Golden age groups flourish there.

The seniors can discuss the weather with intelligence, since State College is not far away. Meteorology is studied there with great seriousness. So is football.

People in Eastern Pennsylvania live in the shadow of New York City and New Jersey. More than a few from the Allentown-Bethlehem-Easton area hop on Interstate 78 and head east for work. A large Edge City awaits in New Jersey at the intersection of 78 and 287.

Many roads in that area lead to Philadelphia, home to 1.6 million people in the city and 9 million in the metro area.

How times have changed there...

Life in southwest Philadelphia used to be so different. It seemed that everyone was Irish. All souls were Catholic. Attending services at Most Blessed Sacrament Church was both a religious and a social must. Irish pastors (named Higgins and Daly) insisted that parishioners pray, pay, and obey. With God firmly housed at MBS, no task in southwest Philadelphia was too small.

Now, however, the story is different, and the tasks are great. The area is black, and MBS is not what it used to be. Sunday donations are now not so hefty. Elderly whites have moved on. The confidence that MBS can outrun all competition is not there.

St. Charles Borromeo (founded 1868) in South Philadelphia is a similar study.

Changing times have impacted Philadelphia a lot, but very little has been done to harm the love of a TV show that started years ago in Philadelphia – "American Bandstand." The show was immensely popular with young people, especially for a young person named Dick Clark (born 1930). He was billed as "America's oldest teenager." In Clark's days over 65,000 songs were played, and each one was nice to dance to and had a good beat.

Another Philadelphia hallmark, although not nearly as pleasant as "Bandstand," is that Philadelphians love to complain. And boo. And hiss. Attending a Phillies game will prove this point beyond a shadow of a doubt. One commentator working for ESPN once remarked that Philadelphians would boo their mother, especially if she did not run out a grounder to second.

How to end this chapter?

Perhaps with the reminder that Pennsylvanians in places like Hazleton and Mahonoy City are still hard at work. The two places years ago shared baseball (in the Anthracite League) and hard work. The baseball is gone, but the need to work hard remains.

Pennsylvanians from the construction site of the CoreStates Center in Philadelphia all the way to the Iron & Glass Bank on Pittsburgh's South Side can relate to that hard work.

Pennsylvania works that way.

Delaware

Pocket-sized

It has been said that the toughest instrument to play is second fiddle, and such might be the case for the state of Delaware. It is the second smallest and, imagine, it takes 53 Delawares to make one Ohio!

If that little item does not make readers raise some eyebrows, then consider the plight of professional baseball's Dallas Green. He has tried over the years to explain that Delaware is just like California, but one seventy-eighth the size!

Making matters worse is the task of doing research about Delaware's vernacular regions. Delaware has no Iron Range, no Bootheel, no Badlands, and no Gateway. There is, however, the wealthy Chateau Country not far from Wilmington.

Maybe the best thing to do is to go to Delaware with any empty tablet and an open mind.

The people? Some Delaware people move to Pennsylvania. Some Maryland people move to Delaware. Approximately 700,000 folks live in Delaware. Swedes and Finns have been seen in the Delaware River Valley where the log cabin made its debut.

The history? Those who love the details of the Civil War can go to North Milford in Kent County. Your mission, should you choose accept it, is to go to the Old Methodist Episcopal Cemetery and study the life of A. T. A. Torbert, who died in 1880. After that, look up Rear Admiral Samuel F. du Pont and Colonel Henry A. du Pont.

Regional matters? Look for a mention of Lower Delaware by those who put out the phone book.

Delmar and Marydel, furthermore, can be found in your road map.

Those into regional studies report that U.S. 40 can be found in Delaware. People from Indianapolis and St. Louis can relate to that road.

Jobs? Study the broiler chicken industry in the Delmarva Peninsula (two counties in Delaware, nine in Maryland, and two in Virginia) during World War II. Climate, economy, and location contributed to some good paychecks.

Baseball? Avoid the temptation of going to Philadelphia, Baltimore, or New York for the big guys, and ask instead about Harlan's Field in Wilmington. Games between blacks and whites used to attract many fans there years ago.

Something to do? Make a dash for Highway 50. It will take a person to Sacramento.

Transportation? Study the important C&D Canal. It was completed in 1829.

Exports? There was and is Teflon, discovered in April 1938 in a lab run by (who else?) Du Pont. Both nylon ("derived from coal, air, and water") and Teflon have had interesting histories.

Demography? There are 300 chickens for every person in Delaware.

Let us do some note-taking in a city or two.

Dover (27,600 people) is the state capital, and the city has a role not described in the travel brochures. Dover Air Force Base received 21,693 dead during the Vietnam era. Some Americans associate Dover with a deceased relative.

Dover is a micropolitan area, of course.

What to do in Dover? Maybe some research at Delaware State University, one of the nation's northernmost black colleges. Ask about the start of the school in 1890. Include a question about where slaves used to live. End with an appreciation for a place once known as the State College for Colored Students.

Homework in Dover will be to explain how and why capital cities differ from other (often larger) cities in the same state. Go to Trenton, Albany, and Annapolis for more information.

If that is too easy, try to find an example of something in Dover that is labeled "backward" and yet is "urban" at the same time. Explain why "backward" and "rural" seem to fit together easily, but "urban" and "backward" do not.

That task will be easier than trying to keep all the du Ponts straight since there are so many in Delaware. One beleaguered writer once had successive conversations with University of Delaware Chancellor Percy du Pont, Highway Commissioner Malcolm du Pont, Chamber of Commerce President Henry du Pont, Rabbi Sheldon du Pont, and Monsignor F. S. du Pont. And to think that at the time the recently retired CEO of Du Pont was Irving Shapiro!

The du Pont name means money, of course, to most people. Those into American fortunes may want to pursue names like Rockefeller, du Pont, and Mellon at the same time.

It may be good to point out now that there is the Tour Du Pont, a must for those into cycling. This is a big deal in Delaware.

A pleasant Delaware diversion, too, is a day or two at Rehoboth Beach. Though not exactly in the same league with La Jolla, California or Key West, Florida, Rehoboth serves as a nice summer playground for Washingtonians and Philadelphians. Each city is less than 150 miles away. Whisper on Rehoboth Beach because a Washington lawyer may be close at hand.

Those sunning at Rehoboth can stay up-to-date by reading the *Daily Whale* newspaper, a fixture in Sussex County.

Another city?

The miracle of neoprene may not be a hot subject today in Wilmington (pop. 71,500 and many poor) but it once was. The "chemical tag" that belonged to the city now has given way to a talk about re-positioning Wilmington as an "ideal business location."

One critic of Wilmington once said it has "the front end of a BMW and the rear of an Edsel."

For extra credit list all the important events that have happened in Wilmington since the Philadelphia, Wilmington and Baltimore Railroad arrived in 1837.

As we go through Newark (not pronounced like Newark, New Jersey), we may as well stop by the home of the University of Delaware Blue Hens.

One might even study why Delaware was made a state in the first place.

No matter.

Take a vacation in Wilmington. Stay at (where else?) the Hotel Du Pont.

Maryland
Much to Do

Did you ever think that dirt can smell nice?

It does.

Just drive your car in July from Gettysburg in Pennsylvania down into Maryland. Roll down the windows. Inhale. Think of Jeremiah Dixon and Charles Mason. The experience can be lovely.

The dirt is mentioned at the start of this chapter because we should not think that Maryland is a "city thing" (Baltimore, Annapolis, Silver Spring) only. Vast open spaces are easily visible in Maryland.

Indeed, Maryland has many sides to it. The state is part Foundry and part Dixie. Black & Decker can be found in Hunt Valley, but the Eastern Shore houses dozens of chicken shacks. Two different agendas.

Authors Neal Peirce and Jerry Hagstrom tell us that Maryland is not "a single portrait."

Consider, too, the many people who have passed through. George Washington and Richard Nixon. Spiro Agnew and George Wallace. Babe Ruth. Cecil Calvert (the Second Lord Baltimore). H.L. Mencken and Marvin Mandel. Quite a list, and we have not yet mentioned Captain John Smith, a man who said, "Heaven and earth have never agreed better to frame a place for man's habitation."

Maryland indeed has endured much over the years, including a debate recently about the state's motto, "Manly deeds, Womanly words". Since 1648 that motto has been fine, but recently the state has been told of its sexism.

Diversity? Talk to the 729,000 people who live in Prince Georges County. They will provide plenty of opinions about everything.

The big fish in Maryland is, of course, the city of Baltimore (pop. 780,000). Where better to start?

Notice the brochures on Pimlico, Little Italy, The Baltimore Museum of Art, Harborplace, Camden Yards, Fell's Point, and Ft. McHenry.

In Baltimore one will see that the words of a student at Morgan State University are true, that Baltimore is "an anomaly – a Northern/Southern place." Northern factories come in contact with Southern accents.

There is also contact between Germans, Irish, and Know-Nothings, as well as between African Methodists, Baptists, and Catholics. Entrepreneurs, privateers, and engineers have been spotted, too.

All kinds in Baltimore remember their Colts playing the famous game with the New York Giants in December 1958 in New York. Colt Alan Ameche plunged into the end zone in overtime for the winning score. The Baltimore quarterback that day was hero John Constantine Unitas.

Memories in Baltimore function well when it comes to Babe Ruth. He was "placed" by his parents in St. Mary's Industrial School in June 1902. He was being trained to be a tailor and shirtmaker, but left school with the following on his record: "he is going to join the Balt. Baseball Team." We are also reminded that the Babe was "the white Josh Gibson," just to keep the record straight.

Make sure you visit the Washington Monument. Not the one in Washington, but the one in Baltimore.

Burned into the memory of many Catholics is the use of *Father McGuire's Baltimore Catechism*. The cardinal virtues were memorized in their entirety. Few today realize the role the Catechism played in assimilating recently arrived (and frequently on-the-move) Catholics for years and years and years. Catholics must have their "thinking caps" on to contemplate all of that.

Some Catholics can describe how Maryland functioned as a haven for them in 1632. That answer is not found in the *Baltimore Catechism*.

Black Catholics know that St. Francis Xavier parish is the oldest black parish in the country. The 200th anniversary is coming soon.

A black man who has been around many years is Sam Lacy, who has been covering sports in the Baltimore-Washington area for decades. Born in 1903, his work on behalf of black people took a nice turn on Lacy's birthday in 1945. That was when a baseball player named Jackie Robinson signed a contract to play minor league baseball.

Baltimore has great history. In 1850 the city was, believe it or not, the second largest in population in the country. Nieuw Amsterdam was first.

Baltimore and Washington are not far apart. The cities are so close that the first telegraph message using Morse code was transmitted between them on May 28, 1844.

Do not think that the differences between the cities do not include jobs. Washingtonians push paper, say Baltimoreans, while those along the Patapsco labor in factories. Not knowing this distinction can get one into a "perilous fight."

Baltimore used to be the nation's capital, of course. Annapolis was at one time, too.

Pleasant Annapolis has been the capital of Maryland since 1694. The streets are Duke of Gloucester, Compromise, King George, Prince George, Shipwright, and Fleet, among others, and the houses are, alas, Georgian. Much history awaits the visitor who can cover considerable distances without a car. The only mystery in town is the name the inhabitants give themselves. Annapolisites? No. Annapolitans!

People into urban studies like to examine the plan for Annapolis in 1718. Notice the two circles and the square.

A side many do not see in Maryland can be found away from Annapolis in tiny Princess Anne. Ask about race relations. Ask about riots in the past. Notice how some "keep on pressin' on".

The hero/villain debate?

How about Edgar Allan Poe? To some he was an opium-crazed, despairing author, while to others he was "a past, with an air of refinement" in the words of a worker at the Poe Museum. A simple place on North Amity Street housed Poe in the 1830's before he died at the age of 40.

An easier example of a man who was a hero might be artist Alfred Jacob Miller (born 1810). He was seen along Colonade Row on Baltimore Street back in 1834. His work on the American West, not the city of Baltimore, deserves serious study by those who love the West. History and art are wedded in Miller's work.

Enjoy Maryland and her history.

The 2.3 million who live in the Baltimore area seem to.

District of Columbia
Supply is Limited

To put words into the mouth of the late Groucho Marx, the District of Columbia is really something. Or could be something. Or should have been something. Or might be some day something. It is the land of paper-shuffling, glasnost, misspeak, regulatory budgets, memorandums of understanding, selective memory, incursions, windows of vulnerability, and unvarnished truth. If you are dizzy, consider it normal. Often in Washington what begins as simple and obvious turns out to be inverted, convoluted, and always costly.

Washington (606,000 people) can be understood at least a little bit by visiting the Georgetown University area. One will notice business people, teachers, politicians, students (often from the heavyweight champion of exporting young people, New Jersey), and movers and shakers of every type. The atmosphere is trendy, cosmopolitan, erudite, and high-priced. If you are now more dizzy, read on.

People in the Georgetown area may reflect a side to Washington which makes the "Style" section of the *Post*, but may not necessarily reflect the rest of the city. The District is over 70 percent black. The chances are that the proverbial "little guy" in the city is black, not so well educated, and not so recently arrived. Set against the embassies and the formal dinners, the scene described above can be a surprise. Cherry blossoms can deceive.

A second side not reported in the *Post* is that all the cards are seldom on the table in Washington. The legal buying and selling of real (not artificial) blood, for example, can contain some "facts" which may differ person to person, consultant to consultant, and meeting to meeting.

The facts in the District will seldom mention the thinking of blacks about shades of black skin color on either side of the Anacostia River. The color has ramifications socially and economically.

The facts will seldom reveal that another "process" will not move the meeting along any better.

The facts will not mention that decisions are often made by default in the District.

There is much "spin" on every issue.

There is doublespeak, too. "I think I do not remember" can take even the most brutal crook out of a problem. Things like "revenue enhancement," "a state of permanent pre-hostility," and "violence processing" (taxes, peace, and war) are important, too. Teachers can relate to the gem which says, "reading is a process of recognizing that printed words represent spoken words and is a part of the total language spectrum."

District of Columbia pols "think they don't remember" that the area's biggest employer only 140 years ago was the building of ships, not the production of paper. Paper was second. Today paper and what goes on it are major items.

Paper and ink weave interesting tales in Washington, but they often neglect the history of the New Negro Alliance (born 1933).

In this mix, too, it happens that cities other than Washington are taking matters into their hands without calling Washington for the answer. Notice life in Atlanta, Kansas City, Detroit, Boston, Miami, Los Angeles, Denver, and San Francisco. The work years ago of engineer Pierre Charles L'Enfant ("to delineate a plan wholly new") does not impress many people today.

Arguing and disagreeing in Washington are as common as rumors at the bars in National Airport, of course. In 1863 Jefferson Finis Davis took a dim view of the Statue of Freedom atop the Capitol. Washington has been arguing ever since.

It is old news, too, that getting things done in Washington is one thing, and working to block other problems is quite another. The war in Vietnam provided many examples of that.

The buck never stops in Washington, either, of course.

Oxymoron is common. Notice the National Air and Space Museum. It has a "conservative modern" style, architects say.

"Conventional wisdom" is tough to pin down, too, not to mention that there is "scientific misconduct" on the part of some who share information about things like health care and other subjects.

One must be careful about confusing the historic with the symbolic in the District. The latter outruns the former frequently.

These notes and cautions are given not to shock but to warn. Moving into and within Washington circles (4.6 million people in metro area) requires that a person proceed cautiously, or his or her name will be (Samuel A.) Mudd, a physician who ended up on the wrong side of the Lincoln assassination.

Everyone knows that Washington seems to have an endless supply of lawyers. "Legorrhea," the excessive and dysfunctional application of laws, is a problem. It is so ordered.

Particularly vexing can be the application of laws to people who feel that the laws are not essential. Is a sound amplification permit really needed to play "No Mas Contigo" outdoors in the hot summer?

Some of the things mentioned above take place because of a basic demographic fact – many people in Washington come from some other place. "Home" is not the District of Columbia. California, Arizona, Alaska, and Hawaii can function the same way.

Capitol Hill is a place where some of the District's gay populace meets, greets, and functions. So is the area around Dupont Circle. (Remember when AIDS was called GRID? The year was 1981, and the term meant "Gay-Related Immunodeficiency Disease.")

Details about the gay community are found in *The Blade* (circ. 42,000). (Some in Washington have calculated the Years of Potential Life Lost [YPLL] due to AIDS. In 1990 the figure was 660,261 years. In 1991 the number was estimated to be 776,240.)

The AIDS problem makes the absence of baseball in Washington look pretty small. For all its legalism and its endless statistics, one would think baseball would go well in Washington. The old Senators, however, moved to Texas in 1971.

The world of baseball blended perfectly with the District's love of statistics in April 1953. At that time Mickey Mantle of the visiting Yanks blasted a homer off of Washington's Chuck Stobbs. Red Patterson, a public relations man, ran off to measure the blast with a tape measure. He returned to say the ball flew about 172 meters. Since that day a "tape measure home run" has become part of baseball talk.

One category in which the District leads the country is the amount of alcohol consumed per person per year. Life in Washington can lend itself to frequent imbibing.

Would some intoxicated people in Washington call the Indy 500 the Indianapolis 804.6? Has anyone ever consumed an 11.25 kilogramer (a quarter pounder)? The metric system is a source, too, of much confusion and anxiety, probably because no one knows when the poor thing will be implemented. Or exactly how. Or by whom.

A smart move on the part of those who run things took place in July 1963 when the Zone Improvement Plan (aka zip code) went into place. One does not have to read *American Demographics* to know that segmenting people ("pools and patios," "shotguns and pickups") is very easy when using zip codes.

Numbers are a big deal in Washington. The Pentagon, the largest low-rise office building in the world, has four zip codes.

The numbers are favorable for those who like to attend plays in the District. Some even remember that Abraham Lincoln was watching "Our American Cousin" in 1865 when he was shot.

Increasing numbers in Washington realize that the District is a treasury of black history. The First Congregational Church, the Duke Ellington Residence, Woodlawn Cemetery, and the O Street Market are but a few important stops. Some will mention that Duke Ellington was a great black musician, while others remember him as a great musician. Learn the difference when you visit.

Learn about Benjamin Banneker, too, the "Afric-American astronomer" who accompanied L'Enfant in surveying the terrain of Washington in 1791.

A final word might be that keeping an eye on Washington is a must. Whether the news is good (the latest call from Atlanta updating AIDS research) or bad (the hoopla surrounding the Susan B. Anthony dollar in July 1979), the living is seldom boring.

In the difficult times, perhaps both blacks and whites can sing part of the (black) national anthem: "Stony the road we trod, bitter the chast'ning rod, felt in the days when hope unborn had died yet with a steady beat, have not our weary feet, come to the place for which our fathers sighed"?

All Washington "operatives" should memorize those lines.

Massachusetts
The Second Glorious Mystery

Massachusetts, the Bay state, is a working mix of the old and the new, the modern and the obsolete, the trendy and the quaint.

The hunt for witches in Salem in 1692, the Boston Tea Party in 1773, the Great Fire of 1872, and the presence of Southeast Asians in racially troubled Lowell in 1987 have made Massachusetts (born 1788) very durable. Even a flood of molasses in 1919 was brushed aside easily.

Boston (575,000 in city, 970,000 in metro area) is the capital of New England, as well as the capital of the People's Republic of Massachusetts. Why not talk about Boston right off the bat?

One feature of Boston life that gets attention and respect early on is the vast number of good academic institutions in the area. Harvard and M.I.T. need no explanation.

Those institutions produce people who can read an article on myocardial infarction or cognitive neuroscience from *The New England Journal of Medicine*. The intelligence is real.

A cute school cheer, by the way, is part of the history over at M.I.T. Here it is: "E to the u, du-dx; e to the x, dx; cosine, secant, tangent, sine, 3.14159; integral, radical u dv; slipstick, slide rule, M.I.T."

Other pretty fair schools are Amherst, Wellesley, Smith, Mount Holyoke. And there's Brandeis and Tufts, too. Did we forget Boston College and Boston University? What about Northeastern?

The world of letters flourishes around Boston. Cambridge gave the world e. e. cummings (not to be confused with t. s. eliot, who was born in st. louis).

Banned in Boston is the feeling that success can be achieved without a good education.

Banned in every way, furthermore, is the feeling that certain

things cannot be done in Boston or in its orbit. The University of Massachusetts hired a black football coach by the name of Matt Bullock in 1904, believe it or not.

Harvard, for the record, is "the white Morehouse College" in the minds of some black people, while the Atlanta school is "the black Harvard."

Some students in the Boston area are the sons and daughters of Erin. Names like Farrell, Flynn, and Flaherty can be found in every corner. In fact, some feel that the Irish in Boston do not have to mind their pints and quarts as other groups have to. The Paddy wagon awaits those who transgress.

Much studying goes on at Boston Latin High, an institution whose name alone inspires many to think of nouns and verbs. Boston Latin considers itself the ne plus ultra of schools. Te iudice.

The use of Latin in Boston, by the way, hit its zenith just a few years ago with the publication of Henry Beard's *Latin For All Occasions*. The author informed everyone, "stadium sedipilae optimum Saeptum Paludosum etiamnunc est." In English, "The best baseball stadium is still Fenway Park."

Artificial intelligence is found along Route 128, New England's answer to the Silicon Valley. New Englanders into biotechnology and AI, as it is called, are grappling with how to forge ahead in a fascinating field and how to monitor the rush of the Japanese into what once was purely American turf.

Both real and artificial intelligence in the Boston area have created a situation that is problematic: dollars from jobs in the high tech field can contribute to outrageous prices for homes and condos. Brookline is expensive. The Back Bay and the South End are also costly.

High prices in Boston invite comparisons with San Francisco. Both cities have water on three sides, a small land area (Boston 45 square miles, San Francisco 47), similar skylines, and, of course, a few hippies wandering around. It costs a fortune to live in these two cities, and both cities complain that there is just too liberal an atmosphere.

More than a few liberals run in the Boston Marathon (born 1897). The distance is 26 miles, 385 yards. A person in the helping professions could have a field day looking at body types and personality types from Main Street in Hopkinton, the starting place, to the very end. In 1941 Ellison "Tarzan" Brown led the race until he decided to take a swim in Lake Cochituate.

The lives of Boston liberals sometimes mirror what happens out West, of course. In 1989 Northwest Airlines filled up a billboard outside Logan airport in Boston by urging Bostonians to "Fly like totally fast to Los Angeles." Gag everyone with a spoon.

John F. Kennedy, a former resident of Brookline at 83 Beals Street, should be mentioned in this chapter, of course. He was a magic presence for millions, whether seen in Dallas in 1963 or even in smaller places like Elgin, Illinois in 1960. Today everything from the speed of the limo (11 mph) to the infirmity from which the President suffered (Addison's disease) has been covered in one place or another.

Some Bostonians rest at Forest Hills Cemetery (pop. 97,000). This "silent city" is a must for anyone wishing to learn about Boston and New England.

So is Mt. Auburn Cemetery in Cambridge. Note how the cemetery had a recreational purpose 150 years ago. Many good biographical studies can be done herein, too. Collect data along Elder Path.

Another subject to study is the influence of race on Boston's professional sports teams. The record shows that the Red Sox were the last team to integrate when they added Elijah "Pumpsie" Green in 1959. Only 34 black major leaguers played for the Red Sox from 1959 to 1991.

On another note it must be said that disappointment in Boston, and in 90 percent of New England, is spelled R-E-D

S-O-X, a team that has snatched defeat from the jaws of victory in 1946, 1967, 1975, 1978, 1986, and 1988.

The Red Sox loss in 1986 was particularly painful since it was in the World Series to the New York Metropolitans.

Suffering Bostonians can always turn to Chicago people for sympathy. The two cities share a dislike for New York City.

It is not so much the Mets that make Red Sox fans ill, but the New York Yankees. The rivalry has something to do with Bosox executive Harry Frazee dealing Babe Ruth to the hated Yanks in 1920. New York and Boston were linked by telegraph wires in 1847, which is probably the last time the cities exchanged pleasantries.

The entire world knows that Fenway Park, mentioned above, is one of the few gorgeous "green cathedrals" left. Fenway was born in 1912, the same day the Titanic went down. Many real heroes have played on real grass at the Fens.

New England beauty continues on Cape Cod for those who like blueberry picking or scallop chowder. Bad features include too many pizza stores and bothersome traffic. If you spend an evening you'll want to stay.

Bring a bucket of money if antique China from 1820-1900 is for sale on the Cape. Bring a lot of money anyway.

Hyannis, some feel, is the ugliest town on the Cape, while Provincetown has the most gays.

Provincetown is where the Pilgrims landed. It is not correct to say they landed at Plymouth Rock. The misinformation began in 1741, long after the deed itself.

Provincetown is a place at land's end, and therefore must be classified carefully. Key West, Florida is similar. One can encounter a variety of things on Commercial Street in Provincetown, he said sexually.

Ride a bike from Provincetown to South Wellfleet. Nudists occasionally cause a flap when they criticize "textiles" who want things covered up in the summer.

Nudists and others know that feet and bike get it done in these parts, not cars.

Around the Cape it is good to know something about what goes on in the water around you. You must know a great white shark from a pretty darn good white shark from a halfway decent white shark. That is New England humor.

A good word must be said about the intense schoolboy football rivalry featuring Martha's Vineyard and the Whalers of Nantucket High. The rivalry makes one think of other fierce football wars (e.g. Massillon, Ohio Washington versus Canton, Ohio McKinley). Take cover at the Jared Coffin House in Nantucket and avoid the throwing of eggs. The winner of the Nantucket-Vineyard game is usually high for months.

A similar euphoria cannot be found today in Lowell, although approximately 100 years ago the Boott Cotton Mills there provided some women with their first paychecks. Single women with French-Canadian surnames, no less.

Lowell may be better known for the bilingual wars that have taken place recently. Spanish versus Khmer might be put in bright lights (with a mention of Greek, too). Just try to explain to Greeks why stores say, "se habla español," but never "se habla ingles." Inquiring minds in the Acre want to know.

Life is calm today in Worcester (pop. 160,000), but its baseball team, a member of the so-called National League of Professional Baseball Clubs over 100 years ago, had its problems. On September 28, 1882 only three dollars were counted in the drawer after a home game. The previous year (September 19, 1881) the club had come under attack for playing a game as President Garfield was being buried. (It is difficult today to believe that places like Worcester, Providence, and Scranton were once homes to the best baseball played in the entire United States. That was approximately 115 years ago.)

Worcester in 1993 was one of those places in which a Catholic church, St. Joseph's, fought to stay open amid bitter feelings between the hierarchy and the parishioners. Were there too few priests? Too much "sameness" one parish to another? Too many old buildings? Too few parishioners? Too much cost? Too much history? Too little commitment? The wrong language? This sociological smorgasbord included a drawing of barriers and boundaries that would made even the most avid legalist proud.

A get-away from such thorny problems can be found on the slopes of western Massachusetts in New Ashford and Great Barrington. To maintain the sanity of the skiers the places advertise that Boston and New York City are only a few hours away in case business calls.

Massachusetts may take a back seat to some places in skiing, but the state will not when it comes to the beginnings of basketball in this country. In 1891 a man names James Naismith, a Canadian no less, put up a few peach baskets in Springfield, and soon some of the boys were shooting set shots and running a few down screens during the cold winter.

In western Massachusetts there is a school of considerable merit by the name of Williams College in Williamstown. A magazine of merit tells us that Williams is a perennial name in the list of top ten liberal arts colleges.

The villages of Lenox and Stockbridge, by the way, should make the notes, since industrialists and bankers once vacationed there in grand style. If you wish to speak to God, it is a local call from this area.

All aboard for Boston.

Connecticut

Nutmeg and Spice

In the writing of this book, certain states like Illinois and Texas had files that were practically exploding, but Connecticut was not like that.

Was that because Hartford was not in the news much?

Were people in isolated Stonington so enamored with their history-filled city that they forgot to make some news?

Was it because Connecticut people were busy arguing over what to call the place, "Nutmeg State" or "Constitution State"?

Was it because the city of New York grabs the attention of many Connecticut people, thereby making for little news back home?

Who knows?

This chapter will try to provide some information so that we all will know that there is more to the state than just Hartford, more to it than life with the rich and famous in places like New Canaan, and more to it than a long day at classy Taft School in Watertown.

Maybe a little relaxing at the start would be good.

A lovely diversion in Connecticut, and in the entire northeast for that matter, is to grab a cup of coffee on a cool fall day and watch some of the longest-running football rivalries on the high school level. An easy example is New London versus Norwich, a feud born in 1875.

Now the cities can be tackled with sufficient energy.

Those who like to study cities can begin in Connecticut with New Haven (21.3 percent poor, 9.3 percent unemployed) and its original "nine squares." Head for the intersection of Grove and Ashmun.

Borders and boundaries are found in the town and gown relationship in New Haven. Those at Yale are aware of the contrast, and recently have made an effort to help the less fortunate.

No mention of New Haven is complete without a word about Grove Street Cemetery. Begin notes at 1797. Notice how the late James Storrs, buried along Hawthorne Path, can watch the students at Yale University Law.

Those into "firsts," by the way, will note that the first black to receive a Ph.D., Edward A. Bouchet, did so (in physics) at Yale in 1876.

New Haven (130,000 people) should be watched for the aging of the people there. The number of persons between the ages of 50 to 59 will grow by 50 percent in the 1990s.

Was it not New Haven that gave condoms to fifth graders recently?

Over in New London there is very little desire to resemble New Haven, especially at 325 Pequot Avenue. The address brings to mind playwright Eugene O'Neill. He loved New London, and he often sketched the windjammers and rigged steamers along the Thames. Many from New London are ambivalent about O'Neill since bars and brothels were on his agenda years ago, too.

New Britain is never to be confused with New Haven or New London, mainly because New Britain has been on television informing everyone about how Stanley tools and New Britain have been intimate friends since 1843. The ads say that New Britain does not hurry to change, and that Stanley does not, either. This theme ("the immutability of lifestyles and screwdrivers") is repeated in countless other Foundry towns in Connecticut. Those who live in New England, a different "nation," are not impressed.

Another place that was new at one time is New Canaan, home to Philip Johnson's Glass House (born 1949). All serious architecture students should visit.

Factory life, not architecture, is understood by those who work for Otis Elevator in Farmington. The company has been a good study about the need to adapt to foreign markets.

If the name Yale (founded 1701) did not get your attention

a while ago, maybe these names will. Taft School in Watertown. Hotchkiss School in Lakeville. Choate in Wallingford. Kent in Kent. The schools are old, patrician, and aristocratic. In the words of one observer, they are "upper-or-upper-middle-class-country club-coming out party-stockbroker-Tudor French Provincial-suburban." Names like Ford and Scranton are on alumni lists.

Successful alumni from the cities of Connecticut cannot escape the traffic in Fairfield County. What was once a very lovely area is now getting near impossible.

Things are getting worse, too. From Greenwich to Westport (a Gold Coast?) there used to be plentiful land, an ample labor pool, very good schools, and affordable housing.

These days, however, the complaining was enough to blow down the tallest building in Bridgeport. A four-bedroom home on an acre of land in Greenwich costs approximately $540,000. The same thing was $86,700 in 1970.

The presence of Fairfield County is not lost on the Federal Reserve, since its "beige book" divides Connecticut into the First District ("Most of Connecticut, Maine, Mass., NH, RI, and VT") and the Second District ("Fairfield County, Conn., NY, northern N.J.").

The wealthy in Fairfield County can see a different world at the jai alai fronton in Bridgeport, not to mention at Cynthia's Rib Crib downtown.

Much of Connecticut, rich and poor, comes together in Hartford.

The city (pop. 139,000) is large, has factories aplenty, and likes to remind everyone that metropolitan New York and New England are two different things. At the Hartford Civic Center notice the people from the Foundry as well as the people from New England.

Some in attendance come from an ethnic parish in Hartford. The ethnicities are Lithuanian, Portuguese, French, "German/Spanish," Polish, and Italian. Notice the walls and barriers erected by some who insist, using data from yesteryear, that their parish is ethnic.

Homework about Hartford should be to study the Cheney Building, given to the world by H. H. Richardson. Mention how the style of the building paralleled the nation's desire at the time for stability and security.

West of Hartford stability is found among Foundry people who work in the Brass Valley (Torrington to Waterbury to Ansonia) along the Naugatuck. Die sinkers and burnishers in Waterbury who visit St. Cecilia's ("German," but changing) can find soulmates in the American Foundry among the tool and die folks in Aurora, Illinois who worship at St. Nicholas ("German," but changing).

A different world, one that relates better to New England, exists in the northeast corner of Connecticut in Putnam, a part of Windham County. This is the "Appalachia of Connecticut" in the minds of some, and just one visit is convincing enough. The *Hartford Courant* barely bothers to report news coming from Windham County.

In Windham County one is in a rare place – a relatively unpopulated county along the megalopolis called "Boswash" (Boston to Washington), where one-sixth of the country's population lives.

Small Moosup in Windham County did its part when it gave baseball the legendary Walt "Moose" Dropo. He is remembered by Chicagoans for his role in the Yankees-White Sox brawl in Chicago in 1957. Dropo's days in Moosup are not remembered as well as the photo of the cap and shirt of Enos Slaughter after the fight.

A mention of small populations can bring us to taking a note or two in western Connecticut, a place where names like Quassapaug and Naugatuck collide with names like Warren and Washington. Some people never saw real estate that they did not like, while other people claim that Colonel John Mason should not have laid siege to a Pequot Indian village back in the 17th century. The crux of the thing centers around who owns the land and whether or not it is possible to own the sky. Tread carefully.

A negative note might be that some things in Connecticut have been changed by the southward and westward rush of millions of Americans. Whale-watching, once thought of only by those east of the Hudson, has firm footing today in California. The situation is a hard pill for some Connecticut people to swallow.

Connecticut can say that it has ESPN (the Entertainment and Sports Programming Network) in Bristol. ESPN had a few brave souls watching Irish hurling in September 1979, but now has millions watching. A popular figure at ESPN is Chris Berman who entertains viewers by using names like Bert "Be Home" Blyleven and Natrone "Refried" Means.

Try at some time to visit what the brochures call CLASSIConnecticut. Both old factories and sailboats at anchor will be noticed.

Many places await the traveler.

As they say, "better yet Connecticut."

Rhode Island

A Fly on the Windshield

This chapter will start as New Mexico and Tennessee did. That is, with a quiz.

Name three towns or cities in Rhode Island.

Providence?

Keep going. Two more names are necessary.

Can't do it?

No one should feel bad. Most Americans cannot get past Providence.

A goal of this chapter will be to inform everyone about life in Rhode Island, a place not everyone will visit.

The size of the state will be talked about first. Four of Montana's 57 counties are smaller than Rhode Island. The Titanic was shorter. The Pentagon is smaller, although its budget is bigger. That should put things in perspective.

Rhode Island is so small that zip codes start in only one of three ways (027, 028, 029). The Pentagon has four such codes.

We are now ready to take up pencil and paper. The big city comes first, and some smaller ones will follow.

Providence (pop. 170,000) contains the Rhode Island School of Design. The school gets four stars, although many will claim they have never heard of the place.

Brown University, an Ivy League institution, does a good job, too. Most have heard of it.

Dropout rates for Providence high schoolers are annoying recently, however. School officials wish that the rates would not be made public.

In Providence visit the homes in the section known as College Hill.

Ask about the Southeast Asians assimilating into the Providence community, but avoid jokes about Italian people.

Those who study American life know that South Water

Street in Providence is important. A few centuries ago there were caves and warehouses containing rum, molasses, and slaves. Notice areas known as Hard Scrabble and Snowtown.

Another city?

For those wishing to find a lovely Rhode Island escape there is Newport, but be careful. There are three Newports to see. First, there is 18th century Newport. Then there is late 19th century Newport. Lastly, there is yachting Newport.

Fans of micropolitan areas known that Newport has 1.8 times as many residents as Rock Springs, Wyoming but only 1 percent of the space. Such things ("factlets"?) brighten the day of urban planners.

More than a few urban planners will shudder when they study the history of Rhode Island. Cotton Mather once described Newport as "the common receptacle of the convicts of Jerusalem and the outcasts of the land."

Some historians have found information about blacks in Newport's Common Burying Ground. Take notes about Primus Gibbs, Neptune Sisson, and Portsmouth Cheeseborough.

Homework will be to write two good paragraphs about how Newport outstripped Boston and Salem as slaving ports about 200 years ago.

Golf and tennis fans love Newport, and some of them go back far enough to remember the start of the Newport Jazz Festival in 1954. The founders wanted to take jazz out of small clubs and put it in front of a large audience.

A wealthy Newport audience witnessed the wedding in 1953 of Jacqueline Bouvier and John F. Kennedy.

Much wealth can be found today at several "cottages" along Bellevue Avenue in Newport.

A third city?

The viewing of bodies is not as great over in Pawtucket, although Hasbro Toys have fashioned some interesting shapes for decades. Hasbro debuted Government Issue Joe in 1964, just in time for the escalation of the Vietnam War. Lincoln Logs sell well, too.

A fourth city?

Central Falls is a place to keep an eye on, in part because its name is on the lips of officials of the Drug Enforcement Administration.

A fifth city?

Bristol was once upon a time a place where a few slaves came and went, too. Newport was not the only fish in the sea in that regard.

Bristol has Hope Street. Historians and lovers of food will have a great time.

People leave Rhode Island on one of three historic roads, U.S. 1, U.S. 6, or U.S. 44. The three are important for those trying to capture the romance of the road. U.S. 1 is a storied route called "the East's Main Street." U.S. 6 runs across the top of Rhode Island. U.S. 44 can be fun, too.

Going from Rhode Island to Connecticut on U.S. 44 will make a person wonder what century we are in, the 18th or the 20th. It seems that there is the need to balance sacred soil with economic growth, as well as Victorian houses and fiberoptics technology. The issue is an important one in much of New England.

Did we neglect to mention the national pastime in this chapter?

Baseball in Providence has a long history. Some will remember the Providence Clams in the days of Babe Ruth.

Pawtucket should get some notes, too. Baseball enthusiasts have known of the Pawtucket team for years.

Enjoy Rhode Island.

It is a well kept secret.

VERMONT

Bellows Falls and Friends

How could anyone in his or her right mind not love Vermont?

There a person finds delicious maple syrup, ample nuclear electricity, excellent skiing, a monster hiding in Lake Champlain, wood piles, folksy bars, on-time child support, a (tiny) black population that is well educated, and hundreds of green herons at Missiquoi National Wildlife Refuge. All of those things are governed by a mind that knows limits and loves to conserve.

However, come to think of it, there is first too much drinking going on in White River Junction. Second, the incoming malls and nuclear power make people mad. Third, it is not looking too good for those who do maple research because of heavy metals like arsenic and selenium.

All is not lost.

Vermont (52 percent unpaved) is really and truly a very nice place, and the state even divides itself easily for those wanting to do more study.

From Manchester down we will use the label Southern Vermont. The area around White River Junction we will call the Upper Conecticut Valley. Central Vermont is Montpelier. From Middlebury up to St. Albans we will use the label Lake Champlain Valley. Lastly, Northern Vermont will be "anchored" by small Stowe.

That was easy, wasn't it?

You were fooled. You probably underlined Manchester, New Hampshire, not Manchester, Vermont. Many people confuse the two states. Mappers do not help, either, since they often put the two states on one page. (If you went to the wrong Manchester with your underliner you may be thrown by natives into Lake Champlain in February.)

On second thought, you can rescue yourself if you can come up with some other labels that map out Vermont.

How about Northeast Kingdom, Green Mountains, the Connecticut Valley, and the Champlain Valley?

Or could we use Green Mountains, Champlain Valley, Taconic Mountains, Vermont Piedmont, and Northeast Highlands?

Did someone throw in the Slate Belt, where many Welsh people used to live?

No matter.

Why not just commit to memory that Barre has Italians and some granite, while Rutland has Poles and some marble? The only people disagreeing will be farmers who are French Canadians.

Dry yourself off and let us get going.

Let us begin with a "big" city.

Montpelier is the capital, and it boasts of only 8,500 souls, the smallest capital city of them all. Such smallness is no problem to Vermonters at all, since quality beats quantity every time there.

Those who rule in Montpelier know they cannot possibly compete with the Bostons and the Clevelands of this world, and they do not want to. Attention is given to staying in school, to being independent (a real Vermont hallmark), and to surviving on an income which will not scare people in St. Armand's Key, Florida or Lake Forest, Illinois.

Being independent is a difficult but essential act in the winter in Vermont, and products at Vermont Castings are named accordingly. The products, wood stoves, are named Vigilant, Resolute, Defiant, and Intrepid. Enough said.

When temperatures rise in Vermont a real treat is Ben & Jerry's ice cream. Addicts over the years have feasted on Chunky Monkey and Dastardly Mash. About 7.5 percent of the company's pre-tax profits are given away. About 99 percent of the customers are satisfied per day.

The mere mention of Ben & Jerry's brings up an important point about Vermont, namely that people expect products and services from there to be first class. Something purchased from House-Mouse Designs in Williston seems to impress Americans from Toledo to Santa Barbara. There's something neat and trendy and classy, the thinking goes, about things from Vermont.

The impressing can get interesting, especially if the product is from Seventh Generation Products for a Healthy Planet in Colchester. For sale are solar flashlights, recycled toilet paper (!), and a trip to a Costa Rican rain forest.

Ask those at L. L. Bean over in Freeport, Maine about the seriousness of blending a little class with a little ecology. Such is life in Maine, in Vermont, and in much of New England.

It is small wonder that Vermont and New England have some important things in common with those who live in Ecotopia, a description of the Chile-like strip on the West Coast. Both New England and Ecotopia like things clean and lean. Imposing limits is imperative, too.

Lean and clean living is done on the slopes by Vermont people who frequent Killington and Smugglers Notch. The places advertise great skiing. Boston and New York City are only a few hours away in case business suddenly calls.

Skiing enables the University of Vermont Catamounts to make their mark in the world of college athletics. The University of Wyoming, the University of Utah, and the University of Colorado all tremble in their boots at the mere mention of having to face the University of Vermont on the slopes. A few years ago Utah was thought to have a home-snow advantage near Park City, Utah as the biggies, including Vermont, faced off in the Wasatch Mountains.

Vermont is not a big player in the world of sports. People at the Final Four ticket booth for the Division I men's tournament in Minneapolis in 1992 reported that only 89 applications were received from Vermont.

Snow arrives in big numbers, though. Burlington gets about 78 inches of snow a year, and Montpelier 98. Those figures make Concord, New Hampshire (63 inches) and Portland, Maine (71 inches) take notice. "Icy finger Vermont," go the lyrics of the song.

Those lyrics can be hummed as late as the first Tuesday in March. That is Town Meeting Day, just for the record, and cold weather can arrive at a moment's notice.

The desire of Vermonters to have things as neat and clean extends to billboards, or the lack of them, throughout the state. Vermonters wish that all places could be that way.

To be on the cutting edge is important when it comes to religion, too. A woman was installed as an Episcopalian bishop in Burlington in 1993. Boston's "limosine liberals" can relate to that.

The lovely landscape in Vermont is good for jogging, although it was in Hardwick where author Jim Fixx died while jogging. On selected fall afternoons in Hardwick one has a difficult time even thinking of death since taking a deep breath can be so exhilarating.

Some choose not to live in Vermont. Only .2 percent of the state's population is black.

The same goes for Hispanics. Only 3,304 were counted a few years ago, the smallest number of any state in the country.

Not many Mormons live in Vermont, either, although both Joseph Smith and Brigham Young were born there.

The smallness of Vermont in some categories is not a big problem, especially in a place like Rutland. With but 18,000 people, Rutland is Vermont's only micropolitan area. Shopping, educated people, and recreational opportunities are easily available. Pay for teachers, however, is not real good.

Low pay was not a problem years ago in Smugglers Notch. History tells us that contraband was moved between Boston and Canada during the embargo period of the War of 1812. Revenuers watched the pints and quarts of everyone.

Life in the city?

Burlington (less than 40,000 people) is besieged annually

by thousands of "leaf peepers" who enjoy the lovely scenery along College Street. Snow does real well, too.

The Burlington metro area, predicted to have 162,400 souls in 2005, has a problem that is a pain in the neck. It seems that students in high school are dropping out to take advantage of the nice wages which some businesses are paying.

How to end this chapter?

With a list.

Purity, wholesomeness, rural values, tradition, self-reliance, trustworthiness, simplicity, hard work, environmental awareness, and closeness to nature.

Use that checklist as you go from from Middlebury to Rutland to Shrewsbury taking notes.

Go, too, from Williston to St. Albans some time, but do not mention Wal-Mart. The company's stores, to hear Vermonters tell it, blight the landscape and hurt downtown business districts.

Think green, if possible.

New Hampshire
Rates May Vary

In order to take no chances, this section will begin with some "musts" to know about New Hampshire, since to many Americans the state may be as well known as Idaho, New Mexico, or Arkansas.

First, New Hampshire is toward the bottom of the list in both square miles and population.

Second, many Massachusetts people have chosen to move to New Hampshire. Learn a little about Bostonians before you move your business to New Hampshire.

Third, a small town atmosphere is found somewhere in each of New Hampshire's 10 counties, guaranteeing at least a running start toward peace and quiet. For more exciting times consult "the youthful giant States of the West," in words dated about 1850.

Fourth, Concord, the capital, gave the world President Franklin Pierce, about whom there should not be any joking.

Fifth, the Seabrook Nuclear Power Plant puts a real damper on a vacation in Hampton Beach.

Sixth, read the *Union Leader* in Manchester (pop. 94,000). The paper once called Ted Kennedy "just plain stupid." The paper once labeled George Bush "a spoon-fed little rich kid."

Seventh, if you love the Oregon Trail, the Natchez Trace, Route 66, elaborate information highways, or reggae music, you will be very disappointed in New Hampshire.

Eighth, like so much of New England, New Hampshire's beauty is found in the simple things in life: quiet walks through virgin snow, covered bridges, and moonlight through the pines.

Ninth, if you love the Appalachian Trail, the Underground Railroad, and an education in an Ivy League school (Dartmouth), you will not be disappointed.

Tenth, keep an eye on the Manchester-Nashua area. For

job growth and business starts it could be a plum. Read the *Nashua Telegraph* for more information.

Those "musts" will make the going a little easier.

Let us go to Manchester.

The city, for the record, was ranked number 1 in lowest rate of violent crime per 1,000 people in 1990. Atlanta, Miami, and Newark (in that order) ranked 1, 2, and 3 in the opposite ledger.

It is only fair to say a few nice things about Nashua, too, so we will say that Nashua people seem to understand other humans pretty well. At least that was the case when the old Brooklyn Dodgers had to place Don Newcombe and Roy Campanella somewhere. Nashua was selected, but Danville, Illinois was rejected for fear of racial problems.

Over in Merrimack County (see Concord, the capital) there are problems, but not necessarily racial ones. The problem is the difficulty of commuting to Boston every day for work. The nice side is an uncongested life upon returning home.

Merrimack's low crime rates are more attractive than living in "Taxachusetts."

It should be said that New Hampshire gets good marks in some other categories.

The state ranks low in infant mortality, low in children in poverty, and low in jobless youth. Mississippians and Louisianans reading this chapter will relate to those categories. A final gem will be to mention that Tax Freedom Day comes quite early in New Hampshire. That is the day on which a person would have met all tax obligations for the year. Nation-wide the day is May 5. Many living in New England know that if business takes you by car from Washington, D.C. to Providence, you are going through about five states and a District that all rank 12th or higher for taxes.

The money one does not pay in New Hampshire for taxes can be used to go skiing in North Conway, Lincoln, and Peterborough. They offer nice slopes, short lines, and romantic nights. The ski places advertise frequently that Boston and New York City are only a few hours away if business calls.

Those into the cold know that in New Hampshire there is serious research about layers of ice that are thousands of years old. Learn the words "oxygen isotopes" as you observe.

An item that New Hampshire has in common with both Vermont and Massachusetts is tasty maple syrup. The syrup can be an experience beyond description. Try Grade A light on some pancakes in Mt. Cube or Sugar Hill, and you may want to move to the Granite State.

If those places are not on your skiing schedule, just take a drive over to North Conway and inspect the train depot there. You will be among tourists who have a difficult time identifying the architecture of the depot. Anyone who can explain the architecture will receive a free trip to Center Sandwich.

While going through places like North Conway and Center Sandwich it may be interesting to visit an ancestor or two in area cemeteries. In Jaffrey, west of Nashua a tad, this epitaph was noticed: "Sarah Averill, 89 years, 5 months, 5 days, She done all she could." Typical New England fixity of purpose!

That same fixity of purpose can be seen in certain schools in the Granite State, like Phillips Exeter Academy in Exeter. The school gave the world John Wilson Irving (class of 1961). Take that, Cheshire Academy in Cheshire, Connecticut!

Heroes and villians?

In a class by himself in the minds of many New Hampshire folks is President Franklin Pierce. He was "loquacious, bubbling over with kindness and beguilingly demonstrative." Add to that description the fact that Pierce was from the backwoods and, voila, we have a real Granite State hero.

The life of Pierce was not easy. He died an alcoholic, and had other problems as well. Few recall that his inaugural address was given on March 4, 1853 amid feelings of sadness for an 11-year-old son who had been killed in a train wreck two months earlier. Pierce gave his address from memory, by the way. He was the first president to do so.

Pierce doubted the good intentions of "the relatively few Africans in the United States."

Some quiet?

Berlin (accent on first syllable) is not in the news much, except if you count smelly cities. Similar to Terre Haute, Indiana, and Missoula, Montana, Berlin is known as the "city that paper built." Efforts have been made to solve the problem, however.

We all know that in New Hampshire the way the wind blows is very important, especially if you are in Dublin working at the *Farmer's Almanac* (born 1792). It reveals when to plant the begonias.

Windy or not, the Mount Washington Hotel in Bretton Woods can provide a nice time away from crowds, or at least Woodrow Wilson and Babe Ruth have thought so. Arrive ready to hike, golf, and enjoy.

New Hampshire likes to think of itself as stoic and conservative, not unlike granite, but such a posture gets jolted a bit every once in a while. The RU 486 abortion pill had the stoics pretty upset with the libertarians, and vice-versa, back in May 1991.

In all truth it may be easy to be a liberal in New Hampshire. Housing for blacks is not an agenda item in Keene these days, but it certainly is in Albany, New York, a part of the American Foundry that lies a short distance to the west of New England.

Ready or not, all aboard for Manchester.

Summer or winter, that is.

MAINE

Here Comes The Sun

As one stands on Main Street in Stockton Springs, there is the feeling that the place is kind of neat. Few cars pollute the air. Garbage up to the ankles is inconceivable. Downtown, if it can be called that, is so quiet that you can hear a pin drop.

The quiet in these parts is a magnet, of course. Some come to Maine for vacation, while others pass through on the way to New Brunswick and Nova Scotia. Even Babe Ruth saw the wisdom of passing through in 1936 when he was persuaded by a friend to visit Nova Scotia.

Maine has only about 1.1 million people (about 37th-38th out of 50), but contains 33,215 square miles. The lovely coastline runs 228 miles as the crow flies. Maine's size and small population, about 37 people per square mile, puts it numerically somewhere down the list with New Mexico and Idaho.

But all was not quiet forever and ever in heavily forested Maine.

Think for a moment what a beehive of activity the state was about a century ago.

Along the Kennebec the ice business was tremendous. Ice was "the crop that never failed."

Cotton manufacturing plants were flourishing.

Potatoes (potatos?) were a big deal in Aroostook County.

Paper in Millinocket was very profitable.

Lobster and canned herring were huge enterprises in Eastport.

Shipbuilding was impressive, to hear those along Front Street in Bath tell it.

The population of the state was increasing.

The Bangor and Aroostook Railroad was humming in 1894.

The Bath Iron Works, which played a role in shipbuilding, had been started in 1884.

The city of Portland, a shining gem in 1895, was watching its population go from 34,000 in 1890 to 50,000 in 1900.

Those were the days.

Today is a new day, however, and some of the agenda has changed.

The state gives thanks that it is not in the nation's top ten in a number of categories: expensive housing, fast-growing cities, gridlock, tardy child support payments, violent crime, gangs, the recruiting of high school athletes, guard/inmate ratio, unwed fathers, and drug trafficking.

Carbohydrates in Aroostook County are still important.

Nuclear warheads and acid rain are a problem, however. So is the smuggling of cigarettes, a million dollar operation annually.

Now might be a good time to mention the various parts of Maine so that a person can embark on learning about this seldom-visited state.

First, there is the Southern Coast (as in Kennebunkport).

Second, there is Casco Bay (see Portland).

Third, there is the Mid-Coast (as in Bath and Boothbay Harbor).

Fourth, there is Down East. That would be Bangor and Machias, to give some examples. This area is so East, by the way, that you have to keep your eye on your watch constantly. The time may change if you're not careful. Those in the Maritime Provinces of Canada already know this. (Maine is like Arizona that way. Both the time as well as the language can change minute to minute.)

Fifth, there is Inland (Bridgton up to Mt. Katahdin). Do not be disappointed if Maine geography gets confusing. John Cabot thought that Newfoundland was really China.

That should do it.

But wait a second. Is it really possible to carve up Maine and do it justice?

Probably not. Those who go "off island" on the ferry to the

mainland probably feel slighted.

Feel free to limit your focus to one facet of Maine life (jobs, dialects, food, politics, or whatever), and get on your way. Have some blueberries from Machias or Union as you select what you want to do.

Main items in Maine would be firewood, dinghies, blackberry cobbler, lobster trap tags, life rafts, mooring buoys, and outboard motors. One look at the *Ellsworth American* (16 1/2 inches wide, similar to the *Lake Geneva Regional News* in Wisconsin) can provide other items for a checklist.

It is essential to understand that Maine can be very poor. Maine in certain places can make Owsley County, Kentucky look like Boca Raton, Florida.

Maine, by the way, ranks fifth in the category marked "highest percentage of homes without plumbing." Alaska, Kentucky, West Virginia, and Mississippi precede Maine on the list.

The lack of plumbing is felt acutely in the cold Maine climate. It was -45 in Van Buren on January 19, 1925.

It gets so cold in Van Buren that burying the dead is a problem for the many French-speaking Acadians who live there. Some choose to spend their final days near St. Bruno's Cemetery. Home is home, after all.

The lack of plumbing in Maine might be most noticeable along the highway 201 near Jackman. The area is close to Moosehead Lake and Moose River. A moose can be spotted easily. Drive with care on 201.

Maybe the most accurate thing to say about Maine and the people there is that minding one's own business is important. Surveys have revealed that people in Presque Isle do not watch televised sports very much. Knitting is preferred.

The calm of Maine's permanent people is disturbed by those labeled "flatlanders." The term is used to describe summer visitors who have fun driving up and down Highway 1 eating fried clams and wishing to see a whale.

Maine may be uneventful when it comes to American regional dialects. There is upper and lower Maine, and that is about it. New England dialects swallow up those particular to Maine, so all a person has to know is that a "top cow" is a bull and a "necessary house" is a toilet.

Should not French be important in Maine life? There is debate both ways. The language breaks down in the homes, not in the schools. There are no small potatoes in this issue. Notice the decline of French in Lewiston. Acadians feel they are losing ground.

Study, too, Maine's "Empty Quarter," north and west of Mt. Katahdin. Pulpwood and sawtimber are there. Look for the Allagash River. Bring reading material.

That material may include an explanation of life in Newfoundland, a part of Atlantic Canada that Americans should learn more about. Newfoundland is 90 minutes ahead of Portland, Maine on the clock. Monday Night Football *starts* at 10:30pm. Airplanes are de-iced on May 25th! (Newfie jokes should be noted, too. They are similar to Aggie jokes in Texas. Why does a Newfie drive a tractor with no steering wheel and no seat? Because that way the farmer gets it in the a** and does not know which way to turn!)

On and on the joking can go, similar to hydroelectric power.

New Brunswick should be studied, too, come to think of it. Prince Edward Island, also.

How would the presence of heroes and villains go in Maine? In Maine there isn't a Bill Cody, a John Dillinger, or a Jesse James.

There was James Augustine Healy, well known in Portland many years ago. The man was born of an Irish father and a black slave mother ("Eliza"). Healy was ordained to the Catholic priesthood in Paris in 1854. He was born in 1830, when the black population was only 18.1 percent in the United States. He fought not against racism, but against anti-Catholicism.

Those from the United States and from Atlantic Canada, too, should study the Aroostook River. About 160 years ago there was serious arguing in the valley of the Aroostook.

Today lobstermen argue because they cannot figure out why 28 million pounds of lobster were taken in during 1991, but only 19 million in 1987. In Boothbay Harbor one will hear many theories for the resurgence. One will hear, too, about flounder, haddock, and cod. Most amazing is how little we know about the much-prized American lobster.

There is the feeling in Maine (and in much of New England) that ecological concerns are extremely important. Disposable containers, plastic six-pack yokes, and "aggressive but voluntary recycling" are frequently on the lips of those who work in Augusta.

A positive note, too, is the presence in Maine of some lovely lighthouses. It boggles the mind to imagine all the people who have been guided to a harbor by a lighthouse. Students of the Sandy Hook, New Jersey lighthouse (born 1764) can explain the rest.

It may help to mention that Maine is both part of New England and the Northeast. The Northeast may mean snow and cold to some, while New England may mean attractive lighthouses near a summer cottage.

Augusta is the capital, of course, and the place is tiny. How tiny is it, in Carsonesque style? It is so tiny that the population of about 21,000 people is one-half the size of the New York City police force. That's tiny.

Maine people do not feel bad about such things, since it is quality not quantity that rules in New England. For the record there are eight capitals that are smaller than the New York City police force. New England has three.

The reference to quality has an interesting side to it, too, since some feel that the name of the game in New England is that many, many people are over-qualified. The situation is a serious problem.

Much of the future can depend on adequate health care in Maine. Just try to find an endocrinologist in northern Maine. The situation is comparable to living in one of the two Dakotas.

Lastly, perception in everything in Maine. To some who live a solitary life the state is a paradise, while to others the place is a rock-filled, jagged hinterland. The difference reminds one of Virginia in 1584 as opposed to Cape Cod in 1620. The former was an immense garden, but the latter was labeled a "hideous and desolate wilderness" in the words of William Bradford.

Come ready to perceive more than 33,000 square miles.

Now have some delicious scallops in Penobscot Bay.

Or visit Monument Square in Portland (pop. 64,000). Have the wild blueberries in August.

Or spend the day in Old Orchard Beach, but dodge the tee shirts and the vibrators.

ILLINOIS

The Lands of Lincoln

The state of Illinois is one which features contrasting people and occasionally contradictory lifestyles, most all of which are shaped (defined?) by the city of Chicago, a northern "anchor," and the city of St. Louis, a "heavyweight" to the south.

We should realize at the outset that Illinois is not as synonymous with farming as it once was. In 1970 there were approximately 123,000 farms, but in 1990 there were only about 88,000. The decrease is still happening today.

Many equate Illinois with the Breadbasket, although certain parts of Illinois are not part of the Breadbasket at all. Both the Foundry and Dixie are present in Illinois, too.

In fact, we might start with an item that distorts the illusion that the fields of corn in Illinois are places of apple pie, the flag, and a sense of order.

There is confusion where the Indiana border touches the Illinois border around Vermillion County, Indiana and Vermilion County, Illinois. The confusion increases since there is a time difference of one hour between the two places, and there is a difference of one digit on the telephone area code. All of this happens among people who do manage to agree on soybeans.

So much for the Breadbasket being a place of conformity and order.

Let us now start in the south and move north.

Southern Illinois contains farms, coal, poverty, "remoteness," a slow lifestyle ("laidback" is too trendy a term), and fear. The fear centers around the idea that the New Madrid, Missouri fault may act up like it did almost 200 years ago. Those in Marked Tree, Arkansas know all the details.

Some counties in Southern Illinois have set the pace for poverty for a few years. Pulaski, Hardin, Hamilton, Clay, and Gallatin (famous for silencing dogs decades ago by saying,

"Hush, puppies" during supper) are easy examples. Dixie values dominate, and many people have a love/hate relationship with the city of St. Louis.

Commercial Avenue in Cairo, a part of Alexander County, may bring us all down to earth as we do our study of Southern Illinois.

Carbondale (pop. 28,000) takes delight in informing visitors that the city lies within a 450-mile radius of Little Rock, Birmingham, Atlanta, the entire state of Tennessee, and Charleston, West Virginia. Notice that Chicago is not mentioned.

Two big rivers meet in Southern Illinois, the Ohio and the Mississippi. A person visits this area with caution if a northerner, but with delight if a southerner. Those who live in Shiloh can explain the difference.

Those who live in Shawneetown reflect the love/hate relation with Chicago. They know that their newspaper, the *Gazette*, once described Chicago as "a sinkhole of abolition."

Many know that places in Southern Illinois like Sparta, Chester, DuQuoin, and Murphysboro are part of Little Egypt. In fact, high schools there are members of the Southwestern Egyptian Conference, and the university (Southern Illinois) has the Saluki, an Egyptian hunting dog, as its mascot.

Modern conveyances have certainly changed lives for Dixie-born and Dixie-bred people. Carbondale to Chicago (via St. Louis) by air takes more time than Chicago to New York. The difference is important. Modes of transportation tend to define lives everywhere, even in Southern Illinois.

The people at UPS know all of this. A package going from Chicago to Carbondale is not as quick a delivery (or as cheap a price) as one going from Chicago to Springfield.

Either Highway 50 or Interstate 64 divides Southern Illinois from Central Illinois. Cases can be made either way. Notice changes in jobs, menus, attitudes, accents, and economy.

Heading north on Interstate 57 beyond Highway 50 calls for some decision-making. Interstate 70 crosses Interstate 57, and some options develop. To the east is Terre Haute, Indiana (former home of basketball's Larry Bird), and to the west are Vandalia and St. Louis. To the north there is Urbana-Champaign.

Let us go north and west a bit.

In Springfield (pop. 105,000) the main emphasis is on getting into and staying "in the know." Government towns seem to work that way.

Two developments that came out of Springfield in the last 25 years are the testing of lite beer (1973) and dwarf-tossing (1989). The former had an impact nationally, but the latter did not.

Hidden today in the pages of Springfield history are the 1908 race riots. It is as though they did not happen.

A big seller in Springfield is anything with Abe Lincoln on it.

Fifty miles west of the Capitol there is Valley City, a quiet place sometimes called "Forgotonia" because Chicago pols and even Peoria business people hardly ever think of the place.

A main stop on the Peoria and Oquawka railroad, the city of Peoria (pop. 130,000) has been the butt of jokes for years.

Redeeming qualities in Peoria are Bradley University basketball, pleasant people, malls like everywhere else, and a fight-back spirit that show that Peoria is not to be taken lightly.

Some Chicago people do not know Peoria from Pretoria because they have never been to Peoria.

Several St. Louis people have visited and even stayed. Notice "St. Louis style" pizza along Adams Street downtown. "Chicago style" pizza gets only a frown.

A good baseball story comes out of Peoria. Hall of Fame announcer Jack Brickhouse, a Peorian who has "scored standing up" in his life of more than 75 years, recalls that one day a heavy-legged catcher ("Ping" Bodie?) was trying to stretch a single into a double, but was tagged out easily at second. A media type was heard to say, "He had larceny in his heart, but his feet were honest."

There has been talk of building a Comedy Hall of Fame in Peoria. Some observers would say that the city gets a few laughs every day without a Hall of Fame, but others would not find that remark funny.

How tough is Peoria? It is so tough that one night two visitors, Brian Yandrisovitz and Jerry Saganowich, had their hands full outside the Civic Center with some hostile Peorians. The two guys were working for the World Wrestling Federation at the time and were known as "The Nasty Boys" professionally.

Komatsu and Kubota are dirty words to Peorians who work at Caterpillar.

Joliet, not part of the Breadbasket like Peoria, is a canal town that became a railroad/steel town that became a gaming town. The city's downtown was once described by an Irish comedian as "a cemetery with lights".

Joliet is the last city in the American Foundry going from east (Syracuse, Buffalo, Toledo, South Bend) to west (Davenport, Des Moines, Omaha) on Interstate 80.

Interesting things take place in Joliet since many locals still think that their Catholic parishes are "national churches," despite the fact that a dominant language (English) has watered down most of the discussion. Let the inhabitant and the visitor beware. (If you want a view of some old-fashioned ethnicity, go up the road to Lemont, and you'll find Irish Catholics at St. Patrick's Church, Polish Catholics at Sts. Cyril and Methodius, German Catholics at St. Alphonsus, and Germans who are Lutheran at St. Matthew's. Look for the corner of Ledochowski and Moczygemba Streets.)

A bright side to Joliet is the Rialto Theater (born 1926). It seats 1,926 people.

Many Jolietans do not realize that a precious history book exists beneath their noses. It is called Oakwood Cemetery (incorporated 1855) on East Cass Street. This "silent city" is fascinating. Notice the different social classes at Oakwood.

Joliet is probably not the quintessential Illinois town or city, but perhaps Pontiac, 50 miles to the south, is. Pontiac is part of the Breadbasket, and has all the right stuff. There are 11,300 friendly people, a high school basketball tournament of considerable merit, an Amtrak depot, and a gorgeous courthouse.

Many Pontiac folks prefer major league baseball in St. Louis (200 miles away) rather than in Chicago (100 miles away). They feel at home with St. Louisans, but not so much with Chicagoans.

Forgive the Pontiac people if they are reluctant to understand newcomers in town, but do not forgive a young basketballer if she misses practice. After all, a big game in the Corn Belt Conference awaits. Take the nearest blacktop to get there right quick now.

Rockford, as in porous bedrock 20 feet below the surface, has 139,712 souls. The city is one where test scores and skin color are at times argued about. This issue is important to the Italians, Swedes, and blacks, who labor, blue-collar style, along the Rock River. The sick head for, appropriately enough, SwedishAmerican Hospital.

Lunch can be a great time to discuss 19th century history over in Galena at the DeSoto House Hotel (born 1855). Highway 20 leading to and from Galena is no bargain. Go carefully by car amid the dangerous roads.

Both DeKalb and Northern Illinois University complain that no one knows exactly where the city and the university are (or how to get there), so here is the solution. DeKalb is 100 kilometers west of Chicago, a stone's throw from Sycamore, a long fly ball from Aurora, and a few miles from Rockford. Use Interstate 88 to come and go.

Using Interstate 88 provides a task for the artists in the group. On a lovely summer night find milemarker 115 going eastbound on 88. Look toward Chicago. The black figures you see are barns and silos of the American Breadbasket. The red you see comes from the lights in Chicago. The white lights in the sky are airplanes leaving O'Hare for points west.

These views are impossible, of course, for those standing in Chicago and looking west. Much poetry awaits therein.

Let us now go to Chicago, and let us start with a well-known man whom many Chicagoans remember fondly.

His Social Security number was 323-07-3515. He was a giant for twelve years (1959-1971) on Chicago radio (WGN AM 720). Many loved his reading of Mary Carolyn Davies ("Why do I love you? I love you for ignoring the possibilities of the fool in me."). His usual occupation, according to his death certificate, was "announcer." Some know by now that the person is Franklyn (H.) MacCormack, the mellifluous voice of the "Meister Brau Showcase." MacCormack was a fixture in Chicago, a city that has had many. He died in 1971.

Discussing "big names" is a good place to start concerning Chicago (2.7 million in city). Many will point out that Philip Armour, Ernie Banks, Daniel Burnham, Walter Payton and many other "heavies" have graced the city's roster.

See the chapter in this book on the East to know that many of Chicago's big names have come from the East. George Washington Gale Ferris ("the man with wheels in his head") came from Pittsburgh. William Wrigley, Jr., who switched at one point from soap sales to gum sales, was the son of a Philadelphia soapmaker. Al Capone was born in Brooklyn.

Being big and tough in Chicago is as essential as bragging about corn in downstate Champaign, by the way.

Big figures accompany Chicago's macho spirit. The Merchandise Mart contains 29 million bricks and has its own zip code (60654). The Sears tower weighs 222,500 tons. Daniel Burnham, after all, once said, "Make no little plans; they have no magic to stir men's blood and probably themselves will not be realized."

Another notable among the millions who have called Chicago home was Anderson "Shorty" Harris, who shined shoes and blocked hats for 66 years. Only 4 feet, 2 inches tall, Harris operated a shop which was patronized by Al Capone,

John Dillinger, and Mayor Richard J. Daley, among others. A joke and a story were free for all who stopped by. "Shorty" Harris was born in Jackson, Mississippi, but died in Chicago in 1990 at the age of 86.

Chicago as a retail center? Just look at your 1897 Sears catalogue to find stove polish, ear trumpets, barley forks, cherry stoners, and Tally-Ho playing cards. What more could a person want or need? A Hopkins & Allen Double Action Revolver? One dollar and seventy cents were never spent so well.

Chicago has been a home for black-appeal radio. In 1929 Jack L. Cooper made his debut on WSBC. Chicago was, after all, "the mouth of the stream of Negroes from the South."

Today maybe a good idea is to mention what Chicago is not.

First, Chicago is not the windy city most people think it is. The term comes from long-winded pols decades ago who tired their listeners by talking endlessly. Chicago has an average wind speed of 11.2 mph. Oklahoma City (14.0) and Great Falls, Montana (13.9), among others, are more windy. Chicago is drafty, yes. Windy, no.

Second, Chicago is not at the bottom of Lake Michigan. It is an above-ground city. Children in suburbs like Hinsdale (the birthplace of Mr. Veeck mentioned above) and Wheaton (remember John Belushi?) seem to picture the city at the bottom of Lake Michigan.

Third, and definitely most important, Chicago is not in the Midwest. It has been described that way for decades, but if one has any proper perspective about Chicago and the country at all, it seems crazy to use that label. The Midwest is where Kansas City and Cedar Rapids and Des Moines are located. Chicago relates more to places involved with manufacturing (that is, the Foundry). People from Syracuse, Detroit, Cleveland, Pittsburgh and Buffalo understand Chicago's sheet metal and glass factories perfectly, while those from Sioux City and Topeka do not and cannot.

There is always bewilderment in Chicago when a *Tribune*

article announces "Midwest Homes Affordable," only to have readers find that the bargains are located in places that do not look, act, or think like Chicago. Terre Haute and Davenport are examples.

The next time someone says that Chicago is in the Midwest, just ask what the city has in common with Wichita or Minneapolis (answer: not much). The understanding is important. This book's chapter about the East has more details.

Fourth, Chicago in the past has been called the "city of neighborhoods," but the term lately is growing stale. Many neighborhoods are changing.

The neighborhoods of Chicago are loaded with people who view the neighborhoods of New York with suspicion, since the two cities love to criticize one another. One should never forget the words of William A. Hulbert, a majority stockholder of the Chicago White Stockings more than a century ago. He said, "I would rather be a lamp post in Chicago than a millionaire in New York." Those words should get the attention of New Yorkers who remember that Chicagoans looked to the East (not the Midwest!) for monies to rebuild after the fire in 1871.

Fifth, countless books have given details about Chicago's macho past (like the railroads), but few accounts have included the "softer" side of the city (like agriculture). The two worlds ("nations"?) come together nicely in Chicago.

More than a few books remind us that the railroads (owned by Easterners!) that came to Chicago from the East found their western terminals in the city, while the railroads coming from the west located their eastern terminals in Chicago. Perfect.

Carl Sandburg was right when he wrote that Chicago makes tools and stacks wheat.

Where better than Chicago to have the General Time Convention in 1883? A standard time was a problem.

Not long ago the *Almanac of American Politics* contained a

great line about Chicago. The book says, "Illinois politics has become a kind of spectator sport – raucous, sometimes bawdy, full of play-acting, on a level somewhere between the Chicago Cubs and professional wrestling." Those words would get a chuckle out of both Ernie Banks and Gorilla Monsoon.

A stop in Chicago few think of is the East Side. Head for 106th and Ewing. The East Side is the American Foundry in triplicate. Those studying the Brier Hill coal mines in Youngstown, Ohio will find themselves very much at home on Chicago's East Side.

Architecture alone provides a person with weeks and weeks of pleasant study in Chicago, in large part due to the proximity of Lake Michigan. One observer has remarked, "the lake is the city's saving grace. It's the quality of the edge. The urban: vertical. The lake: horizontal." For starters, stand with your back to the lake and identify three architectural styles of three Loop buildings. Advanced students are to explain the connection between the Monadnock building and the New Hampshire mountain of the same name.

Architecture students know about the upper deck at the new Comiskey Park (born 1991). The deck is canted at a 34-degree angle, unlike the lower deck which is a 14-degree climb. Get ready to huff and puff.

A final word must be that Chicago very well could be your kind of Consolidated Metropolitan Statistical Area. Long on culture and the arts, heavy with sports and games, and loaded with work to be done, Chicago is indeed a powerful giant.

Those who prefer the Chicago school of architecture (over the Prairie School) and those who enjoy the history of black musicians on the South Side (Earl Hines and Fats Waller) can find an endless supply of people and places to study.

As Hizzoner Richard J. Daley once said, "Chicago looks forward to the future with nostalgia."

Leaving Chicago on the Eisenhower expressway one finds

DuPage County (pop. 816,100), a place that takes the westward "overflow" of Chicago. Wheaton had only 7,700 people in 1940, but has about 50,000 now. Naperville (pop. 101,000) boasts of many residential construction permits. Glen Ellyn, Elmhurst, Lombard, Lisle, and Carol Stream house many corporate executives. Addison, Bensenville, and Wood Dale house some Hispanics who bus tables and sleep in "hot beds" (Spanish "camas calientes") between shifts.

To the west of Chicago, and beyond DuPage County, there is Aurora (101,000 folks). The city was unified in its sadness a few years ago when a radio station (WMRO AM 1280) passed on. The station was a fixture.

Gambling is big in Aurora these days.

Significant to cultural students is Orchard Road on the west side of Aurora. Orchard forms part of the boundary between the Foundry and the Breadbasket.

Beyond Kane County and Aurora there are counties named Carroll, DeKalb, Henry, Lee, Mercer, Ogle, Rock Island, and Whiteside, which feature life on the farm. Ronald Reagan, the polytetraflouroethylene president, was born in Tampico, a part of Whiteside County.

A comical situation developed in 1983 in Carroll, DeKalb, Henry, Kane, Lake, Lee, Mercer, Ogle, Rock Island, Scott, St. Clair, Whiteside, and Will Counties. It was announced that Soviet diplomats and journalists were not permitted to visit those counties, but no one could figure out why not. So much for Soviet and American intelligence.

Illinois is a must in anyone's list.

Start with some Frango mints in Chicago. Head west for Earlville in LaSalle County. Notice the outdoor theater (born 1954) there.

Now start to go south.

Happy trails.

Michigan

Macho, Cold, and Teetering

Michigan has been many things to many people for many years.

The state has been home to several tribes of Indians for a long time, and still is.

Michigan has been a pleasant home for those who love water sports in the summer.

Michigan has been an address for blacks coming "up South." Was not Joe Louis Barrow, prizefighter, from Chambers County, Alabama?

Factories, as well as boxing rings, have attracted blacks over the years to Detroit and other places.

To use the past tense so often tells a tale, however, does it not?

Let us begin with a few cities where some people today still hope that things like steel will turn to gold.

Pontiac (pop. 76,000 and decreasing) is a familiar name. The resume shows some racial problems in the city in the early 1970's. Not good on the resume.

Hard by Pontiac is Auburn Hills, a name that was not even on the map a few years ago. In Auburn Hills is The Palace, which hosts games and concerts. Leaving Detroit to find fun in Auburn Hills seems very easy for many people in the Detroit area.

A short drive from Detroit is Saginaw (population 77,000 and decreasing), and none other than Alexis de Tocqueville once wrote, "It's not only the Indians whom the American pioneers take for dupes. We were ourselves daily victims of their extreme avidity for gain." The Frenchman wrote up his findings when visiting this country in 1831-1832. Saginaw has endured a lot since then.

It may be a long time ago that Indians were ripped off in Saginaw, but in many ways things may not be better today. It is hard to believe that Saginaw was once a lumber capital (1860?-1890?).

We might as well go to Detroit (pop. 1.1 million) now.

No reporting about the Detroit area could be adequate without mentioning an important vertebra in the local backbone – the Polish. Whether protesting exorbitant meat prices, as Mary Zuk did in 1935, or greeting Karol Cardinal Wojtyla, as thousands did in 1969, Polish power has manifested itself in the Motor City for decades. The Poles labored hard "for bread," prayed hard, and contributed heavily to factory and neighborhood life. Panna Maria, Texas and Polonia, Wisconsin cannot make the same claim.

Instead of immersing oneself in the "bitter laments" during the season of Lent, Detroit Poles now dialogue about the racial strife in the city as well as about the Arabs who work in the area at "party stores" ("convenience stores" elsewhere).

Many white people, some of them Poles, have moved to the suburbs. The city knows that it leads the charts in racial polarization.

July 23, 1967 is crucial to the story of Detroit. See Twelfth and Clairmont. The effects are still felt.

Detroit is a good place to test historian Andrew Hacker's research about whites moving when the percentage of black families in a neighborhood reaches 12 percent.

A perception shared by both blacks and whites about Detroit is that some areas are gang-infested drug havens. The Latin Counts, the Cobras, and the Cash Flow Posse were hard at work in Detroit not so long ago.

Detroit is the capital of the American Foundry. The 1963 recording of "Detroit City" by Bobby Bare summarizes what life is like for many Motown people: "By day I make the cars/ By night I make the bars." The words are understood perfectly in Cincinnati, Pittsburgh, Fort Wayne, Syracuse, Chicago, Milwaukee, and other Foundry cities.

For many whites born between 1945 and 1950 the sound of performers on the Motown label is understood perfectly, too. A good word goes out to the Four Tops who in concerts talk about the history at 2648 West Grand Boulevard in Detroit.

Try to sit motionless at a Tops concert when they do "Baby I Need Your Lovin," the group's "national anthem."

Levi Stubbs of the Tops helped with a song ("Detroit For All") a while back in an effort to heal the city of its woes.

How could a person forget the Edsel, a car synonymous with Detroit? The car was born on September 4, 1957. It died on November 19, 1959. Death came after incredible hype.

South of Detroit across the water is Windsor, Ontario. In 1990 a headliner at one of the clubs in Windsor was Suzy Boobies (55 FFF!). Events surrounding Suzy are reported on the Canadian side of the Detroit-Windsor area by powerful CKLW radio (AM 800).

In the Detroit axis, too, is Troy, home to Kmart. The company's vision is that "Kmart will be a symbol to Americans – the place which helps them attain the quality of life guaranteed in the American dream – sooner, better and more conveniently than anyone else." That says it.

When Ann Janette Kellogg and John Preston Kellogg arrived in Battle Creek more than 125 years ago, they believed that "with little prudence any man can soon get rich in Mich-i-gan." Will Keith Kellogg made a fortune in the business of breakfast cereals in Battle Creek. W.K. earned millions, gave away millions, and lived to 91 years of age. W.K. once made the interesting point that even though there were many successes in his life he never really learned to play like other young people.

Grand Rapids, called by some "Bland Rapids," pretty much minds its own business in West Michigan. The city's desire to be noticed became a little desperate in 1989 when Continental Airlines advertised that service to Cleveland would give a person the chance to connect to Tokyo, Mexico, and Europe.

Some would find a recommendation of Grand Rapids ludicrous, but maybe not. Start with some dreaming about the Ledyard Building (born 1874) and end with an evening at the sparkling clean Welsh Auditorium, born 58 years later.

Grand Rapids (pop. 190,000) is part of the Foundry,

although one Foundry trait, a black population of considerable size, seems to be missing. Ponder these things along the streets of Heritage Hill.

Grand Rapidians make a very comfortable contribution to baseball in America, namely ballpark seats. Think of G.R. the next time you see a rear end 22 inches across sitting down in a baseball park.

Luggage going to Grand Rapids is tagged "GRR," a label known best to Tony the Tiger, since Frosted Flakes are "GRReat" over in Battle Creek.

Not far from Grand Rapids is Kalamazoo (pop. 80,270), where a wide and heavy Elvis Presley was sighted (?) at the Burger King on South Westnedge some years back.

To paraphrase the Glenn Miller song, the sweetest gal in Kalamazoo may be the one who brings jobs with her upon arriving and convinces one and all that Kalamazoo is a nice place in which to live.

Western Michigan University in Kalamazoo does a nice job, although the school frequently is just a brief stop on the way up to a bigger university.

This book should not be tough on Grand Rapids or Kalamazoo because the living is very pleasant in those places.

Certainly the wealthy in Grand Beach do not snicker at anything about life in the southwest corner of the state. In fact, they brag that if you squint a little you can see the Sears Tower across Lake Michigan in Chicago. Television signals, values, and attitudes come to Grand Beach from Chicago, one time zone away.

A long way from southwest Michigan is the Upper Peninsula, not to mention deep and large Lake Superior (31,700 square miles). The area receives many visitors in the summer.

The city of Marquette in the UP is not one that makes the news often, but its main value may be religious. If you look out at Superior you may want to say a prayer or two for the 29 men who perished in November 1975 aboard the Edmund Fitzgerald. The gales of November come early, we are reminded.

Lake Superior can be lovely. It can be treacherous, too.

Not far from Marquette is the Michigan Iron Industry Museum, a part of a "world" in Michigan that many Detroit people never see.

The ads have it right about the Upper Peninsula. They say, "If a person is truly a product of his environment, imagine what a week here could do."

To the east of Marquette are Sault Ste. Marie, Michigan and Sault Ste. Marie, Ontario, and the Michigan side has Lake Superior State University, home of the Unicorn Hunters, a group that scrutinizes the poetry of Gordon Lightfoot, every day usage, and technical words not always used correctly. Phrases like "living in poverty," "alternative lifestyle," and "safe sex," they say, should be banished. Bring heavy clothes in October.

Do not snicker at the reference to language in Sault Ste. Marie, Michigan, for there is trouble aplenty on the Canadian side in Sault Ste. Marie, Ontario. The problems are not centered around terms like "safe sex," but have to do with French and English. The reality is that not everyone on the Canadian side speaks French, but French-only laws have created more than a little havoc, since English is the language of commerce, education, the daily newspaper, and youth hockey. The so-called language police might be called in any day to correct this problem.

Down the road from the Soo is Emmet County, a place which once identified itself as part of Upper Lower Michigan.

Upper and lower and up from down are not problematic for the practical types who inhabit Leelanau County, a few bays down from Emmet County. A true lover of Leelanau County and environs writes, "On this back road the land has the juice taken out of it:/stump fences surround nothing worth tearing down/by a deserted filling station/a Veedol sign, the rusted hulk/of a Frazer, 'live bait' on battered tin? A barn with half a tobacco ad owns the greenness of a manure pile." The region

is full of what someone once called "small marginal farms."
Back to a big city?

Enough tears were shed in East Lansing to flood old Jenison Fieldhouse at Michigan State University when it was announced that the Lansing Playboy Club was closing in 1988. Like the Fuller Brush man and the black-and-white television, "Amanda" and "Bobbi" vanished into history. Poor David Olds, photographer, was given the enviable task of photographing "Bobbi" (blond and with a bow tie) as time ran out.

In Ann Arbor the University of Michigan plays serious football. The stadium for football seats 102,501. Sellouts are common.

The words of Fielding H. Yost, who arrived in Ann Arbor in 1901, tell an important story. He once said, "If football answered no other (need) than of drawing the hundreds of thousands into the open air, away from offices and shops, drawing rooms and clubs, for a few health-giving hours, this would be reason enough for its existence." (On the other hand, a faculty committee was raising questions about football at Michigan as far back as 1926. The committee's report said, "there must be no state within the state, no athletic system independent of the educational system.")

As this book went to press the UM football coffers were bulging.

UM administrators have to be on their toes. In 1989 some white students claimed that they needed an alternative to Black History Month, so posters went up announcing "White Pride Week." The occasion was said to be a celebration of "yachts, sailboats, navy blazers, cool white presidents, all the kids we know are our own, polo stuff, L. L. Bean, Land's End, and plantations." The incident made racial and ethnic "experts" run for their desks to study the problem.

Feelings about football between UM and Ohio State University run so high that a mapmaker in 1979 inserted the town of "goblu" on the map near Toledo, Ohio, as well as the town of "beatosu" near Wauseon, Ohio.

Raise your hand if you remember the Ann Arbor debate about standard English and Black English in 1979.

Back to rural life? Return to southwestern Michigan.

Visit the "Banana Belt" (Allegan, Van Buren, Cass, and Berrien counties in Michigan, along with St. Joseph, LaPorte, and Porter counties in Indiana). Skiers invented the term. Notice the Chicagoans in Dowagiac.

Try the apples in Bangor, the strawberries in Hartford, and the wine in Paw Paw. One copy of the *Benton Harbor-St. Joseph Herald-Palladium* will provide sufficient information.

Wall Street in Benton Harbor will never make anyone think of the street of the same name in New York, especially since Benton Harbor always seems to finish so low in *Money* magazine's annual lists of nice places to live.

It is only fair to finish on a positive note about Michigan, so now we will include the state's contributions to high school nicknames. Here are some great names, in David Letterman style:

10 Sun Valley Cutthroats	Ketchum, Idaho
9 Rising Sun Shiners	Rising Sun, Indiana
8 Winters Blizzards	Winters, Texas
7 Tell City Marksmen	Tell City, Indiana
6 Plymouth Rocks	Plymouth, Michigan
5 Bad Axe Hatchets	Bad Axe, Michigan
4 Teutopolis Wooden Shoes	Teutopolis, Illinois
3 Mt. Clemens Battling Bathers	Mt. Clemens, Michigan
2 Hobart Brickies	Hobart, Indiana
1 Granite Falls Kilowatts	Granite Falls, Minnesota

Some will argue that there are other neat names that were not mentioned (e.g. the Cornjerkers of Hoopeston-East Lynn in Illinois), but so be it. Michigan does a nice job nevertheless.

Enjoy Michigan.

Reservations are now being taken for visits to the ghost towns of Wilson and Marlborough.

Did you think that Michigan had so much in it? Bet not.

Wisconsin

Escape To or From?

Quiet, forested Wisconsin is a good place to go for a little vacation.

One can look forward to a time of cold beer, some tasty cheese, and listening to the call of the loon in the Northwoods (e.g. Mercer, in Iron County, a favorite hangout of Ralph "Bottles" Capone, Al's brother).

With thoughts like those swirling in the head, is it any wonder that the heart skips a beat as the plane is landing in Milwaukee?

The Northwoods are, we know, one of the really pretty places in the United States.

Wait a minute.

Milwaukee is not the place to hear the call of the loon. Nor is the city of Milwaukee forested.

What's the problem? What is happening to the nice vacation?

Where is the lacustrine glacial heritage that Wisconsin brags about?

How about the vast fluvial erosion surfaces?

Where is the boundary separating forest from prairie?

The problem is that if a person draws a line from Kenosha to Green Bay (and even beyond), one will notice that one is looking at tool and die heaven (aka the Foundry) on that line and to the right of it. One is culturally removed from the Northwoods. One is not in the profitable "Paper Valley" (Neenah, Menasha, Appleton), either.

What to do now?

Let's make a stop in the restroom at the airport. The presence of Kohler plumbing parts, a familiar Wisconsin "landmark," will make us feel better maybe.

Get in the rent-a-car and head west. Then head north. Then head west, and then head north. At last one finds the Northwoods.

To get a grasp of things in the Northwoods get a copy of *The Clam Lake Papers* by Edward Lueders.
Where are the Northwoods?
Get a Wisconsin map and look for Vilas County.

Or get a map, find Milwaukee, and draw a line from Milwaukee to Wausau to Rhinelander. Continue the line past Wausau, then stop. You're now in the Northwoods, and you will spend a nice time, never to hear the name of the state's most populated city (Milwaukee) or the place where the big university is (Madison). Those places are too wild for people in the Northwoods.

A few days in the woods will be filled with out-of-the-way cabins, pin-drop acoustics, lonely roads, and, in the winter, considerable snow.

Notepads are available for purchase, too.

To the south and west of previously mentioned Vilas County is Rusk County, home to many Chippewa Indians and home to some controversy. It has turned out that Kennecott Copper people would love to do some digging in Rusk County. It has also turned out that the Indians (and some others) would like to live without the digging. The people who oppose the digging do not want to be similar to the many places which dot the Wisconsin-Minnesota border nearby, like Bessemer, Ironwood, Iron Belt, Iron River, and Iron Mountain. In this scene it is farm versus factory, Foundry versus Breadbasket all over again.

It is not far from Vilas County over to Ashland County, a place where Wisconsin logging enjoys a storied reputation. It seems like only yesterday (1890 really) when Henry Sherry formed the Mineral Lake Lumber Company. Then there's the Mellen Lumber Company, too. You have to know your calked boots from your cant hooks in Ashland County, and it helps to know Wisconsin outpaced Michigan and Minnesota in 1899 in lumber production. This Northern Wisconsin-Upper Michigan area can be one for hearty, enduring souls only.

Very tough, too, is the fight between those wishing to keep the mining companies working in Wisconsin and those wishing that they leave the state. Counties like Price, Taylor, Forest, Lincoln, Rusk, Marathon, and Oneida tell us that names like Exxon and Chevron make large profits. Names without much financial backing say that the Flambeau River in Ladysmith will be wrecked. This is old news by now, of course.

Real news may be that the presence of clams in the area will tell the tale. It seems that the creatures indicate a lot about a river's viability by their presence or absence. Second, the arguing may end when someone decides who is telling the truth in their environmental impact statement and who is not.

One door south of Forest County is Oconto County, where picking the Copper Festival Queen is about as competitive as life there gets. Girls are judged on "poise, knowledge of Oconto, and the ability to give directions to people to get where they want to go." The sound you hear is a Stihl saw getting a little oil.

The oil probably came by truck from Milwaukee, home to about 625,000, and a place very different from Oconto County.

Milwaukee is a tool and die town from start to finish, and has some impressive figures. There are 1.6 million people in the Milwaukee-Racine metro area. Cold winters yield only 46 inches of snowfall per year.

Milwaukee's beauty is found in its ability to work hard, its desire to see that life exists beyond bowling "centers" (not alleys), and its use of Lake Michigan.

Milwaukee has a sizeable Polish population. Many remember with fondness the 1948 "coronation" of Frankie Yankovic at the Auditorium as King of Polka.

A short distance from the Auditorium downtown is the corner of Fourth and Kilbourn where blacks once attended church at St. Mark's. Many walk inattentively over the same ground today to attend events at the pretty Bradley Center.

Milwaukee people enjoy a good tussle with those from the

country's "third city," Chicago. History shows that beer barons from Milwaukee expanded their sales because of the Chicago Fire in 1871. Today Chicagoans get even by saying "O'Hare Airport" to Milwaukeeans.

Milwaukee people like it where they are: away from Chicago, away from Madison ("too many freaky college kids there"), and away from Green Bay ("not bad, but too cold").

A positive presence in Milwaukee for many years was Marquette University's Hank Raymonds. He functioned as assistant basketball coach to two men (the late Eddie Hickey and the live Al McGuire), as head coach, and as athletic director, all the while giving Marquette a first class look in all it did. Raymonds retired in April 1987.

Marquette University first opened its doors in 1881, but the first class graduated in 1887. Were the first graduates not applying themselves?

An agenda that is not found at Marquette University is present at the Harley-Davidson plant. Bikers bow when passing by. Happiness is a spin on a 988 Harley-Davidson softail.

Many people forget that Germans in Milwaukee once spoke German fluently and English reluctantly. Many cannot remember that German beer was considered at one time to be far superior to American beer. The reminders are given for those who think that today's newcomers are the only people who do not learn English quickly and "adapt."

Some will remember that Milwaukee, Cincinnati, and St. Louis were part of the "German Triangle of the West" about a century ago. A nice dissertation could be done about how the three shared a pastime (baseball), a beverage (beer), and a language other than English (German).

Delicious brats are obvious in Milwaukee, but not so obvious two hours north in Green Bay (pop. 96,000), home of the famous Packers football team and the "frozen tundra" of Lambeau Field.

For old timers Green Bay was the Beaumont Hotel (1909-

1963) downtown, the Hurlbut clock, and the Acme Packers football team.

For the younger crowd there is the Green Bay Packers team and pleasant, well-behaved people.

For both the young and the old there has been and still is a January high of about 22 degrees and a low of about 5 degrees. Some things never change.

Green Bay is a Foundry town, but a large black community that works in the factories seems to be missing. All rules have exceptions.

The people of Green Bay are well-behaved, especially if you look at the barrels marked "hot coals" at Lambeau Field. Open fires before Packers games are allowed. Such behavior is unthinkable in many other NFL franchises in the American Foundry (Cleveland, Buffalo, Pittsburgh, Chicago).

A Lithuanian Jew (Nate Abrams) was on the ground floor of the founding of the Packers, believe it or not. A Belgian boy (Curly Lambeau) and a son of a prominent family (George Whitney Calhoun) probably were not as instrumental as Abrams in the start-up of the team.

News involving the Oneida Indians in Green Bay will rarely be on the same page as news about the Packers.

Not far from Green Bay is pretty Door County, visited by French trader Pierre Esprit Radusson more than 300 years ago. The French "porte des morts" (English "door of the dead") describes the dangerous conditions caused by occasional choppy waters. Door County can be very nice.

A visit to Door County may allow visitors to see Wisconsinites who have large bodies. The state was ranked "the most obese" (Montana being the leanest) recently. It seems that cheese, butter, ice cream, and brats have made some Badgers a little heavy.

They are not too heavy, however, since they were the first across the goal line in sending in forms for the census in 1990 (Alabama was worst).

Wisconsin people must be pretty good at figures since the folks in Peshtigo, close to Door County, recall the terrible fire in Peshtigo in 1871 with great accuracy. The blaze devastated the town's paper mills, killed hundreds, and was "like a giant fireworks display." Another fire took place in Chicago the same day. The Chicago fire got the headlines, but the Peshtigo fire is well documented, too.

Madison (pop. 190,000) is the state capital, and is the home of the large University of Wisconsin.

Madison and Milwaukee were first connected to each other by rail in 1854.

In 1917 the University of Wisconsin defeated Marquette University 15-14 in basketball. Fireworks usually result when a team from one "nation" (the Foundry) meets a team from another "nation" (the Breadbasket).

Madison (aka "Madtown") is a very nice city, enjoying a reputation for low unemployment, good libraries, and decent public schools. Autumn can be gorgeous. Go to Camp Randall Stadium to enjoy a football game.

The word "isthmus" is a word memorized only in grade school, but it is an important word in Madison if you want to understand the city.

In 1992 the *Chicago Tribune* shared the news that in 1985 UW-Madison had counted 4l,000 publications received that year. The number matched the number of students on the campus, believe it or not.

The last liberal to do poorly in Madison was Abraham Lincoln, who lost the city in both of his presidential races.

Speaking of history, we should do homework about the Northwest Ordinance, not the Declaration of Independence, when visiting the library at UW-Madison. The document (born 1787) is "the highway over which poured the westward march of our civilization," according to Franklin D. Roosevelt.

When in Madison it is easy to get some information about a little-known gem in Wisconsin, the Ice Age National Scenic

Trail. If overnight backpacking is your thing, then several counties (Chippewa, Rusk, Langlade, Marathon) can be heaven. Wisconsin's glacial landforms are an interesting study if hiking almost 500 miles gets too tedious.

Eau Claire (pop. 57,000) is a place where you better know your shorthorns from your charolais from your herefords. That is to say nothing of your hempshires, yorkshires, berkshires, and durocs. On cold winter nights (42 inches of snow a year) the locals follow the very good Blugolds of UW-Eau Claire in the game of roundball.

South of Eau Claire is La Crosse, known to thousands who drink beer. Burned into the mind are the words "G. Heileman Brewing Company, La Crosse, Wisconsin." Those words come easy for people who receive Chicago radio stations.

In Wausau (30,600 folks) there seems to be both a Foundry and a Breadbasket feel to the place. Clues about the former include an emphasis on paper mills and a distrust of minorities. Evidence about the latter is found in a style that seldom intimidates. Contemplating this Jekyll and Hyde situation is best done at a baseball game at Athletic Park (born 1936).

The nice-sounding name of Appleton is synonymous with two of its native sons, Harry Houdini and Joe McCarthy. More current is the arrival in town of the John Birch Society. Watch what you say along College Avenue.

Not taking themselves as seriously as many Appleton types are those who live in Neenah. Everyone knows Neenah. It seems that almost every maintenance hole (not manhole!) cover in the country comes from the Neenah Foundry.

The Birchers in Appleton and the factory people in Neenah join the bib overalls people in Oshkosh at the local bowling centers. There are in the area the "most lanes per resident" as of 1990.

Oshkosh, b'gosh, is home to some "naturists" as well as to many bowlers. The so-called Naturist Society operates out of Oshkosh. "Clothing-optional" is a term to learn.

Would it have been easier to divide up Wisconsin into these

seven areas: Indian Head Country, Northwoods, Central Wisconsin River country, East Wisconsin Waters, Hidden Valleys, Southern Gateway, and Greater Milwaukee?

It matters little.

Let us end with some peace and quiet.

At the foot of Broad Street where it meets Wrigley Drive there is a good view of Lake Geneva (both the town and the lake itself). The most gorgeous time in Lake Geneva, the "Newport of the West," is a quiet fall afternoon, and the most ugly is watching the latest glassblowing shop move in during the spring. Main Street is a place of social conformity and diagonal parking.

For decades Lake Geneva and environs played an important role in the lives of many young people from Chicago. The place was a playground for those under 21 who could drink beer (Old Style?), attend a party, and inch home down Highway 12 back to Chicago. More than a few times the alcohol won.

Lastly, the letters WMMB do not indicate a radio station that gives Packers football updates or news about the latest fire in Milwaukee. The letters stand for Wisconsin Milk Marketing Board. To understand Wisconsin one must know these things. A little bit about screwdrivers doesn't hurt, either.

What is Wisconsin really like? It is probably like a small town of about 5,000 souls who have a quiet life away from the noise of a big city. Such is the case in Elkhorn, where the toughest task all day is finding an empty bench on the square downtown.

Joy in Elkhorn is found in examining the old Sprague Theater (opened 1928). Sadness is caused by fast-talking Chicagoans who talk of staying.

Elkhorn was jolted on July 19, 1933 when Roger Touhy and his boys were arrested after a traffic accident. Elkhorn's own Harry Ward and George "Spur" Wiswell nabbed the bums. The place has not seen such excitement since.

For excitement look for a sale on udder butter.

INDIANA

Wander ...

As this book wanders through Indiana, where English is most certainly the official language, there should be a question first.
Where should one begin?
In the much-publicized urban centers of Gary and Indianapolis?
In the beautiful and tranquil rural areas (e.g. Parke County)?
With the happenings along the Wabash?
Or in some of the southern counties like Gibson or Harrison or Switzerland, where Eastern Standard Time, Eastern Daylight Time, Central Standard Time, and Central Daylight Time cause fistfights among humans and confusion among cows?

Fistfights and confusion should be reserved for those who argue about the borders in Indiana which separate Dixie, the Breadbasket, and the Foundry. Indiana is, after all, "a hodgepodge of contradictory visions," according to Scott Russell Sanders.

Let us proceed alphabetically. That way no favoritism will be given to updated Indianapolis or to gritty Gary. We might learn about Indiana that "lovely are her moonlight rivers shadowed by the sycamores where the fragrant winds of summer play along the willowed shore" in the words of the official state poem.

Anderson (population 65,000) hopes that two events never occur again: the 22 percent unemployment rate in 1980 and the 1983 loss by one point to Connersville on the part of Anderson High. People in and around the Anderson High gym, called the Wigwam, were more despondent over that loss than anyone could ever have imagined. A chance to see the Indians in the future is just a dribble away, however.

Bloomington (pop. 52,000) is a very nice place to attend

college. Indiana University is there, of course, and it boasts of its basketball team under the direction of Robert Montgomery Knight. He has received almost every trophy in sight over the years, but his personality grates on more people than can fit into the Assembly Hall (cap. 17,505). Few remember that a galaxy of excellent basketball minds (Arad McCutchan at Evansville, John Wooden at Indiana State, Piggy Lambert at Purdue, and George Keogan at Notre Dame) knew the intricacies of basketball before Bob Knight.

On a different note, there is an activity around Bloomington (in Monroe County) which also is found in Bedford (in Lawrence County) which is seldom thought of these days, and that is the quarrying of limestone. Notice the Empire State Building in New York, the National Cathedral in Washington, and the Tribune Tower in Chicago. Ask about them in Monroe and Lawrence counties. It boggles the mind to know that when a slab of limestone is toppled to its side, a process called "turning the cut," the stone is seeing the rays of the sun for the first time in 300 million years. The children of "cutters" can be found at Indiana University.

Evansville is pleasant, but for many the city is equated with December 13, 1977 when the University of Evansville's plane crashed and killed all on board. The occasion was "the night it rained tears."

Loved ones buried in Evansville rest in peace at Oak Hill Cemetery (born 1853). Notice names like Goedeke and Heilman, as well as section 75A for blacks with names like Mose Higgins and Lethal Doyle. Put your notebook aside in section 19 in order to study the soundscape of Evansville.

A lot happens close to Evansville (pop. 126,270) but not necessarily in it. The city is not far from Nashville, Louisville, Indianapolis, Lexington, and St. Louis. This situation is well known to rock performers, baseball fans, and the World Wrestling Federation. Evansville's location and size seem to work against it.

Fairmount is the home of the late James Dean (203 East Washington), but the death of the actor does not prevent locals from feeling proud of their man. Dean was a basketball player (what else in Indiana?) for the Fairmount Quakers. He was successful on the forensics team. He was not a rebel in high school in the minds of any of his teachers. He died in 1955, but is very much remembered still.

Ft. Wayne (pop. 165,000) is the home of powerful WOWO (AM 1190) radio and legendary Johnny Appleseed, but there are some problems. The city's population is decreasing. Train service for passengers is a shadow of its former self (32 trains a day in 1956, fewer than 10 today). Big news involves which businesses are choosing to stay in town.

Ironic as it sounds, Ft. Wayne may be one of the proverbial "good place to raise kids" spots. Nature cooperates by sending snow on Christmas 43 percent of the time.

A good way to learn about Ft. Wayne people is to go to the Gun and Knife show at the Coliseum.

Franklin (pop. 13,000) is mentioned only to remind everyone that vernacular names do indeed matter. The Dixie Midwest Trucking Company is located in Franklin. The people there have both Dixie and Midwest values. (Author Nelson Campbell, furthermore, uses the term "Midwest/Near South" for this area. He is correct.)

Since the days of Adam and Eve the city of Gary (pop. 116,000) has been synonymous with steel, and the city will probably always be considered that way.

Gary, of course, is "a city built on sand...made from steel."

White senior citizens will remember steel plants, Tony Zale the boxer, and the old Falstaff brewery, while blacks the same age will recall the plants, too, as well as the athletic prowess of basketball stars Orsten Artis at Froebel High and Donald Crudup at Roosevelt.

The hottest topic for all people in Gary may be the addition of gaming. Drive down Broadway and decide for yourself.

A few Gary people want the world to know that aviation had some roots in Gary before Kitty Hawk, North Carolina. Octave Chanute worked with a glider along the dunes back in 1896, a few years before the Wright Brothers.

A Gary contribution to music has been the Jacksons, of course, who at one time recorded on, appropriately enough, the Steeltown label when they did "Let Me Carry Your Schoolbooks" in 1967. In 1968 they became the Jackson Five.

The black population of Gary is so vast today that it is difficult to picture white immigrants who worked the factories about 75 years ago. Ask about Hungary Row and Hunkeyville. Those who are "mill hunks" from Youngstown and Pittsburgh know exactly what is meant.

Those who love to step back into another time will truly enjoy the Hammond Civic Center, a building that has both rock-hard seats and ghosts. The ghosts look down from rafters made of steel (what else?). At the next quilt show you can easily imagine two young men boxing in the center of the building with the hope of escaping Hammond, a tired town.

Put a pin in the map near Hobart. A few times a year the place gets "six inches of partly sunny." That is a word to the wise.

Was not Huntington the home of Vice-President J. Danforth Quayle? He could tell us about Indiana people farming potatoes. Or was it "potatos"?

Leaving uncrowded Huntington gives a person an opportunity to think of some words in the Indiana lexicon: moonlight, sycamores, the Wabash, rhubarb, and buttermilk. The words bring to mind Hoagy Carmichael. The American landscape that many people yearn for can be found in those Hoosier things.

Indianapolis (pop. 740,000) is a mix of three cultures: Breadbasket, Foundry, and Dixie. Those coming to Indianapolis from the west can discuss corn futures and soybean meal at the Grain Dealers Mutual Insurance Company.

Those coming from the east can relate to Railroadmen's Federal Savings. Those from the south can discuss pushrod engines at the Speedway each May. The three groups meet around Monument Circle downtown.

It is easy to see that Indianapolis has been around for a while. The Madame C. J. Walker Building (opened 1927) and Hinkle Fieldhouse (opened 1928) are two easy examples of how the city has weathered the years fairly well.

All the world knows that Meridian Street in Indianapolis is quite the place today, but few realize that in the 1920's the 800 block of California Street was known as "the black Meridian Street." Colonial Revival homes are found along North Meridian.

Notice Lockefield Gardens, a nice place. Years ago it is where basketball player Oscar Robertson grew up. Robertson, born in Tennessee, tells of an impoverished childhood, but today urges blacks to "position themselves better" in society.

It is not easy to see progress over the years by the black community in Indianapolis, and to this day some still remember the marching and the promises of the 1960's. The city was fortunate to have Bobby Kennedy in town the day Martin Luther King was shot in 1968.

Some blacks and whites still remember *The Searchlight*, an organ of the Ku Klux Klan.

The Indy 804.6 is a big attraction every year. It is still called the Indy 500 for some reason.

Indianapolis for many may be a brief stop before moving up the ladder. A youngster of 17 years of age (hockey's Wayne Gretzky) did well there in the fall of 1978, and countless others have moved through Indianapolis on the way up, too.

Fans of Elvis Presley can't help falling into a mention of the King's final concert on this planet at Market Square Arena on June 26, 1977.

Indianapolis is not "big city" enough? Try to share that

opinion at the Indianapolis Museum of Art (established 1883). That is only 13 years younger than the Metropolitan Museum of Art in New York.

Visit Indianapolis, and you may be pleasantly surprised. Have lunch at the Weiss Deli (since 1920!), enjoy dinner at the St. Elmo Steak House (since 1902!), and watch a basketball game (what else?) at Market Square Arena (since 1974!).

A topic of considerable merit in Lincoln City is the life of Abraham Lincoln when he was 21 years of age. The discussion gets pretty fierce when people from both Kentucky and Illinois start arguing with Hoosiers about Mr. Lincoln. Very little happens in Lincoln City otherwise.

Between Lafayette and Lowell the snow can be brutal. Be careful, since civilization thins out a little. The barns one sees from the car window serve as a reminder that some of the high school basketball games can be "barnburners." (In Logan, Utah "cliffhangers" is the correct term.)

Michiana is another location that one should know about. It is the area where Indiana meets Michigan. Media people covering the area often give "bi-state temperatures." No one knows why "Indimich" is not used in place of "Michiana," but that may be too much for the locals in Sturgis, Michigan to ponder.

Nashville, or as some prefer "the other Nashville," is approximately 45 miles south of Indianapolis, and is a fun place to visit. It is in Brown County, known for its apple butter, and it is a focal point for historians who study a legendary desperado, John Dillinger. He would not recognize "the other Nashville" now.

Visiting Nashville in October is recommended, but be careful. Gridlock is a distinct possibility, and some of the quaint shops catering to tourists might get held up – Dillinger style! He stole $49,000 from banks in New Castle, Danville, Montpelier, and Indianapolis from June to September in 1933.

Newton County is quiet and not well known, which could

be two strikes against it. Not so many years ago some Chicago mobsters, living just a short drive away in Illinois, made an unauthorized deposit of two enemies in the rich soil of the county.

In the Southeast corner of Indiana is Richmond (pop. 38,000). To most people Richmond is a place on I-70 about 75 miles from Indianapolis, but to some others it is the place where Hoagy Carmichael recorded "Stardust". Notice along I-70 that "high up in the sky the little stars climb."

Little Seymour, in Jackson County, has something to make all westerners drool: buried treasure! Supposedly $96,000 in gold, currency, and government bonds are rumored to be hidden in the area. Locals brag about singer John Cougar Mellencamp, a native. Before Mellencamp, Seymour was the site of the first train robbery (1866) in this country.

South Bend is a quiet place except for the presence of the University of Notre Dame du Lac (born 1842). Do some research about the school's founder, Father Edward Sorin. The man was a postmaster, a papal diplomat, a farmer, a clarinet player, a publisher, an actor, and ferociously competitive at marbles.

Surprise your friends by telling them that Father Sorin was all of 28 years of age when he got Notre Dame started.

These days some Catholic conservatives think Notre Dame has lost its religious marbles, but it really has not. Academic life is frequently overshadowed by football, however.

The location of South Bend is important, especially to Chicagoans. It is about two hours east of Chicago, convenient for the many "ethnic Catholics" who love football. Chicagoans can buy the *Chicago Tribune* easily in South Bend, but not so easily the *Indianapolis Star*. It is almost like South Bend is a home away from home for the Chicago people.

Stay in South Bend after the game for inexpensive gasoline before heading back to Chicago.

Notre Dame football, believe it or not, is a difficult sell in much of Indiana, in part because Catholics and football fans are not found on every corner in the state. Only about 13 percent of Indiana is Catholic. Try talking Notre Dame football at the corner of Illinois Street and Ohio Street in Indianapolis. Deaf ears will also be noticed at 7th and Cherry in Terre Haute.

Notre Dame football is a powerful force nevertheless. Many people will pay a good price to see the Irish do their thing. The outcome may play second fiddle to the income.

The need to improve the football stadium is nothing new. In 1927 Knute Rockne wrote to the school's President, Father Walsh, and threatened to resign over inadequate facilities at Cartier Field.

Remember teacher Frank O'Malley at Notre Dame? He taught for decades and often said, "writing is an act of the real tasted with the mind and thought with the fingers." O'Malley's fingers also dealt with cigarettes and alcohol. He died too soon in 1974.

No mention of drinking in South Bend would be complete without mentioning the name of Drewry's beer. Many factory workers in South Bend have guzzled a few bottles of Drewry's.

South Bend's Polish who labor in factories and consume Drewry's can be spotted putting their money with their own – in the Sobieski Federal Savings and Loan.

The influence of Notre Dame is not only in South Bend, but also above it. For airline people the navigational fix for South Bend is "GIPER" (not "Gipper"), referring to George Gipp, the famous Notre Dame student.

The city of Terre Haute (HUF to pilots) reminds a person of a small section or two of Indianapolis, 70 miles away. Both have an Ohio Street that gets a lot of traffic. Both have many people familiar with soybeans. Indianapolis brags about how Highways 31 and 40 form an important crossroads, while Terre Haute talks about 40 and 41 (which becomes Chicago's

Lake Shore Drive up north). Terre Haute goes berserk, too, over basketball. A final similarity might be the presence of Eli Lilly, who mixed elixirs in Indianapolis in 1876.

Terre Haute stands alone, however, for its imposing court house. It will be around long after all of us have enjoyed our final Indiana schoolboy basketball game.

Some in Terre Haute want inexpensive real estate prices. Begin the search around South 13 1/2 Street. Yes, Terre Haute has such designations.

Utopia? No. There is not one in Indiana, although a few Utopian communities have sprung up there over the years.

Vincennes may be as good a place as any to study the Ku Klux Klan, a "patriotic, secret, social, benevolent order" according to its charter.

How to end this chapter? We can end it by adding our own research to the alphabetical list above.

How about touring the round barns in Fulton County?

Don't slurp the apple cider.

Ohio
Big in the Shoulders

Ohio is large.

Maybe the state is not in the top ten in square miles, and big deal if the state does not have as many people as it did years ago. Those things are important, to be sure, but one should not write off Ohio so quickly.

Even in the "remote" West one can see the contributions to American life made by Ohio. A safe manufactured by the Mosler Safe Company was spotted by this book's author in Ft. Collins, Colorado. Wherever one goes there seems to be proof that Ohio has been a major factor in American manufacturing.

Ohio tries to survive despite problems involving manufacturing jobs. The loss of people and jobs to the South and to the West, not to mention decaying buildings which dot Ohio's large cities, are hard pills to swallow. September 19, 1977 was Black Monday when many people lost their jobs in Youngstown.

Now a look at Ohio's cities.

First, there is Cleveland (pop. 505,600 in city), surpassed in numbers not long ago by Columbus (pop. 632,000 in city).

Cleveland is a great ethnic mix. The Hungarian community (Woodland Avenue and East 79th Street) is a good study in how Foundry people learned to be thrifty years ago upon arrival in the United States.

A few Cleveland Hungarians can be seen today spending a few dollars at the baseball games at Jacobs Field. The park is across the street from a Cleveland landmark, the Erie Street Cemetery.

Some might find irony in the name of the baseball team (the Indians) and the monument to "Joc-o-sot," a Sauk chief, in that cemetery.

Clevelanders who run the Rock and Roll Hall of Fame and Museum should remember the "crossing over" between blacks and whites in rock years ago. Elvis Presley sounded black to many listeners, while Frankie Lymon, a black, sounded white. Historians of rock recall a comment attributed to Sam Phillips about a search for a white man who could sing with "a Negro feel."

Very few today remember the newspapers years ago of black Cleveland. *The Gazette* (born 1883, died 1941) contains valuable information about blacks in Cleveland and elsewhere.

Second, over in Toledo (pop. 332,000) there are some of the same problems that Cleveland has, like image, jobs, and economic vitality. The image of Toledo took a blow a few years ago when visitors were handed a brochure listing numbers to call for rat and roach problems.

A good year in Toledo is when the Bassett Nut Company (born 1928) and other manufacturing companies make a few dollars.

A bad year is when tourism lags in the Old West End or at Tony Packo's Cafe.

An in-between year in Toledo takes place when only a few schools and churches shut down despite the hopes and prayers of (holy) Toledoans.

A classy Toledoan, John D. Sabrey, worked at the old Commodore Perry Motor Inn downtown from 1944 until 1965. Sabrey passed away in October 1990 at the age of 91. He made visitors feel at home in Toledo, regardless of the city's problems.

History shows that Samuel Clemens (aka Mark Twain) turned down a chance to live and work in Toledo in 1869. David Ross Locke (aka Petroleum V. Nasby) of the *Toledo Blade* and Clemens would have been quite a pair.

Third, there is Dayton, long a reservoir of inventors, inventions, and innovation. The city has a metro population of more than 800,000. It is an area where southern accents mix with northern ones.

Inventing in Dayton allows some of the factory-worn people there the chance to think of newer, brighter days, simply because inventing works that way. The radio was once thought of as a substitute for the telephone. No one saw the impact that the laser would have, either.

Dayton has a Midwest address, though its climate, time of day, and work force "walk, talk, and smell" Eastern (and more than a bit Southern!).

Dayton brags that it is the 8th largest 90-minute market in the country. A total of 4.1 million people can reach the city within 90 minutes.

A name who started in Dayton back in 1967 was Phil Donahue. His fans remember the show of January 26, 1977. Donahue's guest was future wife Marlo Thomas.

At the drop of a microphone Phil Donahue will relate the difficulties of trying to originate a television show from Dayton. It seems that executives think that only New York and Los Angeles are acceptable. Dayton should not feel bad since some of the high-ranking types also put Chicago in the same category. This is "coastal thinking," one is told.

Fourth, there is Cincinnati (pop. 380,000), not on either coast. The city is like a well-dressed uncle: organized, attractive still, and productive despite the years. The city was once the largest west of the Alleghenies and north of New Orleans.

City fathers and mothers announce that Cincinnati is within 600 miles of 62 percent of the country's population.

Hard work is the order of the day, as coal and other things sail past on the mighty Ohio River. Monies from doing business on the Ohio end up at the Fifth Third Bank at Fountain Square downtown.

That bank has seen a few "Proctoids" pass through. They are people who labor for Procter & Gamble. "Castroids" from San Francisco can understand the terminology.

Many Americans will go to their graves equating Cincinnati with former baseball star Pete Rose. He was known at one time as prisoner 01832-061. He produced 4,256 hits.

"Cinti," as signs call it, brags about its chili, an especially good treat when washed down by Hudepohl beer.

Black Cincinnati can tell us all about having "a fit of the blue devils." The blues (an emotion, a musical structure, a technique, and a way of life) have a long history in town.

How German is Zinzinnati? Ask those at St. Catherine of Siena Church in Westwood. One there will see what look like swastikas in the floor. Notice, also, the rehabbing in the section known as Over-the-Rhine.

A Prussian-born gardener, Adolph Strauch, did not have to rehab the Italian marble 135 years ago at Spring Grove Cemetery, a must for those into urban studies.

Geographer Joseph Brownell was correct in 1960 when he wrote that Cincinnati is part of the "peripheral Midwest," but not part of the Midwest that relates to Des Moines, Fargo, and Kansas City. Cincinnati people spend too much time in factories and in "ethnic churches" to be called real and true Midwest people.

Speaking of regions, Columbus brags to everyone that it is, in its own words, "the fastest growing city in the Northeast." In truth, it is a growing city in the northeast "quadrant" of the country, although Columbus to many people is in the Midwest. Some believe, further, that universities belonging to the Council of Ten Conference are all in the Midwest (including Penn State University?). Pick one of the labels (Northeast/Midwest/Foundry) that you like in order to describe Columbus.

More important probably is that Columbus is, in its words again, "free from recessions and rust." A robust economy is a big attraction. Think of those things as you eat at Wendy's, a Columbus fixture since November 15, 1969.

The fourth game of the 1943 World Series was played in Columbus. Not the game between the Yankees and the St. Louis Cardinals, but the Negro League World Series, of course.

Something smaller than Columbus?

Small Nelsonville is a place which is tied culturally to certain places in Minnesota. The connection is lumberjacking, and you better be pretty good with your Husqvarna 262 XP to impress people.

If you are north of Columbus on the way to, say, Cleveland, know that you are in Mohican Country when you see signs for

Mansfield, Mt. Vernon, or Loudonville. The Mohican area is comprised of five counties (Ashland, Holmes, Knox, Richland, and Wayne). The sound of a canoe paddle on the Mohican River in Loudonville can be lovely.

Mt. Vernon is a quiet place. The only controversy there involves whether or not black Northerners taught the song "Dixie" to a white minstrel, Daniel Decatur Emmett. Historians love the irony as well as the history.

Something larger than Mt. Vernon? The cities beckon once again.

Youngstown, the jewel of the Mahoning Valley and the snowiest of Ohio's major cities, is still feeling the effects of job loss, population loss, and foreign competition. Historians know that the blast furnace has an important role in Youngstown.

Youngstown had about 111,000 citizens in 1982, but only 95,700 in 1990. New ideas are desperately needed in Youngstown, and they will be chronicled in the *Youngstown Vindicator*.

Akron is not much to write home about, except that locals joke that staging a prayer revival (with tent) is a sure way to recoup financial losses. The city needs prayers and jobs.

In 1935 an important part of the history of Alcoholics Anonymous was written at the Mayflower Hotel in Akron. Since then thousands have been helped to sobriety one day at a time.

Down from Akron-Canton are Cadiz, East Cadiz, and Cadiz Junction, famous for very little except perhaps the birth of Clark Gable in Cadiz in 1901. Charleston Street in Cadiz should be noted. Gable died too soon in 1960.

Four people died too soon on May 4, 1970 at Kent State University "when the Age of Aquarius met the Ohio National Guard" at Kent. KSU is a quiet place these days, content to do some arguing about the size and the quality of the memorial to the 1970 happenings.

It is easier in Ohio to talk about professional football than about Kent State problems. Remember the old Portsmouth,

Ohio Spartans in the National Football League? The games today play a major role in American households.

Most know by now that the NFL was born in a Canton Hupmobile showroom in 1920. The American Professional Football Association became the NFL.

College football, a staple also in Ohio households through the years, has been criticized heavily at times for a variety of reasons. In 1894 seven players of the University of Michigan's starting team were not even enrolled as students! In 1905 a total of 23 deaths was tallied on the collegiate level, causing President Teddy Roosevelt to get pretty worried. Ellen Wilson, wife of President Woodrow, reported to friends that Princeton's loss to the University of Pennsylvania occasioned so much grief in her husband that only the election of Grover Cleveland as President that same week was able to take away Woodrow's gloom.

How much is football a part of Ohio life? Since 1941 every down of every NFL game has been played with a Wilson football, and you can see them being made at the plant in Ada.

In 1662 Charles II, King of England, declared that Connecticut should extend from sea to sea, but it did not work out that way. Connecticut's so-called Western Reserve is in Ohio, and the section encompasses 13 counties in the Northeast part of the state. To locate them just draw a line from Sandusky south to the bottom of Huron County. Now draw east to Youngstown. Go up from there to Conneaut, and follow the shore of Lake Erie back to Sandusky. Those who are into quilts and other things will have the time of their lives in Portage, Geauga, and Trumbull counties.

Part of the Western Reserve is Ashtabula. The joke is that a man slept one night with two women at the same time. He retired with his face to Grace and his ass to Beulah.

No laughter, however, was found in the city when Benjamin Ramirez, a football player for the Ashtabula High Panthers, was found dead of steroids in the late 1980's. The death shook the entire community.

Ashtabula must have a tough side to it since Mother

Hubbard's Cupboard is located there. The site was a station on the Underground Railroad. Catherine Hubbard should be studied seriously.

Ashtabula is the home of WFUN (AM 970) radio which says that Ashtabula County is on the "North Coast." This is serious. There is the North Coast Football Conference featuring Kenyon, Oberlin, and Wittenberg, among others.

While trying to learn about southern Ohio, it is best to go to one of the following counties: Monroe, Washington, Athens, Meigs, Gallia, Lawrence, Scioto, Adams, Brown, or Clermont. With a little inquiring one can learn a lot of the large Ohio (River) valley, a 981-mile trip from Pittsburgh to Cairo, Illinois. You'll learn about "where the West began" in Washington County, the old Coonskin Library in Athens, the Bob Evans company in Gallia, and noodle cutters in Scioto.

Finally, if you mix all there is and was up and down the Ohio Valley (a culture that is part Foundry, part Dixie, and always folksy) you get an interesting picture of people who enjoy the simple life by extracting oil (as in Tyler County, West Virginia) and by drinking liquor (as in the city of Bardstown, Kentucky and its famous distiller, E. C. Booz). Whittlers and blacksmiths (as in Jackson County, West Virginia) can be located, too. The Valley has given much over the years, including Mary Marshall.

Who is Mary Marshall? Just a woman who was born in Mason County, Kentucky in 1737. Her tombstone says, "She was good, not brilliant, useful, not ornamental, and the mother of 15."

Ohio, like Mary Marshall, keeps going.

The South

Old Times There

Ah, the South. Land of the largest event in human history, some say, the Civil War. The Late Unpleasantness, some people call it.

Yes, the South. The area that used to provide Presidents every so often.

Alas, the South. Home to the Grand Ole Opry, the Magnolia Trail, the Louisiana Superdome, Monticello, Vicksburg, Staunton, Hotlanta, gumbo, and sitting on the porch.

The South is more than just the land, we are told. The South is the memory, the phrase goes. Oliver Wendell Holmes once spoke of how "our hearts were touched with fire" years ago. There is in Dixie the constant need to remember those who have gone ahead.

The South is the land of myth, too, although scholars have been slow to pick up on that.

This chapter will be similar to the one about the West, wherein there was a listing of several short, snappy statements. The statements are to be picked and chosen for enjoyment and/or study. Do not go to your grave without knowing the American South in detail.

The South has really four subregions to it. Florida is the first. The New South (Virginia, the Carolinas, and Georgia) is the second. The Slower South (Alabama, Mississippi, Louisiana, Arkansas, and parts of Tennessee and Kentucky) is the third. Coal-based Appalachia (West Virginia, western Virginia, and eastern sections of Kentucky and Tennessee) is the fourth. Some will want Texas included herein, while others will want to divide Tennessee a little more.

The South is the land where football is king, although basketball does pretty well in Kentucky.

The South is the place where 20 percent of the state of Mississippi's revenues were spent on artificial limbs during the War for Southern Independence.

The South is the area of poor voter turnout.

The South is the area watched closely by the National Fire Protection Association. Not long ago the top eight states for fire fatalities were all in the South.

The South is the number one region for what geographers call "regional distinctiveness" and a consciousness thereof. New England and the Rocky Mountain West come next.

The South consists of the 12 states where a lady does not shake hands with a strange man. The South is the area of prospering cities and terribly poor countrysides (e.g. Fayette County, Mississippi).

The South is the land of considerable racism, America's

original sin. There are problems of class(ism), too.

The South was and is home to Andrew Jackson and Henry Clay, products of the Golden West of their time.

The South is the place where there were hundreds of lynchings (of both whites and blacks) between 1883 and 1959.

The South is where people vote "according to the way their daddy shot." The shooting, not parenthetically, was done by men in public engaged in war, a "masculine thing." Historians have paid little attention to the women back home who had to fight a different war.

The South is the area from which 1.3 million blacks fled during the 1940's.

The South is the place which says that every idea north of the 37th parallel is bad.

The South is red beans and rice after another football victory registered by Grambling State University.

The South is where a Civil Rights Commission found in 1958 that there were 40 counties in which not a single black person was registered to vote.

The South is home to many Indians.

The South is home to some good schools (Vanderbilt, Tulane, Duke, and North Carolina, to name a few), and some very mediocre ones.

The South is the place where things Southern and things Confederate come together. Realize that all Confederate things are Southern, but not all Southern things are Confederate.

The South is the place where a person bows to a sign saying "Southern Mills" on a laundry hamper featuring old Colonel Cottonblossom.

The South is where you can see cars whiz by with great speed in Daytona, Richmond, Rockingham, Atlanta, Darlington, Talladega, Charlotte, and Bristol. It is imperative to know the difference between the Goodwrench 500 and the

Goody's 500.

The South is the place where there are bitter feelings about how Southern life has been recorded and explained. Blacks see little importance mentioning the auctioning of slaves, while whites do not care to be reminded about who was doing the auctioning. Whites at times write the present back into the past, while the reverse holds true for blacks.

The South is also the place where the work ethic of slavery clashed with the way in which Christian baptism was interpreted. Receiving the sacrament was a renunciation of dance and witchcraft, not a feeling of liberation from the toll of original sin. The difference is significant.

What more can be said about the South?

It all depends on which South one means.

A case can be made that there is the new, romanticized, sanitized South, made immortal in film and music and elsewhere, and it can be said that there is the so-called Old South, filled with mosquitos, segregation, and delicious moon pies.

The discussion (arguing?) goes on and on, silhouetted against a background of change and growth, preference and prejudice, heroes and villains, criminals and victims, class conflict and racial jostling.

Which picture(s) of the South is accurate? It is hard to tell. There is always talk of the "New South" mentioned as far back as 1886 by an editor of the *Atlanta Constitution*.

The South is the area that has been changing so much. It seems like only yesterday when Strom Thurmond said in Birmingham, "There are not enough troops in the army to force the Southern people to break down segregation and admit the Negro race into our theatres, into our swimming pools, into our homes and into our churches." Those words are dated July 1948.

The South is also the area that never changes. It seems like only yesterday when Margie Smith, head of a tenants association, said in Atlanta, "This is a community regardless of the fact that it is public housing. The Olympics are going to be here three weeks. We've been here for years." Those words are dated August 1991.

One should not express shock, therefore, at the words of Ulrich B. Phillips. He has written about a central theme of Southern history, focusing on "a common resolve indomitably maintained" that the South be "a white man's country."

Our last task will be to ponder the talent drain suffered by the South. The area's strong desire to keep "a Southern way of life," joined by the feeling that the "Yankee North" does not have a clue, has created (reinforced?) an isolationism that makes participation in national affairs difficult. Might not the talent drain may be felt less, therefore? It seems that it is.

All aboard for Chattanooga.

Virginia

Residence of Presidents

Virginia is the land of Thomas Jefferson.

Virginia is the state where, if you lose your credit cards, your vacation could be history.

Virginia is a state of much history.

Yes, Virginia, there is much fascinating history to be studied long after this chapter is completed.

Here are just a few historical items about the Old Dominion. Put these in the memory.

In 1607 the first white man was seen in Virginia.

The winter of 1609-1610 was brutal.

In 1617 the first cargo of tobacco was sent to England.

In 1619 twenty slaves arrived in Jamestown.

Also in 1619, approximately 38 settlers gathered at Berkeley, thereby creating the first Thanksgiving. (Some around El Paso, Texas feel that they created Thanksgiving in 1598, while others in Massachusetts think that they did.)

In 1639 "all persons except Negroes" were to get arms and ammunition.

In 1648 missionary John Eliot wrote to London saying, "The Indians are not willing to come to live near to the English, because they have neither tools, nor skill, nor heart to fence their grounds, and if it be not well fenced their Corne is spoyled by the English cattle, which is a great discouragement to them and to me"!

In 1661 a law was passed that "in case any English servant shall run away in company of any Negroes" he would have to give special service for extra years to the master of the runaway Negro.

In 1667 there was inserted into the laws of Virginia an item which read that "...the conferring of baptisme doth not alter the condition of the person as to his bondage or freedom."

In 1676 Governor Berkeley wrote, "How miserable that

man is that Governes a People where six parts of seaven at least are Poore Endebted Discontented and Armed."

In 1691 the state of Virginia provided for the banishment of any "white man or woman being free who shall intermarry with a Negro, mulatto, or Indian man or woman or free."

In 1700 Virginia began a golden century. Names like Thomas Jefferson, Patrick Henry, George Washington, and James Madison will forever appear in our history books.

In 1763 about 170,000 people were slaves. That was about half the population of the state.

On March 28, 1771 a notice appeared in the Virginia Gazette saying, "Just arrived at Leedstown, The Ship Justitia, with about one Hundred Healthy Servants, Men Women & Boys...The Sale will commence on Tuesday the 2nd of April."

In 1788 Virginia became the tenth state.

In 1856 Woodrow Wilson was born in Staunton.

In April 1861 Virginia seceded from the Union.

In 1863 a place called West Virginia joined the Union.

In 1865 Lee surrendered to Grant, ending the War for Southern Independence.

In 1890 there was a baseball player in Richmond named Puss Ellyson. He was, according to local scribes, "all arms and legs like a spider." These days the University of Richmond has Spiders as its nickname.

In 1912 Woodrow Wilson became the eighth Virginian to take on the Presidency.

In 1959 Virginia accepted limited desegregation. The first school integration occurred in Arlington and Norfolk.

In 1968 Justice William J. Brennan, Jr. talked of racial discrimination being eliminated "root and branch."

In 1970 the census revealed that Virginia was about 63 percent urban compared to about 56 percent in 1960. Quite a shift.

In 1979 it was reported that 70 percent of the Old Dominion's mineral output was linked to coal mining.

In 1989 Virginia Military Institute chronicled some pretty ugly arguing about having females in the corps of cadets. VMI leaders felt that the presence of women would soften the training process too much. Even Stonewall Jackson would be afraid of that flammable situation.

In 1993 the Disney people had their eyes on Haymarket. The look was met with suspicion. Imagineering, a neologism for even the Disney people, would make slavery "come alive" (?) for visitors. Many Virginia people had their doubts.

It is easy to get the point now.

There is tremendous historical treasure in Virginia, although some places are being challenged by tourism and dollars. And we haven't even mentioned Monticello, Mount Vernon, Sherwood Forest, and Staunton.

Get a map now. A notepad, too.

Divide Virginia into six parts: Northern Virginia, the Eastern Shore, Central Virginia, the Shenandoah Valley, Tidewater and Hampton Roads, and the Southwestern Blue Ridge Highlands.

The plantations along the James River may be a nice place to start, but do not be shocked by some of the history. Slaves (or servants?) used to transport meals between the huge homes in an underground "whistling tunnel," so named because those in charge wanted to know that the servants (slaves?) were indeed whistling and not eating the food that they were carrying.

Virginia has some cities, too.

Richmond, not the most populated city in the state but the cradle of the old Confederacy nonetheless, has Monument Avenue and Main Street to its credit and some feelings of racism to its discredit. (Some get nervous about the lyrics in "Carry Me Back To Old Virginia.")

Black Richmonders may remember that Lumpkin's Jail, the pen on 15th street between Broad and Franklin, was turned into a school in 1867. The conversion was a high point in "race progress."

By 1903 there were four black-owned banks in Richmond. These days more changes are still happening.

The history of Richmond was changed in November 1989 when a black from the Church Hill neighborhood in Richmond was elected governor. L. Douglas Wilder said upon winning, "As a boy when I would read about an Abraham Lincoln, or a Thomas Jefferson, or a George Mason, when I would read that all men are created equal and that they are endowed by their Creator with certain inalienable rights...I knew it meant me."

An issue in the Old Dominion?

How about the doings at Manassas Battlefield?

Historian Richard Hofstadter tells us that Thomas Jefferson "had an almost compulsive love of counting, observing, and measuring." That talent of Mr. Jefferson would have come in handy when discussing Manassas Battlefield recently. Commercial interests clashed with Civil War history. So what if a mall paves over Stuart's Hill, the site of General Lee's camp back in about 1862? Is not progress more important than history? The fighting was fierce.

The history-development theme occurs time and again in Virginia, of course.

Go to the seven cities of Hampton Roads, if you want, for a more modern "spin" on life in Virginia. You will hear tremendous demographic numbers thrown around, and the living is pleasant.

Roanoke? It is not exactly the Shenandoah Valley, but it is not Surry County, either. Roanoke is pretty nice.

Lexington? Know about Robert E. Lee before entering. Know 19th century history as you walk Main Street.

Lynchburg? The living there is easy. The city is a stop on the Tour DuPont.

Arlington? Conservatives fight daily battles there. Liberals are asked to move on.

Danville? Ask about Ricky Van Shelton.

Staunton? See the Greek Revival buildings. Talk affectionately about the Statler Brothers.

Williamsburg? Be there for an 18th century Christmas. Walk more slowly than you would in Chicago or Omaha. That way you will blend in. (Historians will want to visit Charles City for Thanksgiving and Williamsburg for Christmas.)

Notice the Colonial Revival buildings in Williamsburg (pop. 15,000).

Winchester? Research the life of Patsy Cline.

Need a break from all this movement to and fro?

Take a few days at The Homestead in Hot Springs. The place is very nice, and it is one of many attractive spots to stay in the South. There is "quiet elegance embraced by majestic mountains" in the words of one writer.

Let us go to Charlottesville (41,000 folks) now that we have rested.

A man synonymous with Charlottesville once said, "Give up money, give up fame, give up science, give up the earth itself and all it contains rather than do an immoral act." Indeed the city looks like there has been no lack of morality. Manicured lawns, several rare book stores, a good university, and a busy Route 29 are to be noted. Charlottesville is moving along, thanks to God and Thomas Jefferson.

Jefferson once proposed that new states coming into the union should have names like Michigana, Illinoia, Saratoga, Chersonesus, Assenisipia, Polypotamia, and Metropotamia. Somehow Assenisipia does not make it. And imagine telling people that you live in Chicago, Polypotamia! Every American should thank God that Thomas Jefferson did not get his way with those names.

Every American should realize that history in Virginia pervades everything from cradle to grave. In fact, a funeral home in the Peninsula area brags that it has been around since 1759. (By contrast, the Grinsteiner Funeral Home in central Indiana thinks that it is old since it was established in 1854. That is yesterday by Virginia standards.)

How shall we end this chapter? It will end softly and without disturbance, a gesture no doubt appreciated by those in Virginia who do not want to see the state pushed and tugged beyond all recognition.

We neglected to mention baseball? Thomas Jefferson once wrote to Peter Carr in August 1785 that "games, played with the ball, and others of that nature, are too violent for the body and stamp no character on the mind." Could the history of Virginia not include the game of baseball? God forbid.

A cold apple along a stream in Rappahannock County might be a good ending to this section. Rappahannock hates traffic and air pollution, but loves large trees and non-alcoholic beverages. Quiet conversation does not hurt, either.

The people there? They have names like Hitt and Aylor, and have been in the area for ages. Be nice to them. As long as the deer population increases there will be friendly people in Rappahannock County.

The apples are not bad, either.

Welcome to Virginia.

WEST VIRGINIA
Some Assembly Required

West Virginia, one of the so-called "border south states," is a curious amalgam. There are a few good roads, many coal mines, a few farms, several hollows, two panhandles, many black lungs, a very important river, and, sadly, a future that looks difficult.

Approximately two million people inhabit the state now. The figure may change in the future.

Let us press on, realizing that some people feel that West Virginia may be the closest thing the United States has to a Third World country.

The first thing to figure out is the location of West (by God) Virginia, never to be confused with the state of Virginia.

To some West Virginia is in the East, but to others it is in the South. A disoriented few might even argue it is in the Midwest, but that is difficult.

The Federal Reserve in its "beige book" says that the Fifth District (headquarters: Richmond) includes "most of West Virginia." The Fourth District (headquarters: Cleveland) includes "Northern West Virginia."

Some would argue that West Virginia is to be labeled "South Atlantic," while a few would hold out for "Southeast." And to think there has been no mention of the Dixie/Foundry labels that appear elsewhere in this book.

Public Citizen refers to West Virginia as "Appalachian" when the group discusses low-level waste disposal.

Here's what to do.

Let's think of West Virginia as a little bit Southern and little bit Northern, kind of like the American Petroleum Institute does. The "top 90%" of the state would communicate with Cape May, New Jersey if there is a problem, while the "bottom 10%" would talk to Norfolk, Virginia. That may help.

Another thing that may help is to think that not all of West

Virginia is involved in coal mines. Mine disasters like the one at Monongah in December 1902 (361 people killed) tend to re-enforce the thinking that if one is from West Virginia one is from the mines. That is not necessarily true, of course.

Something from the world of music may tell us about life in West Virginia. Remember the late Red Sovine (1918-1980), a performer who gave us "Teddy Bear" and "Phantom 309"? Folks in Charleston and in Wheeling do, as well as those who listened years ago to the Louisiana Hayride on KWKH (AM 1130) in Shreveport. Sovine sang about the elementary things of life, like a boy needing a father and the need to relax after a hard day's work. Red touched the heart, was not trendy, and celebrated the lives of those who labor and "live hard" in West Virginia.

The relief that music provides is often the last thing on the minds of those who live in Mingo, McDowell, and Wyoming Counties. Paradise they are not. Hundreds have fled, and the forecast is not good. Some in McDowell County think that a landfill or a prison can help a sad economy.

Often a tragedy can speak volumes about the people of a given community, and one can point to Buffalo Creek in February 1972 as an excellent example of that. At that time 132 million gallons of debris-filled muddy water burst through a makeshift mining company dam and roared through the narrow hollow there. The people were tough enough to survive.

Survival is seen again in the words of Virgil Carrington Jones. He once wrote, "along the border of Kentucky and West Virginia, where the Tug Fork flows down to become a part of the Big Sandy, an amazing epic of mountain lore and hatred boiled up in the closing half of the century to leave behind it a trail of graves and burned homes." The words have to do with the Hatfields and the McCoys who know murder, disappearances, kidnapping, hatred, deception, arson, and other dastardly things when they see them. The Hatfields were associated with Logan County, West Virginia, and the McCoys with Pike County, Kentucky. Worth study is the Battle of Grapevine Creek as well as the life of William Anderson "Devil Anse" Hatfield.

The economy, good or bad, in Williamson (in Mingo County) does not get the attention of too many people, perhaps because anyone with ambition moves on after a short stay. Such was the case for a young kid in 1938 who played baseball for Williamson in the Mountain States League. The name was Stan Musial.

From Williamson one can get to places like Institute, Nitro, St. Albans, and South Charleston. The local phone book will show evacuation routes, courtesy of the phone book people as well as the National Institute for Chemical Studies.

The economy of West Virginia seems to need constant help, and the situation is made worse when the state is passed over so regularly. The Atlantic Coast Conference once revealed that Florida State University appeared much more attractive to the Conference than did West Virginia University. The reasons were that in the Mountaineer state there was not a newspaper with a circulation above 100,000, while the state of Florida sported seven with over 200,000 in circulation.

A look at some cities takes us to Morgantown (pop. 26,000). In 1772 Zackquill Morgan had some say there, but today West Virginia University holds most of the cards. Big issues include the fortunes of the Mountaineer football team and the Mountaineer rifle team.

Nothing unites WVU students like a contest against the hated University of Pittsburgh Panthers.

For homework stand in downtown Morgantown at the corner of High and Foundry. Study the old Dering Building (born 1896). One will see a gritty town.

The same is true of Clarksburg (pop. 18,000). Is the place part of the Foundry or part of Dixie? Where did all the Italian people come from? Why is there the big fuss about Stonewall

Jackson, since he is buried in Chancellorsville, Virginia? Why have so many in Clarksburg had such a difficult life? The questions are heavy.

Would a trip using Highway 50 to Parkersburg help our understanding? On the way to Parkersburg, while pondering the future of Clarksburg, try to identify all the roads which cross Highway 50. Raccoon Road. Dark Hollow Road. Bear Run Road. Flinderation Road. Dog Run Road. Dry Run Road. The list goes on.

Parkersburg (pop. 33,800) is having a tough time, too. A visit to the Blennerhasset Hotel may be the only item on the agenda.

No such limitations are found down the interstate in Charleston, the capital. The place has about 60,000 souls, a downtown that is "world class" compared to other Mountaineer cities, and an airport that will take one's breath away.

The airport was opened in December 1947. A car climbs and climbs to get to the parking lot. How the planes do it in bad weather is a mystery. Straight lines are thought to be gifts from God.

West Virginians may be easier to understand than the operations at the Charleston airport. It seems that Wheeling people relate to life in Pittsburgh and Columbus. Harper's Ferry types have been known to exude a big-city sophistication that drops the name of Washington, D.C. from time to time.

Only a few West Virginians can relate to fighting Satan in the mining town of Jolo, a part of much-mentioned McDowell County. Battles are waged with copperheads, water moccasins, and strychnine sipped from a Mason jar. Get ready for culture shock during a session of gospel boogie-woogie.

Where is West Virginia going?

Is the place "almost heaven"?

Will the state ever shed its appearance of being backward,

remote, and unattractive? It is hard to say.

A hero among Mountaineers might be Ana Jarvis. She began a campaign to start Mother's Day. She taught in the public schools. She was a church organist. She was moved by the death of her mother in 1905 to do something to honor all mothers.

West Virginia needs more like her.

Indeed the state's future does not look bright without hard-working people like Ana Jarvis.

North Carolina
Luv Those Heels!

"Ladies and gentlemen, the score is tied 70-70. Only two minutes remain. North Carolina is out of time-outs. Duke has the ball. What will the Tar Heels do? They need this game to win the ACC tournament title. What will happen? Stay tuned. Back after this commercial break."

North Carolina people will certainly give this book their attention after hearing that opening.

That scene, not very fictional, is music to the ears of the thousands and thousands of North Carolina people who love basketball. Every year attention is focused on these titanic battles, and with good reason. The quality of the basketball played is excellent.

Duke and UNC are fine on the hardcourt.

Let us look at some other things.

North Carolina is easily divided. There are the Mountains, the Upper Piedmont, Lower Piedmont, Northern Coast and Islands, and the Southern Coast and Islands. Think of those as you vacation in the Outer Banks or the Crystal Coast.

Let us forget right off the bat that the state of North Carolina is only a reservoir for Southern-born and Southern-bred hillbillies. Although one can still engage in hollerin' in Spivey's Corner, tobacco-spittin' in Clinton, and whistlin' in Louisburg, there nevertheless is a modern "feel" to the state that was not so obvious years ago. Some men sitting at a lunch counter in Greensboro in 1960 may have had something to do with the changes.

North Carolina is to be taken seriously by both the business community and the retirees, two long-standing Tar Heel family members.

Did we say Tar Heels?

Yes. Tar Heels!

History books show that on August 24, 1864 Major Joseph

Engelhard wrote a letter to a friend about a "Tar Heel fight" involving North Carolina troops. Also, none other than Robert E. Lee is reported to have said, "there they stand as if they have tar on their heels." Now you know the rest of the story.

Here are some "vital signs" that should be kept in mind to preserve North Carolina's place of prominence.

First, as the Sunbelt continues to draw people, one should be aware of some upcoming problems. Charlotte by 2005 will be number one in this country in traffic congestion.

Second, the smaller cities of the state may need to prepare themselves for newcomers who are not familiar with the Klan in Greensboro or with the lovely pottery in Seagrove.

Third, high tech and high hopes are making headlines these days, prompting one to ask if poultry barns and manufacturing are to be forgotten about in a state pretty familiar with both.

Fourth, certain cities will fight battles with the EPA, since Charlotte has too much ozone and Raleigh-Durham too much carbon monoxide. Environmental racism, a new term to some, will have to be tackled, too.

Fifth, projects at Research Triangle Park (near Duke, North Carolina State University, and UNC) will continue to make the news, thereby steering attention from rural areas like lovely Cumberland County. (Places like Cumberland may count this as a plus.)

Keep an eye on those five points.

Farming? Sampson County reported 896,710 hogs in 1992. That's more than Sioux County in Iowa or Cuming County in Nebraska.

Minorities? People at Duke University do not realize that Julian Francis Abele, a black architect with brilliant credentials, had a hand in designing some of the campus. These days the 12th Congressional District, mentioned below, impacts minorities, too. The battle continues.

The national pastime? See the corner of Corporation and Morris streets in Durham. The park was born in 1939. Home

runs have been measured at 121.9 meters.
Vernacular names? Ask for Tobacco Road. Notice how tobacco outruns cotton, corn, and soybeans in profitability.
An issue? One very touchy subject in the Tar Heel state is smoking, of course. Billions of dollars are involved. As they say in Pitt County, "tobacco is not just a crop. It is a way of life." North Carolinians point out how history books show that tobacco is as American as apple pie.
Some in (smoke-filled?) rooms along Tobacco Road could write an excellent article about how beer, baseball, and cigarettes were doing back in 1881.
Curiously, the Museum of Tobacco Art and History is not in the Carolinas or in Kentucky. It is in Nashville. Tobacco people there are soulmates of the Carolina people.
Cigarettes are no small item in North Carolina's urban areas.
Winston and Salem cigarettes come from Winston-Salem, a city synonymous with R. J. Reynolds Tobacco. Mr. Reynolds began the cigarette business about 120 years ago, and people in town are either working the second shift or working on the second million.
Cigarettes, however, may look small when compared to the racial gerrymandering in the 12th Congressional District. A drive along its 160 miles will reveal tobacco, furniture plants, retailing, and textile mills. Clear ideas about blacks and whites living near one another will be obvious, too.
Many Tar Heel agenda items meet in growing Charlotte (town) in Mecklenburg County. Cornwallis once remarked about Charlotte, "there's a rebel behind every bush" back about 1780. He was right.
Today Charlotte, a "cousin" of Atlanta, says that no task is too big for those in the area.
The city of Charlotte has 420,000 people and 734,210 television households today. A total of 1.2 million live in the area.
Some people in Charlotte are labeled "new-rich-Baptist-chic."

Sociologist David Goldfield once said that some people claim that New York never sleeps, but those same people should be aware that Charlotte never wakes.

Attracting attention are Charlotte Motor Speedway and the pro basketball Hornets. The arrival of the Hornets made people realize that 5.4 million people live within 100 miles of Charlotte (acceptable for basketball fans) and 9.7 million live within 150 miles (acceptable for football fans).

Charlotte brags that one half of the people in the United States live within one hour's flight time of the city.

What do you call people from Charlotte? Not charlatans, but Charlotteans. Charlatans, the joke has it, are those who sent money to Jim and Tammy Bakker a few years ago.

Considerable amounts of money, some religion, and an excellent education come together at Davidson College. The school is mentioned in the same breath with Duke, Vanderbilt, Tulane, North Carolina, and Virginia for academic excellence in Dixie. Davidson seems very happy to be an academic power, not an athletic one. Some Davidson people will be sad to see the bumper sticker that says, "Duke is expensive. Carolina is priceless."

Away from the cities of North Carolina one can see a return to popularity of the ancient art of storytelling. Although Jonesborough, Tennessee may get more publicity than Banner Elk, North Carolina, it is in Banner Elk where one can hear stories shared by the legendary Ray Hicks ("A girl had let me down. A good-looking girl but she was poor. I fixed her up, bought her a dress and slippers, and then the other boys wanted her...Long courtin' don't prosper, they say in the mountains."). Essential materials for good storytelling include a good memory, a good chair, and some Red Man.

Another complimentary word must go to those who live in Watauga County, home to interesting American folk songs. The songs reflect a world that most people rarely dream about. "Don Kelly's Girl" and "Gonna Keep My Skillet

Greasy" are two examples of the songs known to those in Mabel and in Todd.

The nice times produced by storytelling and singing can make one want to find Comfort, Harmony, Trust, Friendship, Loafer's Glory and Duck. Those places deliver what they say: comfort, harmony, etc. Folks from Rocky Comfort, Missouri can relate easily to the stories, the songs, and the barns.

A rougher time can be found in either Nags Head or Cape Fear when the rains come. You will wish that the National Climatic Data Center in Asheville had tipped you off a little earlier.

Or you may wish that you were living quietly at the Center for Creative Retirement in Asheville.

We might end with a trip to Bald Head Island. Notice the lighthouse. It first functioned in 1817.

Put down the notes.

Enjoy the quiet North Carolina breezes, but please do not come down.

The traffic in Charlotte is bad enough now.

Another (nice) home sold in Raleigh just confuses things.

Tennessee

Easy Does It

In this state both music and volunteers are highly prized, so we will begin with a quick test. Those with a perfect score will receive a free album featuring Roy Acuff and the Smoky Mountain Boys. Match these two columns:

1. "Thank God For Kids" A. written by John Loudermilk
2. "I'm Sorry" B. number 1 in Billboard magazine on July 18, 1960
3. "Then You Can Tell Me Goodbye" C. 1966 hit for Percy Sledge
4. "Crazy" D. written by Willie Nelson
5. "When a Man Loves a Woman" E. written by Eddie Raven

The answers are 1-E, 2-B, 3-A, 4-D, and 5-C.

If you got four correct, you receive a free picture of the Oak Ridge Boys. If you could get one right, you receive the chance to argue about how much money the World's Fair in Knoxville lost in 1982. If you got two right, or three, you receive a free tour of Kingsport and Bristol. If you do not care that much about music, say so now, and thereby forfeit your chance of falling in love with this pretty state.

Tennessee is divided easily into three parts: Western, Middle, and Eastern. Memphis is in the West. Nashville is in the Middle. Knoxville is in the East. Do not ever mix up the three. Many dear hearts and gentle people will become upset if you do.

It may be good here and now to point out that Memphis is in the Mid-South, Louisville in the Upper South, Birmingham in the Lower South, and Biloxi in the Coastal South. There is the Tropical South, also.

Let us look at some cities going west to east, although many people have moved the opposite way over the years.

If you are tapping your feet to Peetie Wheatstraw's "Kidnapper's Blues," you know for a fact that you are in

Memphis (pop. 650,300). The city has been home for many important people, not the least of whom was Ida Wells Barnett (1862-1931), chased from town for writing in a black newspaper that lynching was not a good way to handle social problems.

"In" for Memphians today are Elvis Presley and the desire to have an NFL football franchise. "In" also is a trip to Tunica County, Mississippi for some gambling. "Out" are liquor bottles smuggled around Beale Street (since approval of liquor by the drink in 1969).

Ida Wells Barnett should receive just as much ink as W.C. Handy and his "blue music." Her life seems to have been more difficult than his.

Memphis is the place where Detroit's Wilson Pickett was performing in the 1960's at Stax Records. One's notes also show that Elvis Presley sang Arthur Crudup's "That's All Right," too, in those days. Memphis, New Orleans and Detroit were connected in all of that.

Black Memphians who listened in the early 1950's to WDIA radio ("Dial 73") are familiar with Crudup, Pickett, Rufus Thomas and B. B. King. The station has a great history.

Memphian A.H. "Shorty" Addison deserves mention, too. He worked at the Peabody Hotel, among other places. He knew the high and the mighty (like Victor Borge and Harry Truman) and also knew some people who auctioned mules. "Shorty" died in Memphis in November 1991 at the age of 81. (The Illinois chapter of this book contains details about the life of Anderson "Shorty" Harris. Another cultural clone, if you will.)

Important music and nice people are not the only attraction in West Tennessee, since there was a skirmish of considerable magnitude years ago in Hardin County. At Shiloh National Military Park there are lessons aplenty about the Civil War.

In Middle Tennessee there is the state capitol, Nashville (pop. 516,900). As soon as one arrives at the airport there is notice given to all that Opryland is not far away. Much attention is given to tourists who spend thousands each year buying can openers with Tammy Wynette's picture on them.

Nashville is changing and updating, and has been doing so for several years.

Old Ryman Auditorium downtown is a must. Some students at Vanderbilt University have never let their imaginations go wild at Ryman. It was home to the Opry from 1943 until 1974.

Imaginations can do well, too, at the Hermitage, 12 miles east of town, where one can get a glimpse of the life of Andrew Jackson. Notice, too, the grave of "Alfred," a servant.

Nashville gets high marks for a number of things, not the least of which was the Black Family Summit in May 1984. The gathering was hosted by Fisk University, a school that exists in the shadow of mighty Vanderbilt.

Perhaps there are only two questions for Nashville people. Do we go pop or country, and do we like songs that have three chords or five? Many dollars ($1.7 billion in record sales in 1993) revolve around the answers to those questions.

The popularity of country music is extensive these days, probably as much for the message as for the sound. The statement is clear: a woman should stand by her man, and a man should tell and re-tell his woman that he loves her. That way both, if only for a few minutes per day, can make the world go away.

A good line from Nashville years ago was that Eddy Arnold owned half the place, and that he would have bought the other half if Roy Acuff had been willing to sell it to him. The joke gets a laugh in Branson, Missouri, a cultural "clone," too.

For many years Nashville music people have sung about cheating and drinking, which may make the world go away for a while, but those topics may be more difficult to find in Nashville songwriting in the future. The reason is that MADD and SADD members as well as those who educate about AIDS have asked people to take it easy with lyrics about getting intoxicated and/or sleeping around. The shift is a big change for Nashville, but one the music people can cope with.

Successfully coping in Nashville is Sarah Ophelia Colley Cannon (aka Miss Minnie Pearl). Always looking for "fellars," Minnie has entertained millions for decades. A neat line of Minnie's is that she was stopped by a "fellar" who had his hands all over her in his attempt to rob her. After a few minutes Minnie informed the man, "Keep that up and I will write you a check." Stay tuned for more stories from Grinder's Switch.

For every country singer or sideman in Nashville there are several who get discouraged and quit. The prospect of eating peanut butter and jelly sandwiches on the road for 15 years before making it big is too much for some people to endure. Oldtimers tell some amazing stories about life on the road.

Much of Nashville's music history, by the way, had roots in Chicago.

In the spring of 1924 there was the WLS (AM 890) "Barn Dance" broadcasting from the old Sherman House hotel at Randolph and Clark in Chicago.

However, George Hay, "The Solemn Old Judge," quit at WLS and headed for Nashville. There he started a "Barn Dance" on WSM (AM 650).

Hay proclaimed one night, "for the past hour you've been listening to Grand Opera. Now we will present Grand Old Opry"!

Since that time, of course, Nashville has prospered with country music, but Chicago's WLS has all but forgotten that the music exists. In May 1960 the station started playing rock and roll, only to see a competitor, WGN (AM 720), pick up the "Barn Dance" and stay with it (in one form or another) until 1971 when the show was put to rest completely.

Fans count November 28, 1925 as the starting point for

Opry broadcasts on radio in Nashville, although others count January 4, 1923 at WBAP (AM 820) in Fort Worth as the first Saturday evening broadcast of square dance music. (In 1925 Freeman Gosden and Charles Correll, later known for "Amos 'n' Andy," were working on WEBH radio from Chicago's Edgewater Beach Hotel. The medium was a sensation.)

Heroes and villains?

A curious character in Middle Tennessee history is Andrew Jackson, known as "Old Hickory" to many people and "Sharp Knife" to Indians. Jackson once said, "I suggest the propriety of setting apart an ample district west of the Mississippi...to be guaranteed to the Indian tribes, as long as they shall occupy it."

On the positive side the man was pragmatic, determined, clever, and resourceful.

On the negative he was a person of anger, violence, and self-righteousness.

Jackson was the first Irish Protestant President in history. His parents came from Carrickfergus in County Antrim.

If you are thirsty after studying about heroes and villains in Middle Tennessee, just go to Lynchburg, home to the Jack Daniel Distillery. Lem Motlow, nephew of Jack Daniel, coined the phrase, "all goods worth price charged" in 1907, and the rest is (sippin') history.

Using the same time as New York City, Knoxville in East Tennessee is where three Interstates (40, 75, 81) meet, and the city describes itself as "at the center of the Eastern half of the United States."

If that does not get your attention, then maybe the Fair in 1982 did. No, that did not go over too well, come to think of it.

Knoxville (pop. 165,000) is home to the University of Tennessee. The city and the school boast that about 75 percent of the country's population is situated within 500 miles of the city.

Geographical and/or marketing tidbits take on new meaning if you are in Gatlinburg or Pigeon Forge in October in a car with a non-relative 51 years old or older. That description makes retailers in Sevier County (which includes Dollywood!) drool. In 1990 a total of 553 gift shops were counted in the area.

If you leave Knoxville on Interstate 75 going southwest for about 110 miles you may end up in Onion Bottom, a part of Chattanooga (pop. 160,000). Visit on one of the 213 sunny days per year.

Nice days in Chattanooga make for good baseball weather, especially for the Chattanooga Lookouts at Engel Stadium (born 1930).

The park is named after Joe Engel (1893-1969). He was known as the "Barnum of the Bushes." He believed that baseball belonged to the people, not to corporate moguls. Engel lifted his eyebrows, to say the least, when in 1932 he was informed that Atlanta had passed a law requiring black and white baseball teams to play at least two blocks apart.

Engel Stadium today has it all. Ask about the entrance used by blacks years ago. (The author of this book was talking at Engel a few years ago with some Chattanooga lawyers about life in Dixie. A question was asked about similarities between East Tennessee and southern West Virginia. The lawyers responded that West Virginia is *not* part of the South at all. The author mentioned that only 263 nautical miles separate Chattanooga and Charleston, West Virginia. The men gave no ground at all. They obviously had not heard of the Hotel Dixie in the lives of blacks in West Virginia in the 1920's.)

Everyone knows the line about cotton being king in Chattanooga and iron being the prime minister. How many Chattanoogans, however, can find a maintenance hole cover that says "Acheson Foundry and Machine Works Chattanooga" in the city? Look near Engel Stadium for starters.

Going back to Knoxville for a moment (which many Tennesseeans do daily) one should know that people there love to go to gigantic Neyland Stadium (cap. 91,110) for football when the University of Tennessee Volunteers play. Notice the river. Tailgate there. Or, if you want, "watergate."

Truckers may be the best people to talk to about life in "K-town."

Now, with truckers and football fans happy, our notes are complete.

Maybe this chapter will end on a note that may surprise a few people, and that is that Tennessee and Japan have been seen in public together. Not long ago school children in Tennessee were being asked to write essays concerning the two places collaborating, in their words, "toward a new century." The effort may bear fruit.

Volunteers are being asked to look into the idea.

Kentucky

The Flag Is Up!

As luck or fate would have it, the writing of this chapter was a lot like the state of Kentucky itself. The writing was pleasant, peaceful, and leisurely paced.

Kentucky has good size (40,000 square miles) and is adequately populated (3.6 million folks). From quiet Frankfort, which few realize is the state capital, to grimy Coalgood, the living is, look away, pretty nice.

Find time for a vacation in Kentucky. You'll have a good time "when the corn top's ripe and the meadow is in bloom."

Kentucky cities are worth a look.

Louisville (pronounced LOOH-uh-vuhl) is an Ohio River town certainly, and the city has a Southern feel to it. The south side is really the South End. Notice the mint julep.

One decision in Louisville (pop. 270,000) is crucial, and that is whether to root for the University of Louisville in men's basketball or to root for the University of Kentucky in Lexington. No one is for both. It must be one or the other. Louisville people loved it in 1988-1989 when the University of Kentucky had a losing season. That last happened when Babe Ruth, Calvin Coolidge, and Jack Dempsey were getting headlines in 1927.

The history of Louisville shows that newspapers there were for decades synonymous with the Bingham family, and some very sad tales are found therein. Wealth, power, and large egos contributed to a host of problems, prompting many articles and a few books.

Architecture students will run faster than Secretariat (1:59 and two-fifths over a mile and a quarter!) to study the buildings along the 200 block of West Market Street downtown. Face away from the store which advertises "Drive In Whiskey."

There are some in Louisville who think about baseball,

especially those who think about Louisville Slugger wooden bats. The first Slugger came out in 1884. What could possibly feel better in the hands than a M159 Louisville Slugger, the one Stan Musial endorses? To the chagrin of many Kentuckians the bats are made in Jeffersonville, Indiana.

Not mentioned too often in the Louisville press is that many of the early Kentucky Derby winners were black men, like Isaac Murphy who won the Derby in 1890. The lineage of the horses was well noted then, not the skin color of the jockeys. Blacks were skilled jockeys years ago.

Moses Fleetwood Walker was one skilled (black) major league baseball player back in 1884 in Louisville, although the *Courier-Journal* of May 2, 1884 says that the pressure was too much for him. He now is in a Hall of Fame or two, however.

In Lexington, 75 miles from Louisville, blacks now play basketball in Rupp Arena for the University of Kentucky. Acquiring a ticket to Rupp for a game is very difficult.

The next best thing to do is listen on radio, or just talk to the legendary Cawood Ledford. He remembers it all, from the loss in 1966 to Texas Western College (with its black players) to the winning of the 1975 title. There have been some interesting moments in between, like UK's loss to Marquette in 1969 (with another racial storyline). Ledford stepped down in 1992 after 39 years behind the microphone. When he started there were only four stations carrying UK basketball. A total of 102 were carrying the games when Cawood Ledford quit.

Catching the attention of Cawood Ledford was the addition a few years ago of Bernadette Locke as a volunteer assistant coach. The lifting of eyebrows took place because Locke is a woman, and a black one at that.

Kentucky and Indiana both love basketball, and each place has a sense of humor, too. Kentucky people ask what word describes a sixteen-year-old in third grade in Indiana. "Gifted," Kentuckians respond. Hoosiers retort that driver's education is taught in Kentucky only on Mondays, Tuesdays, and Fridays, since on the other days the cars are needed for sex education. The joking goes on and on, although when it comes to arguing over control of the Ohio River the fighting can be real.

To see a real fight between Bluegrass people and Hoosiers just attend an all-star basketball game involving schoolboys. The sparks really fly. Male High in Louisville, Tilghman in Paducah, and Boone County represent Kentucky well. Indiana can counter with schools like East Chicago Roosevelt and Indianapolis Broad Ripple. Hold on to your seats.

One touchy issue in the Bluegrass state is the "foreign invasion" of the state by those from places like Dusseldorf and Dubai. In the counties of Fayette, Scott, Clark, Jessamine, Madison, Woodford, and Bourbon (the so-called "inner Bluegrass") it seems that Kentucky people get nervous when names like Mahmoud and Moustapha appear in the column marked "owner of the tract." Many Kentuckians consider the change a terrible cultural shift. Cannot owners of horses and land bring in "outsiders" just like basketball coaches do?

No such tensions have been reported over in Bowling Green (pop. 41,000). The city reports that it sits less than 200 miles from Memphis, Birmingham, St. Louis, Indianapolis, and Cincinnati. (Bowling Green, Kentucky is never to be confused with Bowling Green, Ohio. Many living in the former would never admit that they ever even darkened the door of the latter. Dixie and the Foundry do not get along that well at times.)

A trip to the eastern part of "Kaintuck" and the "state" of Cumberland is imperative. The area is made up of three counties in Kentucky (Bell, Knox, and Harlan), three in Virginia (Lee, Wise, and Scott), and three in Tennessee (Claiborne, Hancock, and Hawkins). Locals have been trying to make tourism more popular. If the Derby, Virginia Beach, and the Grand Ole Opry get their share, why can't Cumberland?

Harlan County, named above, is remote, gritty, and unattractive. Many in Harlan County have sold their souls to the company store. Since 1912 more than 1,300 people have lost their lives in the coal mines.

Hazard, a part of Perry County, houses the Center for Rural Health. Staff members report that out-of-work people in Appalachia kill family first and strangers second.

Both impoverished whites and the children of former slaves can excel, however, at Berea College (born 1855). The school is good, but rarely receives any credit.

Kentuckians at times focus their attention on life in small places with interesting names, not schools. Notice Black Snake, Black Knat, Hazard, Paint Lick, Amos, Oscar, Ruth, Hi Hat, Viper, Hills and Dales, and Bugtussle. Texas has Lollipop and Michigan contains Hell, but Kentucky can say it does a good job nevertheless.

Speaking of Paducah, mentioned earlier, native son Irvin S. Cobb, says, "one encounters an agreeable blend of Western kindliness, and Northern enterprises, superimposed upon a Southern background. More chickens are fried, more hot biscuits are eaten, more corn pone is consumed...than in any town of like size in the commonwealth." Correct.

Is the city of Frankfort "an ideal location for those seeking metropolitan access"? Or would it be better to talk to natives on Capital Avenue and Third Street before heading over to see Daniel Boone's grave? Probably the latter, especially if a little bourbon is included.

In Frankfort head for 315 St. Clair Street downtown and sip your coffee slowly. That way you can dream about the thousands and thousands who have passed through the area in Southern, laidback style. Laidback, someone said, "to the point of horizontal."

One more quick stop?

A possum's run from Lexington is Bourbon County, a place that would make anyone think of wooden casks and "white lightning" (the liquid as clear and as colorless as vodka). Have a drink and realize that whiskey which is about half alcohol and half water "proves," by means of a gunpowder test, to be the best proportion for human palates and bloodstreams. Now the word "proof" is understood a little better.

To the south and east of Lexington one can find Clay County. An article years ago described schoolboy basketball there with the words "Hills of Coal, Feats of Clay." That about says it.

The quintessential town in Kentucky?

How about the previously mentioned Bowling Green? Do some research about the Capitol Theatre in the morning. Eat some wonderful Southern food. Locate where people used to go "bowling on the green" at Fountain Square Park, and in the evening see the Western Kentucky University Hilltoppers do battle in basketball against Murray State University. You will know all about Bowling Green when the day is over.

To head southeast out of Bowling Green is to encounter very little except some excellent marble players in Monroe County, Kentucky and Clay County, Tennessee. A game of Rolley Hole can be fun.

This chapter might end with a stop in Eastern Kentucky in Letcher County. There one can look up the description of the 13 states which comprise Appalachia. The 397 counties can be a large workbench for those wishing to learn more about America. Not too long ago Columbiana County, Ohio asked to be included in the official boundaries of the Appalachian region.

Remember the words of Ulrich B. Phillips. He has written that the northern shore of the Ohio River is "American without question," but the southern is "American with a difference."

Look South.

Georgia
On Everyone's Mind

Georgia is well known by now.

The state has done its share over the years, having given the world the sublime (the presidency of Jimmy Carter) and the ridiculous (Atlanta Falcons football), the essential (the peanut) and maybe what is not so essential (Coca-Cola).

This chapter will be an amalgam of many Georgia highlights and lowlights, remembering all the time that Georgia is Dixie, where urban growth, a rollickin' good time, and a cold Doctor Pepper make the day more enjoyable. A game of football does not hurt, either.

Here are some names to put on nine sections of Georgia, with a city in a parenthesis to help things. There are the Magnolia Midlands (Statesville), Classic South (Augusta), Atlanta (no explanation needed), Colonial Coast (Savannah), Historic Heartland (Macon), North East Mountains (Helen), North West Mountains (Dalton), Plantation Trace (Valdosta), and Presidential Pathways (Columbus). The yellow dots should be spread around pretty dang good now.

There are some trails, too, which newcomers should know. They are Blue Gray, Andersonville, Peach Blossom, Chieftains, and Antebellum. Look those up. Now the yellow marker should be functioning real well.

As we head into Atlanta downtown looking for Peachtree Street let us start with some history about an Atlanta fixture, Coca-Cola. The drink has been called the "holy water of the American South."

Back in 1886 John Styth Pemberton concocted a syrup in a brass pot in his Atlanta backyard. Simple enough.

Americans drank gallons and truckloads of Coke.

Coke and Atlanta through the years practically became synonymous, although there were a few years when Wilmington, Delaware was the corporate headquarters.

However, Coke management not so long ago did the unthinkable. It changed the product (with the help of McCann-Erickson New York). The announcement came on April 23, 1985 that "the best has been made even better."

After weeks of phone calls and protests Coke changed its mind, however. On July 11, 1985 the people in charge admitted that they had made a mistake. Americans expressed a sigh of relief. Coke indeed was it(self) again.

The story above is told not to criticize Coke management, but to show that Atlanta and some people in it probably try to run before they can walk. Some think that the state of Georgia frequently does the same thing. Those two points should be kept in mind throughout this chapter.

For the record, and just for the fun of it, Coke is consumed over 300 million times daily. Atlanta likes that.

Big figures are part and parcel of the soft drink world, and large numbers find a home in Atlanta.

Let's take a look.

Atlanta is large (3.1 million in metro area). The city has been called "the New York of the South," and it is the capital of Dixie.

In the 1970's the city of Hotlanta tried everything it could to showcase itself, including the addition of pro hockey (remember the Flames?). The team now plays a bit north of Atlanta in Calgary, Alberta, Canada.

In the 1980's the population of Atlanta and the metro area continued to increase, thereby explaining how so many hotels and lounges in Florida could boast of a group "direct from Atlanta." Atlanta is a major supplier for the southeast.

On the down side, Atlanta is faced with certain negatives from time to time: highway congestion, high crime, and inflated land values. The move from beans and greens to "progress" is a lot for some to endure.

Aside from Atlanta and Georgia moving too quickly there is the problem that Atlanta does not reflect life in Georgia very well. The problem seems to be that some movers and shakers talk about the Georgia Dome, CNN, Underground Atlanta, and a vigorous economy, but seem to be forgetting what the rest of the state is doing. (The same phenomenon can be found in Hartford, Detroit, Chicago, and Providence, where the presence of one large city seems to call the tune for an entire state.)

One Atlanta problem that will not go away is the city's homeless. The situation became difficult during the Democratic National Convention in 1987. Many living under bridges were put out of the way of visiting dignitaries. Figures, of course, are hazy on this subject.

Regardless, Atlanta moves along.

But the rest of the state counts, too.

There is Augusta (pop. 45,000) where golf balls fly to and fro at Augusta National Golf Club ("rolling terrain, clay loam soil with bent grass greens and Bermuda grass tees and fairways"). The place is lovely, complete with great names for the various holes (Pink Dogwood, Chinese Fir, Holly). The Masters is played here, of course, and the event is approached with much care, precision, and love by all those involved. The potential cash value of a putt is played down by announcers. The name of the game is the game at The Masters, although the name itself makes some blacks bristle.

The name of the game along 13th Street in Augusta is poverty. Broken vodka bottles are easily visible. The nice names associated with holes at The Masters will be forgotten quickly after a trip down 13th Street.

The notes must include popular Gwinnett County (72,000 folks in 1970, but 300,000 now), a possum's run from Atlanta. Some notice racism as well as congested roads in Gwinnett.

The same may be said of Forsyth County, a place that may not have the population of Gwinnett County, but certainly the tension.

No such problems are found over in Macon, "the city of

white columns." About 120,000 souls live there amid cherry trees, several aerospace contracts, and a few cannonballs. Macon is in Middle Georgia, just to keep our directions straight.

Macon may jump out of Atlanta's shadow if Macon can take advantage of its music heritage. A "Motown South" may be exaggerating, but who knows? Otis Redding and Little Richard have Macon roots. Singer James Brown was honored by the city in October 1968.

If music history and white columns do not interest you in Macon, then head down Interstate 75 (toward Valdosta) and forget your troubles in Crisp County, not far from Coffee County and Bacon County. The names were picked up on by Rand McNally Company a few years ago, and the names do exist (Crisp and friends, not just Rand McNally!). Part of Coffee County meets part of Bacon County to form the bottom of Jeff Davis County. That's enough history to think about all the way to Valdosta and beyond.

As we go along some will want to play golf on one of Georgia's top 50 public (18-hole) golf courses. Start with Bacon Park in Savannah and end with Wallace Adams in McRae.

If we had moved up the Interstate going north from Atlanta we would have come across Dalton, an unhappy place. The unhappiness is due to so many young people not taking school seriously. The making of carpets provides salaries. Learning about the journals of Colonel William Rattles Plum does not. Some kids in Dalton are dragged up, not brought up.

Learning about how the Dalton area resembles western Pennsylvania may not make Georgians happy, either, but it is the truth. In fact, Walnut Avenue in Dalton is a carbon copy of the main road through Breezewood, Pennsylvania. That fact may make Georgians in Dalton choke on their pecans, not on peanuts.

Notice Royston, where baseball's Ty Cobb is buried. He

had a great career (.367 lifetime batting average), but many people did not like to be around him. Only 400 attended his funeral in 1961. Cobb at times remarked, "the world is lousy."

Today the name of Cobb brings to some people's minds the location where World Championship Wrestling (WCW), headquartered in Atlanta, puts on its "house shows" every few weeks, namely in the city of Marietta, a part of Cobb County.

More important is that Marietta is an "exurban boom town" not unlike Dallas/Richardson in Texas or Herndon/Manassas in Virginia. It is easy to snicker at a mention of WCW, but do not laugh at the letters "WTBS." They stand for the station owned by R. E. (Ted) Turner. Was it not just a few years ago that WTBS was WTCG?

Turner flipped the switch of CNN in June 1980, and the news has not been the same since.

GWTW is not to be taken lightly, either. *Gone With The Wind* is an incredible story, from the writing of it all the way to the author being struck by a taxi at 13th and Peachtree Streets in Atlanta.

Some black people may not be enthusiastic about *GWTW*. The film can be a reminder of some sad times.

Times both sad and glad are remembered by Atlanta blacks along Auburn Avenue, the city's version of Boston's Joy Street and Birmingham's Sixth Avenue North. Still alive are the words of Martin Luther King, Jr. at Ebenezer Baptist Church along Auburn Avenue.

The streets of Atlanta lead to the old Fulton Bag and Cotton Mill. Along Savannah Street life involves gap-toothed smiles, change for a Coke, and talking on the porch after supper. Many of Cabbagetown's residents cannot spell "Appalachian mill village," a tag that fits pretty well. Cabbagetown is similar culturally to Chicago's nearly defunct Mopetown.

Much history is found on Bay Street near the Cotton Exchange in Savannah (145,000 souls), 255 miles from Atlanta. Include Bull Street and Bonaventure Cemetery on the notepad. Savannahians are faced with a crime problem that hurts the good intentions found along River Street.

This book tries to mention some things not said elsewhere, so here and now Moon River, a part of Savannah, can be introduced. Moon River does exist. On Oglethorpe Avenue in Savannah ask about songwriter Johnny Mercer, born in Savannah. Ask also about the story of re-naming a river in order to honor the song. Decide for yourself if the river is wider than a mile.

In Savannah, too, visit Temple Mickve Israel, founded a mere five months after the founding of Savannah herself.

Visit Georgia real soon now.

From the old courthouse in Decatur to tennis on Jekyll Island one can have a real nice time.

Visit Atlanta, too. It calls the tune.

Alabama

White Bathroom, Colored Bathroom

Do you remember the year 1966?

Music was going from Liverpool to London to New York to San Francisco. The Baltimore Orioles were winning the American League pennant going away. Those born during the first half of the baby boom (between 1946 and 1955) will remember the details well.

As exciting as 1966 may have been for some, it is safe to say that the entire country was not enthralled with the Lovin' Spoonful on the Kama Sutra label.

In Alabama, to be sure, there were more serious issues to be considered.

A talk in Washington, D.C. in 1963 involving a dream stirred up the minds and hearts of some Alabamans.

There had been the Freedom Summer of 1964, when many Jews stood side by side with blacks to fight oppression and prejudice.

There was a Civil Rights Act in 1964.

There was the Economic Opportunity Act in 1964.

There was the Voting Rights Act in 1965, a year which had Jim Crow on the run, some say.

Was it really true that in 1965 there was not one registered black voter in Lowndes County?

Were not the ramifications of Brown v. Board of Education of Topeka (1954) played out at least a little in Alabama in 1966?

Author Mark Childress is correct when he says that Alabama is "afflicted with history." The state these days plods along, quietly and with a certain seriousness.

Who could blame the state for having a heavy heart these days?

There have been beatings, marches, whips, clubs, tear gas, insults, and hatred. The seven national football championships at the University of Alabama since 1960 look small next to such things.

Should we divide up Alabama in order to understand the state a little better? No. Dixie is a good label. Heart of Dixie may be better.

Let us start with some cities.

The term "Southern college town" fits Tuscaloosa, former capital, like a glove. From the historic Gorgas House to the Moody Music Building, the city (pop. 75,000) and the University of Alabama neatly overlap. The history alone is worth the trip, not to mention the biscuits, the football, and the ribs.

The biscuits are needed for strength when the Alabama Crimson Tide take the football field to administer a licking on visitors. Paul ("Bear") Bryant, a legend, coached the Tide from 1958 to 1982. The pressure on others to be as successful has been tremendous.

Next to Bryant-Denny Stadium there is a cemetery in which many former Alabama fans are buried. Even the dead must root for the Tide.

Those who survive must realize that a black homecoming queen is a possibility at the University of Alabama. There was some debate about that a while back.

All within Alabama must root for either Alabama or Auburn, by the way. Not both. One or the other. Kind of like Lafayette-Lehigh and Kentucky-Louisville.

A few brave souls say that they do not care for football in Alabama, and they point out that being ranked 49th in child care does not seem to penetrate the brains of those who are into football rivalries.

Auburn University is located in Auburn (pop. 34,000), and the school is into football, too. All hell breaks loose when students and others jam Jordan-Hare Stadium (cap. 85,000).

The ultimate game in the minds of many took place when Auburn defeated Alabama on December 2, 1989. Details are recalled easily over a can of soda.

Ask for the location of Toomer's Corner in Auburn when the Tigers win, and then get out of the way of those celebrating.

Why the mention at length of football?

Because the University of Alabama was winning Rose Bowls back in the 1920's when many Civil War veterans were still alive. Winning football games meant everything. Football gave the state something to be proud of.

Celebrating football victories at Auburn or at Alabama may look small when compared to celebrating gains in civil rights in Birmingham (pop. 266,000).

The city has been trying to catch up.

In the words of Martin Luther King concerning Birmingham, "fear and oppression were as thick in its atmosphere as the smog from its factories" back in 1963. One can learn a lot about Birmingham by reading the April 3, 1963 *Birmingham News* which shouted "New Day Dawns for Birmingham." A book or two can be written about that "new day."

Diamonds are not forever in Birmingham. Rickwood Field (born 1910) was the site of Willie Mays' first non-Negro league game in 1948. See Rickwood quickly. It may not last much longer.

Things that last may be a good subject to pursue in Selma (pop. 24,000). Memories still function concerning the struggle for voting rights. Photos of the beatings at the Pettus Bridge still exist. The life of William Rufus King, vice-president under Franklin Pierce, is well noted. Look for the corner where Dr. Martin Luther King Jr. Street meets Jeff Davis Avenue. Historians will love Selma.

In Montgomery (188,000 souls) one can read of history, too. Notice the plaque which quotes the Secretary of War of the Confederate States of America who spoke of "an effusion of blood" in April 1861 if the states were to fight one another.

Research in Montgomery reveals that there have been some

uneasy times there, going back to the visit of Alexis de Tocqueville in January 1832. He was told at that time, "there is no one here who is not carrying arms under his coat. In the smallest dispute, you pull out a knife or a pistol."

For homework in Montgomery find the place where Jefferson Davis was inaugurated President of the Confederate States of America in February 1861.

Montgomery has given the world several significant people in the modern era, including Nat "King" Cole. Aside from his nice music ("Unforgettable," "Smile"), one is well advised to remember what he said concerning the need for television to find sponsors many years ago. Cole told his wife, "Madison Avenue is afraid of the dark." He knew well the turf of which he spoke.

Nat Cole, in the words of the black Montgomery newspaper, "leaves to cherish his memory" thousands of people who enjoyed his singing.

Montgomery plays baseball at Paterson Field (born 1950). Across the street from the diamond is Oakwood Cemetery. Many fans watch the games in total peace.

The peace of Mobile gave way to the whirr of the cotton business years ago. Hiram Fuller in the 1850's noted how people there were encouraged to "buy cotton, sell cotton, think cotton, eat cotton, drink cotton, and dream cotton. They marry cotton wives, and unto them are born cotton children."

Mobile has given the world good baseball players in addition to good cotton. Satchell Paige was one. Everyone knows Paige's advice about diet ("avoid fried meats which angry up the blood"). Only a few are aware of his perspective about the anxiety of having to pitch a baseball ("if your stomach disputes you, lie down and pacify it with cool thoughts").

Some blacks who have passed through Mobile have not had the luxury to think about sports and games. E.M. Jones arrived in 1859 as a child to be sold for $800 in gold. A debt had to be paid. Jones' mother was heard to say at the sale, "Be good." The record shows that the Calhoun family was the new owner. Such stories are plentiful in Alabama.

Learn about Mobile by studying the court case labeled City of Mobile v. Bolden (1980). Compare and contrast indirect and direct discrimination.

Look at the history of hiring blacks in Mobile for shipbuilding jobs over the years. White in-migrants were faster hires than blacks at times.

Mobile (pop 197,000) may be a good place to increase one's awareness of the complex nature of the history of slavery. The record shows that slavery differed from place to place and from time to time. Not all slaves worked tobacco fields. Not all owners were profit-hungry savages. American-born slaves were frequently treated differently from African-born slaves. Some felt that slavery was certainly morally wrong, but not economically wrong. Investigate these things before tee time in Mobile.

Some success stories were born at Tuskegee during World War II. Many remember July 1948 well. That was when President Truman signed Executive Order 9981, officially integrating the military.

Some Tuskegee people remember the days when blacks had syphilis, but were told that they had "bad blood." The distrust of doctors continues there.

Where to end and how to end this chapter on Alabama? It is hard to say. Maybe one should remember the words above about the state being "afflicted with history."

Start the notes in Birmingham.

South Carolina

Historical Treasure

Remember those syllogisms taught in Logic class many years ago?

One syllogism might go like this.

South Carolinians are in love with the city of Charleston.

The tall man cutting grass at the Capitol in Columbia is one of about three million South Carolinians. Therefore, the tall man in Columbia is in love with Charleston.

Something like that.

There has to be a subject (the people of the Palmetto state), a predicate (working with rice? cotton? factories? tourism?), and a copula (a verb denoting progress? something that means jobs for everyone?).

But one must watch out for the dreaded thing called "the undistributed middle" (the Lowcountry versus the Upcountry?).

Unlike the perfect syllogism, South Carolina was not and is not perfectly ordered.

Years ago life may have been pleasant for those who supervised cotton mills, the allocation of welfare monies, and defense budgets, but life was not so pleasant for those in the rice fields and in the prisons. Poor S.A.T. scores have been noticed, too, in all of this.

There were "the rag tags, lintheads, and poor farmers," to use an old phrase.

There was "cultural strain," too, for those who said that rice could hold its own with cotton. English-born planters learned about growing rice by brushing shoulders with skillful slaves (who proved that acculturation goes two ways!).

Race, not to be confused with rice, has played no small role through the years in South Carolina.

In fact, race, class, role, jobs, status, and a smorgasbord of things (gender, too) come together easily in South Carolina.

Writer V. O. Key offers this scene involving cotton mills over the years. The owner first builds a church for his workers. Second, the owner puts the pastor on the payroll. Third, the pastor preaches about how the meek shall inherit the earth! (Small digression: a similar atmosphere has been noticed when studying Native Americans in the West. They claim that the Good Book was in the hands of the missionaries years ago, and that the land was in the possession of the people. Now, however, the people have the Book and the missionaries have the land. Another good "syllogism"!)

Religion in South Carolina deserves more mention. Not so many years ago the words "Catholic" and "immigrant" did not go over too well. One evangelist, Baxter F. McLendon, said that the recent arrivals were "a foreign brood of vultures with the smell of steerage on their carcasses."

Now for some cities.

Charleston (pop. 80,400) is big on fertilizer, history, architecture, and tourists these days, but has survived fires, storms, and some war in the past.

Charleston may be running behind the rest of the country, someone said? Perhaps the reason is that the city has been bypassed by "towns with 'Yankee' stamped on them."

Where better than in Charleston to contemplate the difference between dealing with the North by rail from Charleston versus dealing with the South by schooner 145 years ago? Those in Savannah and Norfolk should know the difference.

Author David Lamb once said that Charleston people "seem to stroll, not walk, and steep their accents in vats of honey." Check this out during a next visit to St. Michael's church, completed in 1761.

The pews and spires of Charleston are worth serious study. Notice pew number 43 in St. Michael's. George Washington prayed there in 1791. Robert E. Lee did so in 1861.

We should all pray that South Carolinians get along together. Africans and Europeans arrived in South Carolina at the same time. We all know the words of Mayesville native James McBride Dabbs. He has said, "through the process of history and the grace of God we have been made one people."

One people, girls and boys together, should arrive at the same time for class at The Citadel in Charleston, too, although the issue is not an easy one. A young lady was labeled "Mrs. Doubtgender" recently as she tried to be a part of the Corps of Cadets.

A walk in Charleston along the harbor on East Battery will make a person forget about gender issues at The Citadel. After the walk describe how Charleston is indeed an island, not attached to much of anything.

Great poetry can be written at the confluence of the Cooper and Ashley Rivers. Does the water really act like a mirror?

In Camden (pop. 6,600), for those who wish something smaller, both Sherman and Cornwallis have visited. The history of Camden begins in 1733. A hero is the late Richard Kirkland who lugged water to fellow soldiers after the Battle of Fredericksburg, Maryland.

Greenville (pop. 58,200) topped the charts recently in cocaine arrests.

A different story is noticed over in Columbia (pop. 103,000), home to the University of South Carolina Gamecocks. The city seems to be a good place for black businesses.

In Columbia do some research about Bantu place names in South Carolina (Lobeco, Wimbee, Cheeha, Wappoo, etc.). Ask why they are on some maps, but not all maps.

Business and pleasure are on the map near the golf courses of nice Myrtle Beach.

The gentle winds that move a golf ball can become powerful blasts occasionally. Talk to the people along King Street in Charleston about Hurricane Hugo for some grizzly details.

The weather is important in South Carolina.

In 1886 dozens died in an earthquake that visited Charleston. Keep that year 1886 in mind. The middle and the end of the

1880's are as far back as some blacks can trace their personal histories in the area. A warehouse in Charleston or dirt atop a levy over in Mississippi will probably be mentioned in the tracing.

At times over at Clemson University the yelling and screaming at athletic contests give way to quiet solitude. The quiet comes as people try to locate the graves of slaves. Similar studies take place in rural Jasper County, too, with the hope of piecing some items of black history together.

There is history in Ninety Six, a place mentioned by author William Trogdon (aka William Least Heat-Moon).

Baseball?

There is some in Spartanburg (pop. 43,700). (While guessing the humidity at game time, it may be good to realize that the level at which baseball is played usually matches the size of the local market. For example, Springfield in Illinois plays A baseball and has about 100,000 people, but Binghamton, New York plays AA with approximately 150,000 souls. Omaha is AAA with about 350,000 people. Prices increase accordingly.)

A South Carolina name "rediscovered" recently has been that of "Shoeless" Joe Jackson, born in Brandon Mills. He was a great baseball player, but was involved in the scandal of 1919. His batting (.356 lifetime average) overshadowed his limitations away from the diamond. He never won a batting title.

Do we look in vain for heroes and villains in South Carolina?

No.

None other than John C. Calhoun, born of Scotch-Irish parents, will more than suffice. He had quite an ego and loved a good verbal battle. Students should remember the words of William P. Trent. He has said that Calhoun "started with the conclusion he wanted and reasoned back to the premises...."

Kind of like the syllogism that opened this chapter, isn't it?

Enjoy the Palmetto state.

Mississippi

A Forest of Chimneys

Mississippi is perceived by some people to be a place that is quiet, poor, unskilled, and unattractive. Although most know that the capital is Jackson and that a good golf game can be found in Biloxi, there nevertheless seems to be a reluctance on the part of some to think of Mississippi, never mind to visit it.

Do humid days and old clapboard houses have something to do with that situation?

Did the fight for civil rights years ago in Mississippi make the hearts and minds of potential visitors weary?

Who knows?

Weary still is life today for many people in Mississippi. Getting a job can be difficult. There is prejudice, too. Memories recall the 1955 beating and death of Emmett Till, not to mention the reasons surrounding them.

A goal of this chapter will be to increase awareness a bit about the state, and maybe a little weariness will be lifted.

Several people who left Mississippi years ago for the North and have returned can tell us that Mississippi may be progressing, however slowly.

We will walk slowly in this section. Mississippians would like that.

Let's start our trip by getting a mention of poverty out of the way.

Memorize the following: "big critters have happily issued jagged knives leisurely (and) nimbly, proving quickly (that) sharp sticks touch Tony willingly yonder." The sentence means nothing, except that the first letter of each word stands for a poor county in Mississippi. The counties are Bolivar, Coahoma, Holmes, Humphreys, Issaquena, Jefferson, Kemper, Leflore, Noxubee, Panola, Quitman, Shatkey, Sunflower, Tallahatchie, Tunica, Wilkinson, and Yazoo.

Expect at least 33 percent of the residents of those counties to be living in (suffering in?) poverty.

Some writers have pointed out that Maine is poorer than Mississippi. Many Northerners always answer that Mississippi is the poorest state. Argue if you want.

On the heels of the mention about "serious poverty" one might as well say that poverty contributes to the state leading the nation in the category marked "deaths due to fires." Georgia, South Carolina and North Carolina join Ole Miss in this bad scenario. Too many 55-gallon drums of motor oil and too many portable heaters filled with wood, one is told.

It is almost impossible to overlook the dreadful figures that describe Mississippi's infant mortality rates. The score is perennially disturbing. Georgia, Alabama, South Carolina, and Louisiana should hang their heads in shame with Mississippi in this area.

Those from Mississippi who think that this chapter so far has been too critical should not run to the phone to complain. The facts are that 12.6 percent of Mississippi households do not have a telephone.

There must be a way out of these problems.

Could things change for the better if there were more black professionals in the state? In McComb, a part of Pike County, there is the feeling that professional role models are essential if a "new Mississippi" is ever to arrive. Locals report, however, that there is not a black doctor in the town (46 percent black), and it is frowned on when people try to recruit one.

Might gaming help?

Some people down in Harrison County and Jackson County have the opinion that the life labeled "beach tacky" is preferred over gaming every time.

Those in the north end of the state in Tunica County (the poorest in the nation?) will have a more positive opinion about gaming. The damage of wetlands is a sore subject, though.

Would leaving and coming back help?

Heading north for Memphis would look pretty good to a young man with musical talent. A guy could then head to Detroit and hope to latch on with the music people there. Add a few twirls and microphone flings to the choreography, and you never know what might happen. Money will take care of itself, the theory goes.

The journey above is not fiction, since the details mirror the life of Davis Eli Ruffin (aka David Ruffin, 1941-1991) of the Temptations. He was born in Meridian, Mississippi but died in Philadelphia (Pennsylvania, not Mississippi).

If the name of David Ruffin makes you take notice, then just consider these Mississippi names who excelled in music. Muddy Waters, Howlin' Wolf, Bo Diddley, Otis Rush, B.B. King, Elvis Presley, John Lee Hooker, Albert King, and Jimmy Reed. Those names make both a sideman and a headliner drool. They all moved on.

Moving up and moving on are suggested in the lyrics of the "blue music" that one finds in the 16 counties of the Delta. In places like Clarksdale, Indianola, Greenville, and Ruleville one can enjoy both Little Milton Campbell and pit-cooked pork. The history of the blues ("a botheration on your mind") is available on request in these parts as well as in Helena, Arkansas across the border. For the record, George Gershwin's note of appreciation to W. C. Handy is dated August 30, 1926.

The importance of the blues and the details of the lives of Mississippians who have moved out are known to some Chicagoans. Many blues performers have headed up Highway 61 to Memphis, and then proceeded (on other roads) another 400 miles to Chicago. Theresa's Lounge at 4801 S. Indiana (from 1953 to 1986) in Chicago hosted a great list of blues people. Junior Wells and Homesick James are examples. They got out, and some did not come back.

Do some research about what the term "black and blue" means in black autobiographies, by the way. The autobiographies may give some understanding about those who go and those who stay.

Getting to Chicago is easy, of course. Hop on the City of New Orleans train as it goes through Jackson, Durant, and other stops. Those who used to ride "two to a mule" will know the train schedule.

Above the hum of the train everyone should listen to the music of Bessie Smith. George Hoefer was correct when he said that one cannot listen to Bessie without hearing the reasons why Martin Luther King did not want to wait any more.

Some who waited, and got little for it, are buried in the Delta area. Some of the graves now sprout cotton.

What is one to do?

What would be reasons to stay?

Schools may be one reason, at the University of Mississippi, Mississippi State, Southern Mississippi, and Jackson State, located in Oxford, Starkville, Hattiesburg, and Jackson respectively. ("Ole Miss" refers to the University of Mississippi, of course, but the term was used by slaves for the mistress of a plantation. The plantation owner's daughter was "the young miss," and his wife was "the old miss." "Ole Miss" is, they say, the most deeply Southern way of saying "alma mater." Some minds wanted to know.)

Those four schools may be a firm first step toward a better life, and they sure can help everyone understand Mississippi life, although history may show us a thing or two we might not expect.

That history will mention the owning of black slaves by blacks many years ago. William Johnson was a businessman in Natchez in the 1840's. He sold a slave ("Steven") for $600 in 1843. Johnson was murdered in 1851.

Wait one minute.

There is a battle going on about the schools in Mississippi? Some claim that the schools could undergo some merging?

Would Mississippians profit from this?

Would not black schools would be "submerged"?
Are we to segregate? Desegregate? Integrate?
Here comes the weariness again.

Extra credit will be given for explaining the words of Joseph Lowery of the Southern Christian Leadership Conference. He said, "they seem to define desegregation as the systematic movement of all things black to all things white when we prefer to see it as the emphatic movement of all things wrong to all things right." Be specific in your answer.

Students of Brown v. Board of Education (1954) will jump in at this time, please.

All of the above can give a person a severe case of dizziness, if not a case of the blues.

Get ready to hear some insults, too. One is that NAACP stands for "niggers, alligators, apes, coons, and possums."

No one said a certain group would keep their activities klandestine.

The scene can be enough to make a person wish that the soon-arriving "New Mississippi," part of the much talked about "New South," would get here in a hurry.

That "New South" will have to come to grips, too, with the Mississippi Delta, a place called "the most Southern place on earth." Rev. Jesse Jackson once used the term "America's Ethiopia" when referring to certain parts of the area.

Maybe a few smaller things should be introduced to get our minds off all the serious stuff.

East Tupelo gave the world Elvis Presley. Many remember the day when the radio reported that Joe Esposito, road manager, could not revive Elvis in 1977. The King lives on, in a manner of speaking.

A place with a long history of both good and bad is Neshoba County, in the east-central part of the state. In 1840 there were 2,683 whites and 744 slaves living there, but by 1860 those figures were 6,131 and 2,212. Those who have studied Plessy v. Ferguson (1896) would be wise to visit

Neshoba County.

Although Neshoba County produces a young person of note from time to time (e.g. Marcus Dupree of tiny Philadelphia who played football at the University of Oklahoma), there is the feeling that Neshoba County experiences growth without change, and, on other occasions, change without growth. At times Neshoba County, known to have "mysterious" suicides in jails, has neither.

Jackson (pop. 197,000) has cultural and educational amenities, as well as some beauty. An unattractive side, however, is a closed public swimming pool here and there.

Jackson's public schools are usually indicative of what is happening in town. Watch them carefully.

Jackson is not that well known. The city is frequently missing from your local newspaper's listing of home prices across the nation each quarter. Biloxi does make the list, however.

Jackson's Farish Street is popular for those who like the blues. Enjoy a sardine loaf there.

Over in Gulfport it is best to spend a week at the beach and a day with the President. That's President Jefferson Davis, of course.

Vicksburg (pop. 21,000) and Natchez (pop. 19,400)?

The two do not care for each other that much, but both are full of history. The cities were seen years ago stealing goods from boats passing by on the Mississippi.

Did the two cities know what they were up against? Have the times not changed that much from then to now?

Is Mississippi (the poverty, the desire to leave, the schools, and the music) easy to figure? No.

Many issues overlap.

Start to sort things out along Catfish Row in Vicksburg.

Arkansas

A Quiet Paradise

Arkansas, long on fishing-filled vacations and short on national attention, is a state which has been trying to catch up to the rest of the country for years.

This "land of opportunity," however, seems to be on the move these days, accomodating retirees in Mountain Home, wealthy Texas businesspersons in Little Rock, collegians in Fayetteville, and visitors to Ft. Smith. Duck hunters in DeWitt are happy. So are bass anglers in Pine Bluff.

Those places are located in a state that contains quiet prairies, too. Thomas Nuttall once remarked about them, "no echo answers the voice, and its tones die away in boundless and enfeebled undulations."

The state seems to be busy, but at the same time quiet. Or maybe one should say quiet, but busy. The peace and quiet are important, no matter the vernacular region (Delta, Arklatex, etc.).

Could there really be swamps in Arkansas? Yes.

People at MCI can tell us a little about the swamps of Arkansas. MCI reported that pulling fiber cable through a swamp in Arkansas was a greater challenge than dragging the stuff through the tunnel under the Hudson River in New York.

Stereotypes? Yes again.

Visitors ask Arkansans, "how many kitchen appliances are on the front porch of the average Arkansas home"?

Approximately 2.5 million peoplc (Arkansans or Arkansawyers) find very little humor there.

History? There is much.

Let us walk slowly some more through this chapter. The people of Arkansas, some of whom were once labeled "a saucy set of Negroes," seem to prefer things that way. Move the underliner and the pen slowly, too.

Let's see...

In the northern part of the state, a place where the name

"Ozark" is seen frequently, there are counties named Izard and Stone. There one can dream about activities on and along the White River. In this region there have been quail hunts by torchlight and fist fights on horseback!

The existence of a rough side to Arkansas should not surprise anyone. References to "the Bowie Knife state" go back more than 100 years. The knife (aka the Arkansas toothpick!) was very useful for "duellists" years ago.

Something more sedate?

Hot Springs (pop. 33,000) will do.

People in their seventies these days will recall that Hot Springs once offered anything a person could imagine: sex, liquor, gambling, hot baths, and so forth.

Today Hot Springs comes alive when thoroughbred racing cranks up at Oaklawn and when stressed-out Americans need a bath. The guest list is impressive.

In the Springs one should include a mention of history-filled Central Avenue. Research there reveals the presence of good biscuits.

The bad news about Hot Springs is that schooling does not mean much, or at least the emphasis on teaching does not mean much. The crime rate is not good, either.

Hot Springs receives many Texans each year. The border between the two states is not formidable. The Dallas newspaper can be bought easily in Hot Springs.

That border between Arkansas and Texas may be small in miles, but that did not stop a man named Harold Jenkins from noticing that there is a Conway in Arkansas and a Twitty in Texas. The late Conway Twitty earned a lot of money singing to both Longhorns and Razorbacks.

Do not laugh at the reference to Conway (pop. 27,000). The place is home, along with Chicago and New York, for Infobase Services, a company that thinks Arkansas is a good place in which to do business. The *Log Cabin Democrat* (circ. 10,000) verifies all of that.

Very serious business takes place when mentioning Texas, Arkansas, and football in the same sentence. Memorize that mixture when in Arkansas as you attend the game between Rison High and Fordyce High. Emotions will run high.

Today's exciting football game can distract a person nicely from the relationship through the years between blacks and whites in Arkansas. Certain economic historians (aka "cliometricians") have found fertile soil in Arkansas on the subject of slavery, farming, and the profits therein.

Fertile Arkansas soil for Civil War students is found at Pea Ridge, of course.

Some in Chicot and Phillips counties have noted that the Civil War in Arkansas could use additional study. A good start would be to find out how the war was "a rich man's war and a poor man's fight."

Chicot County is a good place to study dogtrot houses, never to be confused with shotgun houses.

The mention in this book of heroes and villains might include Franz Sigel, born in Germany, but a member of the Union Army. The record shows that his authority exceeded his ability. He was a German officer in an American army. Return to Pea Ridge for more information.

Go to Pine Bluff (pop. 58,000) for information about John Rust, a relative unknown, who gave the world the mechanical cotton harvestor. He died in 1954. His invention created the second great emancipation, freeing southerners, black and white, from the oppression of King Cotton. Cotton went from being a labor-intensive crop to being a capital-intensive one. *Much* history rests therein.

Cotton is known well along Highway 61 near the Tennessee border, and many blues musicians who "look up at down" have used Highway 61.

When jobs open up around Mississippi County (in Arkansas) one must remember that the blues can be celebratory as well as sad.

When sad times occur see if it is possible to notice how some people "fear God and the Mississippi River."

Better, happier times in Arkansas are found in a new pair of pants purchased at Wal-Mart. The business was started in 1962 by Sam "Made in America" Walton.

Wal-Mart knows the value of keeping things simple in Arkansas. That is the way the people like it. Any other way is, in the words of the late Conway Twitty, only make believe.

Something smaller?

There is Delight, a small place that simple folk can relate to. The place gave the world singer Glen Campbell.

Something larger than Delight?

There is Helena (pop. 20,000), home to some good blues music (born 1900?). Listen to KFFA radio (AM 1360).

Larger still is Little Rock (pop. 393,400 in metro area), the place many choose for both business and pleasure.

Let the imagination go wild at West End Park. Can you see a meeting of the Ex-Slaves Association taking place there in the 1890's?

Names like Ish, Gillam, and Sanders were once part of the black aristocracy in town, although one is well advised to know that last names of slaves were not always available. Owners did not want to emphasize family ties among blacks.

In the fall of 1957 the mix and blacks and whites in Little Rock grabbed the headlines of many American newspapers. Some readers of the *Arkansas Gazette* still remember the headline, "Troops Take Over at Central High; Negroes Told to Wait."

Newsman John Chancellor has said that Little Rock in 1957 was in a time warp, fighting the Civil War (again) on the city's streets while at the same time watching Sputnik taking people to outer space.

Times have changed, and Little Rock now glories in its opportunities, not in its past so much. Business opportunities are good. Costs are manageable, and so are the quiet nights, the friendly people, and the warm weather.

Some Little Rock people rest at Mt. Holly Cemetery (born 1843), overlooking downtown. Notice the grave of (still another) Jefferson Davis (1862-1913). The noisy soundscape makes concentrating on the Davis grave difficult. The words say, "to live in the hearts of those we love is not to die."

The highways through downtown Little Rock will take you over to a city with a western flavor, Fort Smith (pop. 73,000). One is warned that "there is no Sunday west of St. Louis, and no God west of Fort Smith." Think about that while buying a saddle in Ft. Smith, not a fiddle. The western flavor of Ft. Smith gets a boost from the weather. The city receives less precipitation than Little Rock.

Another world exists in Eureka Springs. The place is, man, somethin' else. People arrive there to avoid stress, overwork, and chaos. They leave when the words of poet Crescent Dragonwagon get stale. (Study "hippie time" in the Springs. Those in the Haight in San Francisco, of course, know all about it. This book mentions at least three "times.")

Some in Arkansas get away from it all by going to Onyx Cave. Spelunkers and speleologists find peace and quiet there. Define karst for homework.

Did we forget to mention a school nickname or two, as we've done in other states? How about the Southern Arkansas Muleriders and the Arkansas at Monticello Boll Weevils? Hold on to your hats when they meet.

Let us leave now. Quietly. That is the way Arkansans would do it.

Who said there was nothing of note in Arkansas?

Pass the catfish.

LOUISIANA

The Devil May Care

It may appear to some people that Louisiana pretty much has everything under control. The state has alligators and shrimp boats in good supply, skilled musicians everywhere, plenty of tourists, abundant sunshine, romantic bayous, and the mighty Mississippi. The Annual Louisiana Shrimp and Petroleum Festival, as odd as that may sound, is always a nice time.

But caution may be the best advice.

Louisiana is the land of the diminishing shoreline. The 1984 World Expo was a financial flop. Several people are on death row. The "Houstonization" of New Orleans is enough to make a grown person cry.

What is going on here?

The answer is a clear "business as usual" for this Sunbelt, fun-loving, growing, laidback place. For every oldtimer who remembers the days of cotton production there are two young people who wish to have fun in New Orleans ("south of the South") on a Friday night, and for every one person in Lafayette who wishes to polish the use of French, there are two people recently arrived in Abbeville who want to make a living using perfect English in the oil business.

There are troubles, however. Louisiana is a medical disaster in the minds of many people. There are chemical plants in Ascension Parish and in Iberville Parish. There is putrid water in many areas. There is soil erosion in LaFourche Parish. The distance between Baton Rouge and New Orleans has been called Cancer Alley (aka "the deadly Delta").

No one should act surprised when still another insurance company says that Louisianans have the shortest lifespan in the country.

Perhaps the best advice is to spend a short time, like four years at Louisiana State University in Baton Rouge, and leave.

Let us go to New Orleans (pop. 496,900) first.

Most people are already familiar with the obvious things about New Orleans: jazz, Bourbon Street, alligator on a stick, the Superdome, the Riverwalk, St. Louis Cathedral, and so forth.

"Nawlins," furthermore, calls itself "The Big Easy." It is easy to have a great time in the French Quarter. It is easy to embrace the leisurely pace of both the tourists and the permanent residents. It is like taking candy from a baby to be a conventioneer for a week or so in the Crescent City.

But all is not so wonderful in New Orleans, either.

It is not fun to see life in the Desire and the Saint Thomas projects. A popular tactic for drug dealers there in the late 1980's was to tie drugs with duct tape to the waists of little children, so that the little ones, for a dollar, could act as runners. Broken glass and broken homes dot the landscape.

Not facing the rough areas of the city can be done at the immense Superdome on Poydras Street. It boggles the mind to imagine the noise levels reached when the Rolling Stones came calling years ago.

Major league baseball is not played regularly in the Superdome. The game may be too sedate for people in the Crescent City. It took "base ball" (two words decades ago) until July 1859 to arrive in New Orleans.

The city and music have made for great history. In the 1920's dozens of black musicians hopped the Illinois Central in order to get work in Chicago. A key date is 1902 when the first black local of the musicians union (Local 208) was established in Chicago. Louis Armstrong arrived in Chicago in 1922. We all know the line that jazz was born in New Orleans, but it grew up in Chicago.

Nawlins has been called "a city of sounds," and in Storyville 100 years ago the sounds existed next to a little vice. Jazz, of course, was once scorned by purists and banned by moralists.

Duke Ellington has said that jazz has no specific geographical location. It is "anywhere and everywhere, wherever you can hear the soul." A book or two can be written about that line.

Outside New Orleans, away from music and before another cold hurricane drink, one can get an education by visiting the Vacherie area in St. James Parish. On the way to Oak Alley Plantation, where the live oaks are live due to their green color for 365 days, there is St. James Parish Junior High on Highway 18. The motto of the school is, "everybody is somebody." Black men sit on porches nearby and drink Coke. It may be a while in Saint James Parish before everybody becomes somebody.

Perhaps one help in all of this would be to ask Louisianans to try to understand one another. It is a fact that people from Shreveport and Monroe see "Southerners" from Lafayette and New Orleans as gumbo-eating, hurricane-drinking good old boys, while those from the South see the "Northerners" as Bible-toting, chicken-and-dumplings-eating folks from the piney hills. One side is Baptist, the other Catholic. One is French-speaking Cajuns, the other English, Scottish, or Irish. One is traditional, the other not. These differences can be explored by using Interstate 49 between Lafayette and Shreveport.

Between Lafayette and Lake Charles one's notes must say that both tourism and "modern things" may not go together. Since the discovery of oil in 1901 near Jennings there has been an "invasion" of Cajun culture by outsiders. All of this is too much for some to endure.

Homework will be to draw the line east to west in Louisiana that the Federal Reserve System uses in order to distinguish Districts 6 and 11. The "capital" of the former is Atlanta, and the "capital" of the latter is Dallas. Find where the line is drawn and you will be smarter for it.

The line drawn by television is important, too. Those west of an arbitrary line on a Saturday afternoon in the fall will receive the Texas-Oklahoma game while those east of the line will will receive, for example, the Auburn-Mississippi State game.

A line somewhere in Louisiana denotes differing burial practices. There is burial beneath the ground or above the ground. The presence or absence of crosses is another important feature. So is the direction the deceased is facing. Differences in life are one thing, but in Louisiana differences in death are significant, too.

The mix of peoples in Louisiana should never be taken lightly, since things like jazz, mentioned above, come from the mixing. Creoles and "American Negroes" were influenced by French and Spanish songs and dances so that an amazing music and history were born. Add some voodoo and the situation becomes even more interesting. The mix is important.

There was some awkward mixing not long ago in little Bastrop. Seems that the prom at the high school was a problem. The students voted for an integrated prom (240-229). The white prom committee, however, announced it would hold a white-only "spring formal."

The Saturday religion in Louisiana is football. To follow the Louisiana State Tigers in the fall is to touch base with the Divine. The late "Bear" Bryant of the hated University of Alabama once said that the toughest place to win is Baton Rouge, the home of the LSU Tigers.

A real Louisiana treat is to face the drive home after the football game with some red beans and rice in the tummy, having washed everything down with a cold one while listening to the Grand Ole Opry on WSM (AM 650) in Nashville. If a person does not enjoy that "menu," then in Southern minds there is definitely something very wrong.

Returning to religion and raunch in the same paragraph, someone could ask how they can exist side by side. The answer is amazingly simple. They ignore each other. If someone wants to do some voyeurism one minute, and then commit to being a "faith partner" the next, what is so bad about that? Has no one ever heard about the beauty of changing one's mind? Louisiana bills itself, after all, as the "dream state," does it not?

Religion and football are both found in the life of Eddie Robinson, the football coach at Grambling State University. The school is known well by those who follow football. Football stars include Charlie Joiner, Buck Buchanan, Ernie Ladd, Doug Williams, Willie Davis, and Tank Younger. Did we forget Frank Lewis and Willie Brown? Robinson coached them all.

Important, too, is the opinion that many blacks never had the chance to showcase their talents in the collegiate ranks for a long, long time. This is heady stuff for fans of football.

Grambling was started as the two-year Colored Industrial and Technical School in 1901, but was called the Louisiana Negro Normal and Industrial Institute when Eddie Robinson was hired in 1941. The school has survived pitifully small budgets, rickety school busses, and more than a little discrimination. Even today, sadly, many whites fail to see the distance that Grambling has come.

Race is no small issue in the Bayou State, of course. Documentation abounds.

Ethnicity is also part and parcel of much of Louisiana. Knowing French is highly recommended in Lafayette. Report cards at Tulane University in New Orleans are in English. Speaking Spanish is helpful in certain parts of Baton Rouge.

Whether the discussion is about ethnicity or about racism, some terms must be learned in order to know about Louisiana life: Cajun, Creole, bouree, roux, Klan, and zydeco. The first two in the list are easy, and everyone knows of the Klan. The third and fourth are words associated with cooking food. What does zydeco mean? Pick up your accordian, get ready to tap your toes, and ask about "a lively variant of Cajun music." Get ready to have some fun.

Laissez les bons temps rouler.

Florida

Minimum Purchase Required

What could be nicer than a cold beverage after a walk on the beach at Longboat Key?

Is it not lovely to dine with friends after a tough day trying to purchase a condominium (meaning "joint agreement" to lawyers) in St. Petersburg?

Is not the Greek food delightful in Tarpon Springs?

What could be better than doing business in Jacksonville and getting back home the same day, knowing that snow and sleet will never be a problem?

Is not dreaming fun, and part of life, in Florida? Is Florida not Paradise itself? It seems that we were all told as much since infancy.

In truth many different stories exist in Florida. This chapter will mention only a few of them.

Maybe this chapter should be written in Spanish, not English, since Spanish is such a big part of life in Florida. In Miami, after all, some use the term "xeroxear" and "taipear" to describe certain office tasks.

This chapter will start with eleven paragraphs whose purpose is to convince everyone that Florida is indeed a delicate place with a colorful past. We are all reminded that the fun and the amenities of today may often deceive, however.

First, Florida for many people is supposed to be Paradise, but other states can warn Florida about how problematic such a label can be. The Hudson River Valley in New York had patroons, while Louisiana counted several privateers long ago. Utah had pioneers, but Boston boasted about pilgrims and patriots. Colorado has prospectors. Hawaii has palaces. Arizona makes only promises. Florida has its hands full trying to be Paradise.

Second, Florida would be well advised to learn of the ways and the means of its pirates and prostitutes. Persuasion and dialogue do not go far. Violence is popular south of the "Smith and Wesson" line.

Third, many retirees come to Florida for their final days in Paradise, but the stay can be difficult. Some have worked up north for decades to pay off a mortgage, only to find that the etymology of the word makes a day in the sun a little sadder.

Fourth, Florida does not understand the desire for steak and ale. Try squid, rum, and Key lime pie.

Fifth, Florida sells "land by the gallon." Such a concept is incomprehensible to those in Omaha and Denver.

Sixth, there should be no unnecessary fuss about the "tropical depressions" that visit Florida from time to time. If the hell gets kicked out of everything the name "hurricane" should be used. Know that a Category 1 hurricane (minimal) is different from a Category 5 hurricane (catastrophic).

Seventh, the Apalachees, Calusas, and Ais should be studied right along with the Seminoles and Creeks, especially if the reader wants to brush up on what happened in 1763. Red syntax and white syntax, interestingly, were "translated" by blacks back about then.

Eighth, Indian names and terms are important in Tallahassee, the home of the Florida State University Seminoles. At last look tickets were being "scalped" there for the school's football games.

Ninth, Ponce de Leon and his fountain of youth are quite a story. The man was a seasoned soldier, not a sauna-sitting adventurer. History shows he had his hands full on the southeast coast arguing with residents in the Land of Mayami.

Tenth, Florida and New Mexico, not Virginia and Massachusetts, boast the oldest Christian churches in the United States. That is a fact. The use of English, or the lack of it, might have something to do with how this situation has developed over the years, he said historically.

Eleventh, one must divide Florida in order to study it properly. How about Lamb-choppers and Pork-choppers? How about Dixie and the Islands, the categories of Joel Garreau?Jacksonville and Gainesville are in the Northeast. The Northwest contains Tallahassee and Cedar Key. Orlando and Ocala make up Central Florida. The Southeast in Miami and Ft. Lauderdale, while the Southwest is Naples, Ft. Myers, and Sarasota, among others. The Keys are from the Overseas Highway to the end. That should make it easy for your yellow underliner as you do lunch in South Miami Beach looking at art deco(ratif) buildings.

Now for some cities and a major issue or two in them.

Down in Key West (pop. 25,000) there is much to do and much to think about, not the least of which is watching the sun set (with a drink in the hand of every watcher). Do not places at land's end seem different? Avoid the sword swallower.

A person who did some humor at one time was Lincoln Theodore Monroe Andrew Perry, born in the Keys in 1902. We knew the man as Stepin' Fetchit, an early performer in the (now developing) history of black comedy.

In Key West notice the cemetery near Olivia Street.

Notice, too, that Key West, a Conch Republic, is closer to Havana than to Miami.

The Keys make one want to take up pen and paper along with a cold lemonade. Jonathan Raban has described the Keys as "the great American haven of un-American activities." He continues, "if there was any place on the map of the United States where the elevated ideology of being American finally unraveled, it was on the Keys. Morally and geographically, the Keys were terminal." Right again.

There is much to think about in these parts. The mind can wander concerning the millions in buried treasure that may be uncovered by a diver. In 1985 the Atocha was found with about $400 million in coins, silver bars, and other pieces hidden in the deep. Let your mind wander as you sip your drink.

Let us go north with our notepads.

When you get to Orlando (pop. 165,000) be ready for a fun day at Universal Studios, a horrible day trying to drive, and a good day for the guy taking your money at any number of places in Orange County. In 1979 only about 5.3 million tourists came through. In 1990 the figure was about 11.9 million. The driving can be brutal. It makes no difference who you are.

Those figures really should not surprise the whole world since in 1990 there were 75,134 hotel rooms available for visitors to use. The number is the envy of many in Reno and Atlantic City.

And the numbers are very important to those waging "airline wars" in Orlando. The Southeast is fertile ground (air?) for airline profits.

Some in trendy Orlando can tell you about "virtual reality" since they have friends in Southern California who understand the term perfectly.

See the hurricane map in your phone book, too, as we are leaving Orlando.

We all know that Florida is the land of the hurricane myth, so now here are three. First, hurricanes are becoming more severe. Second, the most severe hurricanes are related to global warming. Third, hurricane severity will increase in a warmed world. Memorize this on your way to a nice afternoon on Marco Island.

Over in Ft. Lauderdale ($102,800 median price for a home) the only problem is trying to distinguish FLL from FTL. The former is what the airline luggage tags say, while the latter is the ticker symbol on the stock exchange for Fruit of the Loom, Inc. Under a warm sun with a drink in hand that distinction is about as heavy as life gets in Ft. Lauderdale.

Life became heavy in St. Petersburg (pop. 240,300) when it was announced not long ago that the Suncoast Dome (cap. 43,000 for baseball) would be used for baseball. Ranked between 13 and 17 in various people's television market listings, St. Pete is one place where the saying "if you build it, they will come" may apply, too.

The absence of baseball, however, has not discouraged too many people from coming to Pinellas County (pop. 900,000). In a period of ten years (pick just about any ten) a growth rate of 20 percent is not unheard of. The huge population of Pinellas County may love golf more than baseball.

When you combine that number with those down the road in Hillsborough County (read: Tampa and environs) the number gets to approximately 2 million people. That is impressive if you are talking sports, soft drinks, religion, recreation, and land values.

Tampa (born 1824) is a city of "Anglo cool and Latin heat." Festivals, Cuban coffee, and November temperatures between 59 and 82 degrees are always on the menu. Bring lots of money.

Land values? They are outrageous just about anywhere in the state of Florida. Bring more money.

That brings to mind another "l word," limits. Many in Florida think there should be none, but some feel there should be (strict) limits to development of subdivisions, the use of wetlands, etc. On and on goes the battle.

Imagine, too, for a moment that some of those playing leading roles in Florida's future are not Floridians, but "imports" from cold, snow-laden Northern places. These outsiders, the argument goes, are unfamiliar with what needs to be done in Florida.

Those from Cuba will tell you that they know what needs to be done in Florida. Some "permanent residents" disagree. Hurricane Andrew may have been more tranquil.

Where does Florida go from here?

To trying to keep shiny cities like Tampa still shiny.

What is Miami (358,000 souls) like?

It is like any other city that tries to play down its role as a supplier of drugs and guns, while at the same time featuring articles in the *Miami Herald* about how easy it is to counterfeit money. (People from Virginia, too, know about the selling and movement of guns, come to think of it.)

Miami is like any other city where *El Herald* is read faithfully. There is much diversity in Miami. Nicaraguans. Cubans. Millionaires. Venezuelans. Catholics. Jews. Haitians. Gays. Calle Ocho (8th Street, for those into English only). New Yorkers. Homeless. Colombians. Even some who claim to be "natural-born" Floridians.

A Cuban who came through Miami years ago was Desiderio Arnaz y de Acha III (aka Desi Arnaz), who once cleaned bird cages for a living in order to improve himself.

Many in Miami today forget the striving some people have had to do.

Miami is part of the Sunbelt (a term born in 1969), and is the economic and cultural capital of the entire Caribbean basin, of course.

Miami is "a capital in exile," to hear some tell it.

Many Miami blacks feel that they are on the bottom of the social ladder, although some have been in the city longer than some "newcomers." This is old news to the black community.

More recent news may be the treatment of women jockeys at Tropical Park in Miami in 1969. A male rider uttered the immortal words, "If you let women ride, we're all dead." To this day women are a problem to some in the profession.

Some of those "newcomers" who are not black make good money from the import/export business in Miami. The pages marked "Import" in the Miami phone book number about three or four. The "Export" pages number about 136.

Cuban-Americans know that the hyphen can either separate or divide. The hyphen is important.

Miami and Dade County should be watched closely, too, because of the presence of the gay community. Remember June 1977 when Anita Bryant was on her rampage?

Watch Miami and Dade County, too, for news coming out of the Jewish community. Jews have been in Florida only since 1763.

Jewish Miami can recall the days of being "permanent tourists in a community of strangers." The feeling was odd. Some who grew up in New York thought that the whole world was Jewish. William Zuckerman has said that Jews are "Americans by birth and instinct, not by nationality and gratitude." Discuss that quote at the pool.

A few Miami Jews today recall that people once buried meat in the ground to keep it cold!

The food in Palm Beach (9,800 people) is well taken care of. Playing polo and attending the Palm Beach Opera Debutante Cotillion must not be done on an empty stomach.

Jacksonville, where $75,200 is the median price for a home, is big in area, and has about 944,000 very humid people in the metro area. Television households number about 470,950 (54th in USA). Those figures impress sports franchises looking for a better deal. Japanese imports and Latin American exports are big deals in "JAX."

In 1764 Pensacola was "a huddle of huts" and little else. In 1821 Andrew Jackson, the first Irish Protestant President, called the city "filthy and disgusting."

In 1926 there were a few paved roads.

Today Pensacola has 289,000 souls. Many know the city as part of "the Redneck Riviera." For homework name the three flags that have flown over Pensacola, a part of what some call the "Wild South."

Tallahassee (pop. 125,000) has antebellum mansions and occasional snowfall, white gloves and parasols. Who could forget the Secession Convention of January 1861? Those who go to Florida Gators football games in the fall sure can forget, since the atmosphere can be pretty rowdy.

Name the four flags that have flown over St. Augustine. Now find St. George Street and count from 1565 up to today.

Just about anyone in Daytona who knows about racing remembers the late Bill France, Sr. A favorite story about Bill is that one day the chaplain was running late, and there was no one to say the opening prayer. Bill said it himself, asking the Almighty to keep a watchful eye on the cars, the drivers, the infield, the sparkplugs, and the finish line. Puzzled about what to say at the end of his praying, Bill took a deep breath and said, "Sincerely yours, Bill France."

Speed in Daytona has had a long history, including the days when Jackie Robinson raced down the basepaths in the spring of 1946.

A summary statement about Florida?

The Land of Flowers is proof that a delicate cultural and historic smorgasbord still exists. Snowbirds, rocket ships, refugees, Klan hoods, plastic crocodiles, immigrants, senior citizens, drug trafficking, and Goofy live among exiles, the Florida Citrus Commission, Cuban cigars, and Seminole Indians. One should throw in bilingual education for good measure.

Paradise can make a person dizzy.

Perfection, always the expectation from Pensacola to the Keys, is never easy.

The Breadbasket

Play Ball!

To learn about this area some touring is necessary.

The Breadbasket goes from (roughly) west of Indianapolis to Denver's eastern doorstep, and from (roughly again) central Texas up to the Canadian border. Life involves farming, needless to say.

What about the people?

Four ideas must be kept in mind.

First, farm people are serious, almost bland to some observers, since they are not as loud or as outspoken as someone from Cleveland or Miami.

Second, farmers are specialists in getting things done.

Committees, boards, and councils are fine, but farm people are good leaders without them.

Third, and somewhat contradicting the first point, the folks in this area can be very funny, although in a dry way ("My neighbor is crazy. The other day he was cutting some wood. He thinks that a saw is an axe with teeth," Ottawa, Illinois, 1983).

Fourth, Easterners must resist the word "backward" at all costs when visiting the Breadbasket, because frequently the word will be used incorrectly. We all should memorize that what is rural is not automatically out of date, and what is urban can indeed be out of date. Eastern city folks frequently get those two perceptions mixed up.

All of us know that the ground rules have long been established in the Breadbasket. There are few minorities. Most all the faces are white. English is spoken, and not much else. Conformity is the rule of the day. Sameness, a characteristic that humans enjoy, is found easily. The 1990's talk about diversity doesn't bake much bread. These "rules" explain the area's efficiency. (Those labeled "minorities" do exist in the Breadbasket. of course. See Marathon County, Wisconsin, for example, which counted 111,270 residents [110,470 whites]. Making a dent were many Hmong living in the area.)

Too, there is an attitude that is discriminating as far as marketing a product is concerned. If you cannot sell a John Deere product to a St. Joseph, Missouri person, you better abandon the idea. If you can sell the thing, give it a try in Atlanta or Boise.

Some have described how the Breadbasket functions as the superego morally as well as politically in the United States. The area really does.

All of the above has been said without mentioning food, an essential item produced by the region. Who could blame Minneapolis for boasting about Wheaties (born 1924)? General Mills in 1933 wedded breakfast cereal to baseball (the Minneapolis Millers) and to radio (WCCO AM 830). A new era had dawned.

A noticeable chink in the armor of the Breadbasket, apart from a little clannishness, may be that several places are losing population. The bailing out of a local bank and the closing of a school are pretty good indications that life in the Breadbasket may be undergoing more "cultural strain" than anyone thinks. Those who do cattle ranching in Arthur County, Nebraska (population 462; 0.7 people per square mile) can explain all of this. Let the marketer beware.

Marketers should also know that numbers sometimes deceive in the Breadbasket. Mental illness in this part of the country may be easily noticed because there is not much of it. The same with jobs, because those who do not work, although small in number, are spotted instantly. The same with people on drugs. This phenomenon ("Ward's Theory"?) should receive four stars in notes about this region.

It is interesting to note that some nutty things can be found in this area over the years, most laughably some of the early days of professional wrestling. Notables have included female champ Mildred Burke (of Coffeyville, Kansas), Martin "Farmer" Burns (Cedar County, Iowa), "Gorgeous George" Wagner (Seward, Nebraska), and Frank Gotch (Humboldt, Iowa). Some of the grapplers toured with the old Sells-Floto Circus.

Names are important in the Breadbasket, because to be accepted it helps to have the name of Merle or Bud. Virgil and Mildred are popular, too.

Going by air may be difficult for Virgil. Just try getting a convenient flight from Fargo, North Dakota to Sioux Falls, South Dakota.

When in the Breadbasket (Manhattan, Kansas, for example) try tuning your car radio to different stations. You will find that signals from immense distances can be received with relative ease. It is not impossible to get KSL (AM 1160) in Salt Lake on a nice Kansas night. Such is not the case in Camden.

Your radio can receive signals moving through the star-filled heavens clearly visible above the Breadbasket. In the words of W. P. Kinsella, "the stars have moved in close enough to eavesdrop." The scene is ideal for those who have a 1957 Chevrolet.

Another hallmark of the Breadbasket? How about that birds know the difference between the Breadbasket and the Foundry! Incontinent pigeons decorate buildings in the Foundry, while graceful blackbirds survey the lonely highways of the Breadbasket.

Architecture? Examine the Paramount Arts Center in Aurora, Illinois, and then the Adler Theater in Davenport, Iowa. One notices circles and curves in one place, straight lines in the other. Ludwig Mies van der Rohe once said, "God is in the details." The differences are in the details, too, in the Foundry and the Breadbasket.

Certain subjects do not receive much positive press in the Breadbasket. Saying that the phrase "under God" should not have been added to the Pledge of Allegiance in 1954, for example, will not get you too far.

Scoring points with people can be done by mentioning the efficiency of Breadbasket businesses like HOK Sports Facilities Group in Kansas City. The people there have been the architects for several red-blooded, American baseball parks (Comiskey in Chicago, Jacobs in Cleveland, Camden Yards in Baltimore, the Suncoast Dome in Florida, for example). Where better to have architects for baseball than in America's Breadbasket?

Where better to witness the standardization of American values (referred to above), especially when the process involves a pull to the right? Such is the case in Peoria, Illinois, a town that always loved a good fistfight, a bottle of whiskey, and a deck of cards. Pulling to the right lately is Catholic Bishop John J. Myers, who wishes to safeguard orthodoxy throughout the Diocese of Peoria's 28 counties in central Illinois. The vote here is that Breadbasket Catholics will find Myers a little too traditional and off the mark. The Bishop is worried about "the private witholding of assent from received teaching."

A more pleasant item is that the pace of the Breadbasket allows a person time to think about life's real issues. After the event at the Myriad in Oklahoma City ponder how night and day are being changed daily by Americans. Notice the appointment book of the farmers. Try to buy milk at midnight in OKC. Filling the dark hours with (more) activity is not done so easily in the Breadbasket.

The hours are less expensive in the Breadbasket than in the Foundry. You will get more for your money at the Savoy Grill in Kansas City than you will at Tony Packo's in Toledo. (Is not a differing economy a proof that American life is regional in nature?)

Realize, too, that there can be surprises within the various regions of this country. Rockford, Illinois walks, talks, and smells like the Foundry, but the city is encircled by farms, farming, and farmers. Rockford's Coronado Theatre (born 1927) may look similar to the Paramount in Aurora and the Rialto in Joliet, but other things along the Rock River make Rockford a little different from Aurora and Joliet. Beware.

Lastly, it should be said that the Breadbasket's universities get high marks in many categories which may surprise savvy Easterners. Whether the focus be architecture or football, one better know dentils, fluted shafts, and cyma recta from an end around and a flying wedge. Breadbasket universities (Kansas State, Iowa State, etc.) are good.

Kansas City awaits.

Minnesota

Modern, Renewing, and Improving

Life in Minnesota is nice. People pretty much mind their own business. Schools are good. People clean up after themselves, and a drive to the Twin Cities can put a person in touch with a place that is well organized. Lo and behold, even a rough Minnesota winter or two can be tolerated after some practice.

Minnesota can be divided like other states are in this book, although one must say that the labels really do not provide much information. Vikingland, Heartland, Arrowhead, Pioneerland, Hiawathaland, and Metroland are labels some people use. One could throw in Red River Valley and Sioux Valley, too.

Minnesota is a land to which many people go, even to retire.

Minnesota is not an old place. Statehood came in 1858.

Minnesota has clean politics as well as more than 10,000 clean lakes. Everyone is pleased as punch to know about the politics.

Minnesota has dozens of small cities (New Ulm, for example) where life is pleasant.

Minnesota seems to be a place where progress, quality of life, social order, and good fishing co-exist delightfully.

What possibly can be said of Minneapolis and St. Paul (358,000 and 272,000 folks respectively) that has not already been said? All reports are true about the folks "up there" having it together, although "up there" really is not so far up. Schools, politics, jobs, recreation, and you-name-it seem to go pretty well.

Minneapolis people may get a little upset, however, when North Dakota people come to Minnesota for some fun, get drunk, and then cause some social havoc by running red lights, cursing big city life, and leaving. If Cleveland and Chicago had such tiny social problems the world would probably come to a halt.

Just to show that hard-working, conforming people can make a mistake, visit the Hubert H. Humphrey Metrodome in downtown Minneapolis. The dome was given to the world by Skidmore Owings & Merrill of Chicago, and the building may be in the same class as the Rosemont Horizon in suburban Chicago. The Metrodome has been called the Rollerdome, the Thunderdome, a covered dish, and a livestock pavilion.

Those within earshot of the Twin Cities gave the world the wonderful Burma-Shave ads from 1927 until 1963 (e.g. "He played a sax/had no B.O./but his whiskers scratched/so she let him go/ Burma-Shave").

The ads are fading a bit in the American memory perhaps, but the name of the football team in the Cities (Vikings!) is not. The club was purchased in 1961 for a paltry $600,000 by Bill Boyer, Max Winter, H. P. Skogland, Bernie Ridder, and Ole Haugsrud (a real Minnesota name!). The team has a large following in the so-called Upper Midwest.

Those who live in the Minneapple metro area (pop. 2.6 million) talk of a "cold nose, warm heart" disposition during the cold months. One gets that way after fishing outdoors in the winter and watching baseball indoors in the summer. Have a Pig's Eye beer while trying to figure that out.

There is relief indoors at the Mall of America (born 1992). Notice the 4.2 million square feet.

We all know that Minneapolis and St. Paul get on each other from time to time.

A look into the 1890 census will reveal some interesting things. First, the census was Census XI (not unlike a Super Bowl number today). Second, when not bashing heads, the two cities counted them, coming up with 182,967 folks in Minneapolis and 142,581 in St. Paul. Third, in an apparent effort to duplicate Chicago's politics, the "teams" got into some serious name-calling. Fourth, things got so bad that William Henry Eustis claims in all this that he was kicked "for at least sixteen feet." To this day the Cities get on one another.

A larger, more serious item is the quality of the advertising agencies in town. Carmichael-Lynch and Fallon McElligott are two easy names. In 1993 Ameritech signed on with Fallon McElligott, and Continental Bank in Chicago was already in the portfolio (to the chagrin of many Chicagoans). Clio awards seem to find their way to MSP, possibly saying something for hard work, humility, a grasp of the language, and throwing image and frills to the cool Minnesota wind.

Another Minnesota success story involves 3M's Post-it notes. The little things are now both famous and handy. A sidebar to the story is that their design involved thinking about what is "permanently temporary." Creative thinking (typical of much of Minnesota) enabled Post-it people to escape traditional paradigms and come up with the little notes.

Score still another one for the Cities when St. Paul started the first hotline for battered women in 1972.

Score a point, too, for the University of Minnesota. It beat California at Berkeley by two years for having a multicultural requirement in order to graduate. UM students can compare and contrast the East's Ellis Island with the West's Angel Island.

Away from the Cities one can find peace and quiet in Chisago County. Charles P. Pierce once wrote, "The summer people go home before the sky grows all muscular with the clouds that will bring the first snow down upon Chisago County. They are all gone by then — all the happy children, and the men in battered hats as thickly stuck with fishing lures as Moby Dick's hide was with harpoons. They come in the summer to fish the lakes for muskies — there is even a muskie painted on the water tower that greets you as you drive into Chisago City — and they take their leisure and the fish together, and they leave before the lake turns to deep, black ice.

They leave and the farmers stay." That about says it.

In the other direction from the Cities is quiet Red Wing, home to the old but venerable St. James Hotel, built in 1875. After a long day of cross-country skiing the St. James looks great.

English is the official language of Minnesota, of course, and one is well advised to talk like the natives. Here are the things to use in everyday conversation: yep, you bet, yeah but, if you feel like it, if a guy, a lotta guys, a guy could, if it's not too much trouble, whatever, and that's different. Using a few of those little things can fake out even a Minnesotan. Just say at the airport to a redcap that "a guy could get stranded here in the winter months for a long time. Whatever." No one will know that you are a visitor. That's different. Yep. You bet.

Religion is no small issue in the Gopher state, either. Being Lutheran helps. This ditty should be committed to memory: "Irish are Catholic we're told/Lutherans, they walk streets of gold/so convert them, my friend/to a more blessed end/before they are dead and go cold." Martin Luther died in 1546, be advised, but you could never tell by listening to the many, many Lutherans who inhabit Minnesota.

If the death of Martin Luther in 1546 sounds like long ago, then try 1362. That is when a group of Scandanavians came through central Minnesota. Do not sell the Scandanavian people short. They will remind one and all that Columbus was discovering the Bahamas in 1492, a long time after central Minnesota was abuzz with religious fervor.

At the top of the Gopher state, and some would say at the end of the world, is Koochiching County, home to International Falls. If you think it gets rough in January in Boston, Dayton, or Green Bay, you have not seen a thing yet. Only about 15,000 inhabit the entire county, and just 6,000 live in cold International Falls. The Falls has had a running feud for some time with Fraser, Colorado about who is to be labeled "Icebox of the Nation." The vote here goes to Zerexloving International Falls.

One door to the east of Koochiching County is very large St. Louis County (as in Duluth, Hibbing, and Ely). Local history was changed in 1887 with the discovery of iron ore on the Mesabi Range. Today if there is any conversation at all about the area it is about the weather (17.6 average daily high in January). From 1980 to 1990 the county lost 22,800 people, the most in Minnesota.

Did we forget to mention that there are some wonderful families in Minnesota? There's the trouts, panfishes, pikes, salmons, walleyes, basses, and the catfishes. You will meet them all in Minnesota.

Duluth, the snowiest of the state's major cities, had 107,000 souls about 30 years ago, but only 88,000 now. The place is cold, but bills itself as "the San Francisco of the Midwest" for the bay, the fog, and the hills.

That label may point out two mistakes, by the way. Duluth is not similar to San Francisco, and, secondly, it seems difficult to call Duluth part of the Midwest. Iron ore shares top billing with grain in Duluth.

Notice, too, the clothes worn by people at Duluth's Wade Stadium (born 1941). Anything goes. The atmosphere reminds one of the Empty Quarter of the United States, not the Foundry or the Breadbasket. Make up your mind as you tour the lovely Union Depot (born 1892) downtown.

Maybe Bob Dylan, a native son, best described Duluth with "honkin' foghorns...the rainy mist...an' the rocky cliffs."

Something that Duluth people do these days is examine the ancient and fascinating dark gray basalt rocks that are remarkably similar to parts of the moon. In fact, if the day of farming on the moon ever comes (with a harvest Earth overhead), then Duluth may get some credit for successfully studying what is around it, beneath it, and below it.

Over in Hibbing (18,000 souls) conversations center around the mixed feelings for Bob Dylan and the activities at the Hull Rust Mahoning Mine. Simple as that.

Bemidji is Paul Bunyan, so much so that the local high school is called the Lumberjacks (or, if female, the Lumberjills). Sparks usually fly when the Jacks or Jills play Moorhead.

A negative word about Minnesota is sort of rare, but the truth must be told about life in Lincoln County. The place is west and south of the Twin Cities, and is supposedly in the nation's most rural Congressional District. Lincoln County may re-define the phrase "peace and quiet." In fact, the pace of the "town" of Ivanhoe can hammer home the notion that one can be too removed from the rest of the world. It is easy to locate Lincoln County on the map. It is right below Yellow Medicine and Lac Qui Parle Counties.

Parts of Minnesota are so empty and quiet that "there isn't even a thing that one can hide behind," in the words of Ole Edvart Rolvaag.

If you think Yellow Medicine and Lac Qui Parle sound funny, consider Otter Tail County, home of such newsworthy places as Elizabeth and Fergus Falls. That is right. There is not much there to consider.

On second thought, someone doing research could be pretty happy in Otter Tail County. Years ago a guy found that Otter Tail residents of German descent were not similar to people around them. Swedes, Norwegians, and Scandinavians were in the majority, not the Germans.

That same research about Minnesota's people might reveal the the terrible hanging of some Sioux in Mankato, a part of Blue Earth County, the day after Christmas, 1862. President Lincoln was told that "everything went off quietly."

Did a skeptic say Minnesota needs some things on its agenda these days? Well, go to the Norske Dag in Dalton, Belgian-American Days in Ghent, the Wood Duck Festival in Fulda, Lefse Dagen in Starbuck, or Buttered Corn Days in Sleepy Eye. You will have some things to do.

Recreation meets religion in Finland, Minnesota, by the way. There one can take part in the St. Urho's Day Celebration. St. Urho rid Finland of grasshoppers a long time ago. The Finns, by the way, are no trivial item in Minnesota. They are people who work very hard. Some joke about their speech with the gem that Finns like to ask, "How you kum tis kuntri? Pick sip? Chet blane? Lirrol pote"?

In southeast Minnesota there is nothing but peace and quiet over in Rochester (pop. 58,000). Peace and quiet provided, that is, that you have just toured Mayowood and provided that you are a graduate of Mayo High. Rochester is one of the proverbial "good places in which to raise children."

Rochester has baseball at, you guessed it, Mayo Field. Off the left field line some fans rest quietly at Oakwood Cemetery (born 1862). Edwin C. Cross (1824-1894) has the best view of the action.

Rochester's Mayo Clinic has been ranked number one in cardiology, endocrinology, neurology, and gastroenterology across the country. And the place is in the top five in orthopedics, psychiatry, and otolaryngology. Not too shabby.

Finally, how could a mention of Minnesota be complete without including the Minnesota Multiphasic Personality Inventory (first published 1943)? Well, the MMPI is alive and well, just like some of the Minnesotans who first devised statements like "I am afraid of losing my mind" and "There is something wrong with my sex organs." We all got a chuckle out of those years ago.

The MMPI just keeps going and going.

Not unlike the sturdy Norwegians whose opinions were asked when the thing first got started years ago. You bet.

Change the fan belt in the snowmobile and get going.

Yep.

North Dakota

Remote and Quiet

A person sitting in Beulah, North Dakota is soon hit with two very clear impressions. First, the place is a long way from anywhere. Second, not many people choose to live in Beulah or in North Dakota.

The population of the entire state is only 638,000, roughly the same number as the city of Milwaukee.

The state of North Dakota is 17th in land area. A human gets to feel in a hurry that he or she is a small fish in a very huge pond.

The figures above, combined with winters that terrify even natives like the late Eric Sevareid, make the state a quiet, yes lonely, outpost. Those from Northern Maine and Northern New York can relate to that.

However, there is evidence that the "flip side" of the life described above can be encouraging. There is not much divorce in North Dakota. There is excellent voter turnout. There are not many school dropouts. Drug use is not as plentiful as other places one can think of.

Other places one can think of have houses that cost more than those in North Dakota. Some houses in North Dakota can almost be put on a Visa card.

Another plus is that quiet North Dakota may be an excellent place to study how geography, history, and theology come together in the lives of Indian people. Ask about how history is cyclic, not linear, before digging up graves. Ask about how land is shared, not owned. Make sure you know how Christian religion and the idea of history in the Western hemisphere are not easily separated. Some eyebrows will be lifted, and perspectives will be changed.

North Dakota's "removed" status may make abortions difficult to get. A few years ago there were only about 1,200 physicians in the entire state. People in the western end of the state may have to drive about 350 miles (one way!) to get service.

Driving long distances can be difficult since temperatures can change very suddenly. A few people who are reading this book will recall relatives talking about February 21, 1918 when the mercury jumped from -33 to +50 in Granville. To farmers, visitors, and others this item is not trivial.

The remote and quiet nature of North Dakota life can contribute to a sense of humor, too. North Dakotans simply say, "Stay in North Dakota – Custer was healthy when he left." Montanans do not see the humor.

No one should say that North Dakota has not contributed to American life, by the way. Angie Dickinson and Shadoe Stevens both came from the Flickertail state.

Now for some cities.

Fargo (pop. 75,000) may not have much in common with Miami, except that the two cities are at the opposite end of the spectrum for stress. Fargo was at one time calculated to be the least stressful, Miami the most. The two cities in the mid-1980's talked to each other about respective strengths and weaknesses. In the words of one person, "Miami vice met Fargo ice."

For those who use Amtrak, Fargo is simply FAR on the ticket identifying one's baggage. To many Americans the city is simply FAR from civilization.

Amtrak goes through Fargo, Grand Forks, and other places, but not to or through South Dakota. There may be a message in that.

Fargo is not that bad a place, especially if you remember that its neighbor is Moorhead, Minnesota, across the river. Schools, hospitals, and even a few universities dot the two cities which make one Standard Metropolitan Statistical Area.

Fargoans joke about the weather. A temperature of -35 "keeps the riffraff out," they say.

Famous people from Fargo include the late baseball star,

Roger Maris (correct spelling: Maras). Many from both Fargo and the baseball world considered it the ultimate insult to have Maris' record (61 homers in 1961 for the Yankees) in the book with an asterisk (*) for so many years. Few remember that Maris was an accomplished schoolboy football player. He is buried in Fargo. He is spoken of highly.

A study of the "moral geography" of Fargo may include asking if there is a gay bar in town. Do not laugh. Ask at nightfall. Note the thickness of the walls and the boundaries put up by both the gay and the straight communities. Never think such a geography cannot take place in these parts. The Breadbasket is often a barometer for such things, in fact.

That barometer in North Dakota will not measure how things involving blacks and Jews are going. The NAACP (founded 1909) and its black/Jewish roots are not major items for conversation in these parts.

Details about the lives of the homeless ("better garbage is found at major airports than along Main Street") are not, either.

The populations of Mandan (15,100) and West Fargo (12,200) make it difficult to prove or disprove the theories of Sociology 101. Living in Cleveland does have its advantages.

Fargo and Moorhead (on the Minnesota side, remember) were to have been a stop on the Winter Dance Party in 1959. The record shows that the plane carrying Ritchie Valens and friends never made it out of Mason City, Iowa. The guys were supposed to play in Moorhead on February 3, but died on February 2.

Jamestown, large by North Dakota standards, has about 16,000 people today, and it gave us author Louis L'Amour on March 22, 1908. L'Amour died in 1988, having reached the age of 80. Life expectancy in this country was about 50 when he was born.

Rugby? Know what is going on in Winnipeg to impress people.

Zap and Pick City? Compare and contrast them with Keokuk for isolation.

Bismarck (pop. 44,485)? It is the capital. Ask about the difference between East and West there. Notice the different grass and the different landscape.

Williston? Ask about oil and coal as you detrain there 21 hours after leaving Chicago. Eastbound from Seattle the trip is only 23 hours.

Finally, something that absolutely, positively must be explained is the "image problem" of North Dakota. "Nodak" jokes are a popular way for Minnesotans and Montanans, among others, to tease about the Flickertail state. One joke is, "What is the official tree of North Dakota? The telephone pole."

On a serious note there is more than a little disgust on the part of Minnesotans who notice that "Nodakers" hop on Interstate 94 and journey into Minnesota to create a little havoc from time to time.

Amid the havoc it may be a good time now to mention the three suits of Scandinavian-American fashion in North Dakota — pants, leisure, and snowmobile.

Dress appropriately in North Dakota.

In August, that is.

South Dakota

Thirty Days Same as Cash

This chapter was written with at least the faint hope that some of the information provided could prevent a person from getting socked in the mouth.

The reasoning is that many people confuse the two Dakotas, and more than a few people get mad about the confusion.

The two Dakotas do have more animals than people, but that should not get in the way. Seven other states are in the same situation.

Let us just say that the two states are indeed similar in certain things (like R-values in homes), but each should be studied separately.

Let us start by mentioning someone both states can relate to so that no one will be assaulted.

One important person who is shared by both Dakotas is Sitting Bull (Tatan'ka Iyota'ke, if you will). In 1953 some irate South Dakotans crossed the border and stole the remains of the great Sioux warrior from his grave. Many North Dakotans took a dim view of the theft. These days the two settle their differences on the football field when the University of North Dakota and the University of South Dakota play for the Sitting Bull Trophy.

North Dakotans sure know how to get under the hide of South Dakota people. One mispronunciation of Pierre ("pier"), the capital of South Dakota, is all that it takes.

South Dakota is easily divided. Use the same underliner that was used to do the underlining in Montana. South Dakota, and the large states in general, divide themselves easily.

South Dakota has four areas that are simple to draw. First, there is the northern tier (from Milbank to Aberdeen to Mobridge to Bison). Second, there is the central corridor (Brookings to Huron to Pierre to Union Center). Third, we have the southern tier (Sioux Falls to Mitchell to Wall).

Lastly there is the Black Hills section (from Buffalo on top to Hot Springs on the bottom, with Rapid City, Deadwood, Lead, and Spearfish in between).

Pretty easy, wasn't it? The underlining was easy because the state of South Dakota is uncomplicated, pleasant, and not a burden to anyone.

In fact, there is a real easy way to divide South Dakota, come to think of it. There's "Eas Triver" and "Wes Triver." The names describe the two sides of the Missouri River. Some would argue the only thing the two sides of the river have in common is area code 605.

Remember the difference between a rancher and a farmer, too, as well as the difference between ample water and insufficient water. None other than Charles M. Russell may have said it best when he remarked, "The grass was knee high. Cattle would fatten on it. Ever'body was happy. An' then came civilization and law an', last an' worst, the farmer ... He plants corn and gets tumbleweeds. Damn him. It serves 'im right." Write those words in your notes as you remember the time change in the state.

A trot down memory lane in Turner County, in the southern tier, can show how life was, and in some ways still is, in South Dakota.

One hundred years ago houses were made of sod. The mention of typhoid fever was enough to scare anyone. The big event of the year was the bowery dance. The *Turner County Herald* of April 1, 1885 reported that "a terrific fire swept the bluffs of Turkey Ridge. E. J. Jenks lost his barn and all out buildings, besides lumber and shingles, and only hard fighting saved the house."

People living in Turner County then had names like Goettertz, Georgeson, Dangel, Weier, and Schweitzer. Life was not easy. Places like Viborg, Menno, and Freeman were venues for a big night out for those from the tiny "towns" (like Idylwilde).

So what? So someone can make the case that South Dakota has not changed that much, and that the lack of change is something South Dakotans want anyway. Farmers still fear fires. Typhoid has been replaced with some other ailments. Television has informed people of life in Kansas City. Names like Dangel and Schweitzer still are found in Turner County. Interstate 29 can get you to Sioux Falls for a night out. Maybe things don't change that much, and maybe that is fine.

One problem in South Dakota is that finding a doctor can really be a challenge. People in Little Edgemont (in the southwest corner) who need a full-service hospital may wish they lived elsewhere. "Physician's assistants" fill in when needed.

It is no secret that the loneliness of South Dakota life can lead to large social problems not restricted to cities alone. Alcohol abuse, drugs, economic hardships, and depression dot the landscape in counties like Corson, Dewey, and Ziebach. Talk to anyone there who works with youth for more details.

Life can be lonely, indeed, if you are black. There simply are not many blacks who live in South Dakota. Only 94 were counted in the 1870 census. The census in 1990 did not do much better. The King holiday in January goes by with hardly a word. The old line is that people of color in South Dakota are Italians who have moved in from Cleveland or Syracuse.

Even in "big city" places like Mitchell, home of the Corn Palace, life can be kind of slow no matter what the skin color. Try a few nights at the Chief Motel in Mitchell as you research the term "Middle Border" before lunch. The search for the meaning of the term may be all the excitement Mitchell sees that day.

A large city?

Sioux Falls (pop. 100,800 folks) is located in County Minnehaha, and is big by South Dakota comparisons. The place has lovely quartzite buildings, a nice baseball stadium, and incessant train whistles serenading downtown. Forgive the cars that have not been washed since statehood in 1889.

All of the above takes place in Sioux Falls amid a Breadbasket culture that is a little bit Western in flavor.

Newspaper sales in Sioux Falls keep people aware of what happens in Minneapolis.

Non-stops to Chicago from Sioux Falls every day provide a connection to the East, too.

Ask in Mitchell (pop. 13,700) about differences between East and West.

Better, go over to Chamberlain. There hay grinding and full-energy soybeans are big items. So is a payment to Deere and Company. Who will be crowned Snow Queen is important, too.

Going west some more, it is obvious as the nose on one's face that Pine Ridge is different from Chamberlain. In the Pine Ridge-Porcupine area you will notice names like Eli Feather Earring, Loren Two Crow, and Loren Kills Small. They were high school basketball players not too long ago. Schools like Crazy Horse, Little Wound, and Crow Creek dot the sports schedules.

Indians and those who are not Indians were involved not long ago in "1990 – Beginning Reconciliation," an attempt in South Dakota to get people to understand and appreciate Indian life, lore, mythology, religion, and government. Some people read *Bury My Heart at Wounded Knee*, while others examined Vine Deloria's *God is Red*. The history and the heritage, please note, can be two different things.

Indians have a sense of humor, of course, and here is a sampling of both Custer and Columbus jokes, two favorite categories for the Indians. "What did Custer say when he realized he was surrounded with no hope for survival? Well, it's better than going back to North Dakota." "What did the Indians say to one another when they saw Columbus land?

Well, there goes the neighborhood." On and on the jokes go.
To too many people, unfortunately, Native Americans are similar to the ones in John T. McCutcheon's 1907 cartoon, "Injun Summer." Autumn is "when all the homesick Injuns come back to play." The leaves become red "when an old Injun sperrit gits tired dancin' an' goes up an' squats on a leaf t' rest."
There is not much levity, although there is "political correctness," when it comes to the mention of the place where the Sioux Indians were victorious many years ago. Is it "the Custer Battlefield"? Or is it "The Little Bighorn Battlefield"? General Philip H. Sheridan in 1876 referred to "Custer's battle." Let us move on, political correctness to the side.
The thinking of South Dakotans in Deadwood is focused not on political correctness as much as on legalized gambling in town. Seems that Wild Bill Hickock was shot in Deadwood in 1876, and there appears to be a desire to create a similar carnival-type atmosphere in Deadwood these days. Ask for Calamity Jane's.
South Dakotans with good memories will recall January 22, 1943, when the temperature went from -4 to +45 in Spearfish in a few minutes! It is a record. A similar warning is given in this book to those visiting North Dakota.
The cold weather of South Dakota is remembered easily by those who attended school in a real Breadbasket hallmark — the one-room schoolhouse. There were 3,300 such things in the state in 1967, but only 98 in 1990. Many people tell incredible tales about trekking to school in the morning through brutal weather.
No matter what the weather in South Dakota, certain people want little or no part of it. People who run Super 8 Motels, Fairfield Inns, Bob Evans restaurants, Econo-Lodges, and Hilton Hotels do not vend their products in South Dakota.
Life is so simple that over in Pierre (pop. 13,000) the three "r words" are ride, riding, and rode.

There are not megabucks to be earned in South Dakota, and such a condition is known to drug dealers. In 1990 a survey by the Senate Judiciary Committee said that South Dakota ranked last in cocaine addicts (D.C. was first, New York second). The numbers are just not there in South Dakota to enhance significantly the profits of the drug people.

If people want to spend a few bucks at the immense Crazy Horse Memorial a short distance from Mt. Rushmore, that's just fine. The Memorial is something else. It is 563 feet high and 641 feet long. More significant than the size of the Memorial is that it is a statement about the place of Indians in America. The struggle continues.

Of course, it is obvious that South Dakota is not in the center of the universe, which suits the folks at Wall Drug in Wall (1,500 motel beds in town) just fine. The store has progressed nicely since 1931 when free ice water was given to thirsty tourists. Over $8 million was grossed in 1990 with the sale of everything from postcards to bull harnesses.

Mount Rushmore is really something. It is hard to believe that work ended there on October 31, 1941. It is also hard to believe that four politicians could look out on the American people for so long and still have their mouths closed.

Enjoy a South Dakota vacation.

During July, of course.

IOWA

Really A State of Mind

If Vermont is green, and if California is golden, then we should probably color Iowa red, provided one is looking at the terrain photographed by a Land-Sat camera from 80,000 feet up. The red indicates that agriculture is the order of the day.

Iowa is agriculture.

Small Burlington (pop. 27,000) is a place where one can see some agriculture and the people who work therein. Let us begin there.

The city has attractive old churches like First United Methodist and Christ Episcopal, as well as the old (in Beaux Arts Classical!) Free Public Library, proof of the importance of education to Iowans. Burlington has good potato chips (Sterzing's), too. Did we neglect Memorial Auditorium on the river with the Ten Commandments near the front door?

Mark Twain was correct when he described Burlington as "a very sober city." Burlington, by the way, may be the only place where you see the word "criterium." Pedal your bike toward Snake Alley.

Wait one minute.

Why not get to the heart of things in this chapter as quickly as possible, since Iowans seem pretty good at that anyway?

The beauty of Iowa is found in its gentle pace and in its willingness to work. A certain "sophistication" is noticed, too.

One must clarify by giving some background.

First, Iowa is not as isolated as some Easterners would have one think. Des Moines is a plane trip of only 45 minutes from Chicago. Cedar Rapids is not difficult to get to, either. Sports fans know that living in Des Moines can put a person near three major collegiate sports conferences (Big 12 in Ames, Missouri Valley in Des Moines, and Big 10 in Iowa City).

Des Moines is not far, either, from a major league "cousin"

to the south (Kansas City) or from a jewel sitting to the north (Minneapolis). Business can be done to the west (Omaha), too.

Second, Iowans take work seriously. The reason the streets roll up a little early in Clinton after the minor league baseball game is not because the locals are backward or puritanical. It is because there is a lot of work to be done in the early morning.

That hard work is visible to motorists who move along I-80 seeing signs for Delhi, Colfax, New Sharon, Mingo, Tama, Montezuma, Amana, and What Cheer. (To Westerners heading for Chicago or for Easterners thinking of the slopes in Colorado an appreciation of the work necessary to run a farm may be lost.)

Third, certain places in Iowa may have more in common with life in a "big city" than one thinks. A place like Iowa City, home of the University of Iowa, has some things in common with large American cities, although not necessarily with small Iowa towns a few miles away. The doings in Ames at Iowa State University look like the doings at "fancy schools" in the East, too.

Schools in Iowa are good. That is where the sophistication comes in. Skills, too.

So there.

No one should be shocked at how Iowa is not so "hick" after all. Not isolated, either.

Are there ethnics in Iowa, like in Chicago? Notice the Czechs and the Lebanese in Cedar Rapids.

How about the category marked "other"?

Hoboes have gathered each year in Britt since 1933. The "convention" attracts names that would make a manager of a professional wrestler proud. Inkman, Seattle Slim, Cardboard, Lord Openroad, and Slow Motion Shorty are but a few names. Seattle Slim informs the world, "a hobo is someone who works and wanders. A tramp is someone who dreams and wanders. A bum is someone who drinks and bums."

Hoboes dislike "bulls," who are police, as well as "citizens," who are non-hoboes. Hoboes, who are not to be called homeless, just kind of "motivate" around. Iowa is good to them. Are there poor areas? Go to Gravity. Not much happens there. Many have left. Those who have stayed see closed stores and young people leaving. Elderly? Age is important in Iowa. Many retirees are noticed, not to mention that the state has several centenarians. Those from Florida and Pennsylvania can verify this. A person of note in Iowa? A hero?

Roger Peterson always took his job seriously, and he worked in Cerro Gordo County (seat: Mason City). On a winter night years ago he was told by his boss to fly the company's plane to the Fargo-Moorhead area so that the three passengers in the plane could perform there. Peterson was only 21 years of age in 1959.

The story about Peterson should sound familiar, especially if you think you know the history of rock and roll and its connection to Iowa. The passengers on February 2, 1959 were Ritchie Valens, Buddy Holly, and Jiles P. Richardson (aka the "Big Bopper"). All perished when the plane crashed. The three had performed at the Surf Ballroom in Clear Lake. Tickets were $1.25. Some still remember Roger Peterson's name, and almost everyone in Cerro Gordo County remembers some details about the disaster on Albert Juhl's farm "the day the music died." Only a handful remember who the "added attraction" was that night (Frankie Sardo!).

Seldom mentioned in this Iowa-Peterson-Holly story is that Holly's career was not going so well at the time of his death. Spring Valley in Illinois was another place on the tour in 1959, to give an idea of the size of the "cities" he was playing. Fort Dodge in Iowa was another.

A Breadbasket city with some history is Sioux City (pop. 80,000), known more for the packing of meat than anything else. Names like Cudahy, Armour, and Swift ran their affairs in Sioux City with much success for many years. Seek out the 1912 Sioux City Livestock Exchange building and try to imagine all the history.

In Sioux City make sure you visit the Coney Island restaurant (since 1921!) on Nebraska Street. Information will be given free of charge. Buy a few Siouxvenirs to help the economy.

Waterloo (66,000 souls) is the place where those at the Waterloo Gasoline Engine Company once put their heads together with the folks at Deere and Company around 1918. The rest is (tractor) history. (Ask a Waterloo person why 1837 and 1874 are important. Someone there should know that the two dates correspond to the advent of the self-polishing steel plow and the invention of barbed wire respectively.)

If anything gets under the skin of an Iowan, by the way, it is an Easterner with a large mouth and a big agenda. In January 1977 Drake University in Des Moines was losing at the wire at home to Al McGuire's Marquette team. McGuire walked onto the court at the tail end of the game to tell his players where to stand. The radio people (WHO AM 1040), the Drake coach, and 10,000 Drake Bulldog rooters howled in disapproval. Be careful about coming on strong in the Midlands.

Those who do not come on strong enjoy life in the southwest corner of the state in the small but friendly burgs of Clarinda, Atlantic, and Shenandoah, each within earshot (or "radioshot") of the race results of Ak-Sar-Ben racetrack in Omaha. Tiny Winterset gave us Marion Robert Morrison (aka John Wayne, American), and from Clarinda came Glenn Miller.

Some relaxation in Iowa?

For many places which cannot pay the high price necessary for major league athletic franchises, there is minor league baseball in the summer. Iowa has such teams in Burlington, Clinton, Cedar Rapids, Des Moines, and Davenport. Rocky Colavito and Harry Chiti, two old names, polished their skills years ago in Cedar Rapids and Des Moines respectively. Minor league baseball may be cheaper for a young man than drinking beer at the local Knights of Columbus Hall.

Relax at Riverview Park (born 1937) in Clinton. The person next to you may choose to bring a pitcher of beer purchased at the park to her seat. There is no way that would happen at Engel Stadium in Chattanooga (for religious reasons) or at Tiger Stadium in Detroit (for safety reasons).

Did we not elaborate about Des Moines?

Des Moines had only about 20,000 people in 1865, but that's not bad when you consider that mighty Seattle had only about 25,000 in 1887. The two places are mentioned together because their numbers were similar many years ago, and both today have a lot of well-behaved, hard-working types.

The only hint of trouble in Des Moines is found in the boxes that vend the Omaha newspaper to gamblers following the ponies and dogs in Omaha. The Nebraska city is only about 135 miles from Des Moines.

In Des Moines the Principal Building (630 feet high) is Iowa's highest. Comparisons with New York, Chicago, and other cities prove very little. Iowans feel no need to apologize.

As you lean against the sign that says "Sbrocco Fruit Company" along Court Avenue in Des Moines please realize that time moves slowly in Des Moines, or so it seems. That may be because a person can get more done in two hours in Des Moines than in four hours in larger cities to the east.

Des Moines is a good test market. If you can sell a product to Des Moines people, then you can pretty much take it anywhere. If the sell is tough, forget it.

Do not forget that Des Moines behavior was argued about in the case labeled Tinker v. Des Moines (1969) involving student rights about free speech.

Des Moines is easy to find. Go to where the Des Moines River meets the Raccoon. Then have a cold one along Court

Avenue to celebrate.

Dubuque?

Dubuque was the site years ago of a great lead rush, not a gold rush, and a few (German farmers?) put their money in the German Bank on Main Street.

Small efforts are made today in downtown Dubuque to preserve a sense of local history. There is reference to William "Hog" Ryan, a founding father who sired 10 children a century ago. Perhaps he had his money in the Harvest Savings Bank.

Could this chapter end without mentioning Davenport, home to 100,000 people?

Davenport people claim to have a "personal relationship" with the Mississippi. Building up walls to stop flooding does not seem to be a good idea.

Davenport reports that 34 million people live within six hours of the city. At least that is what Iowa's director of riverboat gambling was saying in March 1991 as the area was gearing up for tourists. The odds today are 3 to 1 that raising kids in Davenport is a good idea. Those kids can see baseball at adorable John O'Donnell Stadium (dedicated 1931).

Finally, historians should locate the August 9, 1941 issue of *Wallace's Farmer and Iowa Homestead* magazine. In it one will see that Iowa people are asked to be people of "good farming, clear thinking, and right living." Also in that issue is the lead article "When It's Judging Time in the Hog Ring."

Need more be said about Iowa?

Yes, but there is not room here.

Come visit.

A pleasant surprise awaits.

Nebraska

While Supplies Last

Most Americans are probably more familiar with a mention of hunting witches in Massachusetts than with life in the Sandhills of Nebraska.

Many people can get through a few names on the 1960 New York Yankees (Bobby Richardson, Elston Howard), but how many can name the current governor of Nebraska?

All those who visited Nebraska during its quasquicentennial a few years ago may be more familiar with Nebraska than before, but the state remains unknown to millions.

Nebraska is home to 1.5 million people. The state is not visited by hundreds of thousands annually.

But all is not lost.

The people of Nebraska work hard at providing food for others. The people are models of efficiency in areas like paying bills and being on time. Many are well educated. Many live to a ripe old age.

How to learn of Nebraska? Go and visit.

Tourists should head for Omaha. Then Lincoln. Then to points west, like Window Rock. Sterile buildings and pink phone messages back home will be a thing of the past.

A glance at the nearest map will allow us to see some "big" places on the Cornhusker landscape.

Notice Kearney, where you may feel a mix of the Midwest and the West. A change in air quality may take place, too.

Notice the Platte River.

Be aware that the quiet of Nebraska takes on a dark side in the northwest corner of the state along Highway 20. Several towns there are fighting to stay alive with populations of about 1,300 (as in Rushville). Gordon, Cody, Valentine, Hay Springs, and Chadron all can relate to the difficulties of small town survival.

Some places will stop at nothing to find an advantage, and

such is the case in Cozad, a place that says it is the "100th Meridian City." The idea may be a profitable one since the 98th meridian has marked the beginning of the West for many people for years.

How might such "dots" on the map survive in the future? Geographer Frank Popper says there should be an area called the Buffalo Commons, stretching from the 98th meridian over to an arbitrary line running over the top of the Rockies. In those lands, home now to many elk and bobcats, there could be more national parks and other attractions. So, Popper argues, the area(s) can survive. Stay tuned.

Omaha (400,000 people) certainly is surviving. The city is only about 10 percent black, but that does not stop the black community from feeling proud about one of its own, the late Malcolm X (born Malcolm Little). His birthsite is 3448 Pinckney Street. His life and legacy cause some whites in Omaha to cringe, although many blacks there feel proud. About such a situation Malcolm X would probably say, "Think – it's not illegal yet." (Study his life "by any means necessary." Don't be surprised to hear that he was the grandson of a white man. The story may be especially meaningful for those who are "ex-Christians and ex-slaves".)

Omaha was special on June 19, 1977. As people sat waiting for the concert to begin, sweat was on the hands of everyone. Several patrons made a run to the bathroom out of sheer nervousness. The 240-pound superstar was soon to make his appearance. The headliner was not a chubby Kenny Rogers. Nor was it an overweight Roy Clark. The star was none other than Elvis Presley. Elvis huffed and puffed through the concert like a horse in the last race at Omaha's Ak-Sar-Ben race track. The night is remembered, of course, since Elvis passed away such a short time later. (Chicagoans have similar memories of sweaty palms with Elvis on March 28, 1957, when the singer swiveled away in Chicago. What a difference 20 years, 65 pounds, and an electric guitar can make.)

January, 1957 was an important time in Omaha history, too. That is when someone started to monitor things in the war room of the Strategic Air Command (SAC). Similar "command consoles" are found in Ft. Richie, Maryland and Colorado Springs, Colorado.

Omaha has Boys Town, founded at 25th and Dodge on December 10, 1917. The school now accepts girls, and the phrase "there are no bad girls" seems totally in line with what Boys Town hopes to accomplish. Few realize that Fr. Flanagan once worked with alcoholic men before working with young boys, and even fewer realize that St. Vincent's in Marin County, California claims to be "the first Boys Town," since 1855 marks the beginning of St. Vincent's. That is 31 years before Fr. Flanagan was born.

Corn-fed Omahans like to narrate details about an economy that is recession-proof, the Union Pacific railroad, ConAgra projects, and 800 phone numbers. The gist of the 800 numbers is that the city is the 1-800 "capital" of the United States. Omahans have no discernible accent on the phone.

Omaha has excellent numbers. The number of people multiplied by the number of square miles times the degree of difficulty in finding Dodge Street equal a lifestyle that is the envy of those in Newark and Santa Barbara.

Another big city in Nebraska? Is there one?

A rousing time for Cornhuskers is found on fall Saturdays in Lincoln (pop. 191,000), the capital. The University of Nebraska puts the hammer with regularity to Iowa State University, Kansas, and Kansas State, among others, to the absolute delight of 75,650 boisterous patrons. As if by magic, the red of Nebraska football turns to green in the cash drawer at kickoff time.

Let us now do some (big) driving after the football game, remembering the line about the football stadium being the third largest "city" in the state on game day.

Sidney, not big by anyone's measure, may be one place in

rural Nebraska that reminds a person of the Breadbasket at its best. With a population of about 6,000, Sidney suffered a lot when it lost in 1984 the last cord-board, operator-run phone system. AT&T was the culprit. Ella Runge, operator from 1920-1927, was heard to say the immortal words, "I hate to see it go." (In 1990 the last hand-cranked party-line phone system was disconnected in North Fork, Idaho.)

Changes in phone service over the years should be expected, given the few Nebraskans one finds in some regions. Seven counties in Nebraska have less than a thousand people, and there are only about sixteen such counties in the entire country. The seven in Nebraska are Arthur, Blaine, Grant, Hooker, Loup, McPherson, and Thomas.

Memorize those names while in Scottsbluff watching the plane above going between Sacramento and Chicago. The pilot will be mentioning that Scottsbluff is below.

At Scottsbluff adjust the wristwatch. Scottsbluff as well as Cozad do serve a purpose.

One worthwhile activity when walking in Scottsbluff is the study of the Oregon Trail (born 1843). Those who undertake such a study should memorize these words: "this stretch has not changed much in 150 years." The meaning will be clear to all.

The change of time on the wrist is important for the farmers who go all the way from Sidney to Lincoln (345 miles!) in the fall for college football and return home to Sidney the same day. Such is the price one pays for living in western Nebraska.

If one wants to talk about sheer size, then consider Cherry County. The place is immense.

Immense, too, is the interest in Red Cloud about author Willa Cather. (Remember that in the Introduction it was said that there would be a mention of some heroes and villains? Some of her work has angered and puzzled many observers of Hispanic life in the Southwest. Those at the Millicent Rogers

Museum in Taos, New Mexico can supply other details. Those at Third and Cedar in Red Cloud, Nebraska, however, will remind all that Cather was inducted into the state's Hall of Fame in 1962.)

A more recent Nebraska contribution who has become a part of the American scene is comedian Johnny Carson, who at times used to mention his roots in Norfolk, Nebraska as well in Corning, Iowa.

Many Nebraskans are like that. They remember the good times.

Giddy up!

Kansas
Former Desert, Current Oasis

One of the easiest ways to get someone's attention is to shock him or her, so this chapter will begin with some things which most people would not associate with Kansas.

First, there is a nuclear plant in Burlington in Coffey County. The plant is big.

Second, a famous prostitute once worked Dodge City, "Squirrel Tooth" Alice.

Third, there is much history in "Bloody" Newton.

Fourth, Wichita State University is a real university, although Kansas and Kansas State alumni might think otherwise.

Fifth, be nice to people from Kansas. Kansans provide food. Detroit and Knoxville cannot make that claim.

There.

We now have our attention on a place, Kansas, which many probably will not visit.

The notepad may have to work overtime in this chapter to make up for that.

Let us go from east to west, starting in Leavenworth (born 1854), the first city of Kansas. We will then use I-70 in order to go west. Wichita and Kansas City (Kansas) will be mentioned toward the end of our trip.

By the way, the first note may be to warn everyone that Kansas at five in the afternoon in late April may not be a good idea. That is when tornados come calling. Many Easterners may find that alarming.

Leavenworth (population just under 30,000 now and forever) is the land of Guenthers, Larkins, and Willcotts. All three families remember German social organizations in town. Sociology majors will enjoy studying the Untestuetzungs Verein years ago at St. Joseph's Church.

Some Leavenworth Germans know their cards. It helps to

be able to play some sheepshead. Know a maurer from a schneider.

Know about the miltary in Leavenworth, too, especially at Leavenworth National Cemetery. The markers there are interesting. One says, "On fame's eternal camping-ground/their silent tents are spread/And glory guards with solemn round/the bivouac of the dead."

Stump those in the military by asking them the "historically correct" name of the GI Bill. It was the Servicemen's Readjustment Act of 1944.

Some who survive in Leavenworth are doing time at the prison along Metropolitan Avenue. John Grindstone, a Native American, was the first inmate, "received" in 1906. (Mr. Grindstone was doing a little "devilment," to use a word from the local lexicon.)

After a cheeseburger at Homer's in Leavenworth one can head south on Fourth Street and get on Interstate 70.

Let us go west (as Horace Greeley told us), heading for Lawrence, Topeka, Manhattan, and Goodland (near the Colorado line).

Lawrence (established 1854) was a cherished stop along the Underground Railroad decades ago. Now it is a typical college town: fast food, rowdyism, eager-to-move-on students, and money to be budgeted everywhere. Detractors of KU call it "Snob Hill."

Many moons ago Lawrence was "beset by Indians, cholera, and starvation," but today research on both the Oregon and the Santa Fe Trails can be done there. Visit right quick now.

KU people like to mention that the crimson and blue colors were chosen because the founders of KU had Harvard and Yale connections. An 1856 graduate of Harvard, Daniel Webster Wilder, was the father of the Kansas Historical Society, for the record.

The inventor of basketball, Doctor James Naismith, coached at KU. Few remember that Naismith was ordained to the ministry in 1916. Practically no one remembers that he did not think too highly of his invention of basket ball (two words then).

Next on the westward trek on I-70 is Topeka (pop. 119,000), the home of the award-winning *Capital-Journal* newspaper. Unlike most Breadbasket cities, Topeka has a sizeable Mexican population. Agenda items there include: 1) the future of mining in the state, 2) the effects of liquor by the drink, and 3) the "hayseed" image of the state.

A copy of Brown v. Board of Education (1954) should adorn the coffee table of all serious students of American life. Ask in Topeka for someone who remembers the words "Negroes and Mexicans served in sacks only" in the city's restaurants.

Manhattan, the home of Kansas State University, is the land of the exciting basketball game and the lost football game. The university dominates the local scene. The school is called "Silo Tech" by its detractors.

Near Manhattan is Junction City, where many a lad working for Uncle Sam lost his sobriety and his virginity often on the same evening.

Beyond Junction City there are places like Salina (pop. 42,100) and Hays (pop. 17,000). Life is quiet in both. Notice the plane heading from Chicago to California in the blue sky above Salina and Hays.

Highway 81, by the way, connects Salina with Wichita and Concordia. Eastern and Western Kansas are defined thereby. Altitude, climate, and perceptions differ one side of 81 to the other.

At the end of the Kansas westbound portion of I-70 is Goodland, which has a lot of good land, just like Richland County, Illinois has a lot of rich land. Colorado is close by. The border is pretty transparent. Kansans and Coloradans both operate farms.

The farmers in Goodland know that it is a long 405 miles

to Kansas City (in Kansas, remember). Our "switchback" to KCK will make newcomers run for a map, if not for more water.

KCK (pop. 150,000) knows about the life of the late jazz giant Charlie "Yardbird" Parker.

KCK's biggest plus may be its proximity to Kansas City, Missouri (the one with the Savoy Grill, Hallmark Cards, and Swope Park).

About the only newsy thing from KCK in recent days was a good fight over some land in the Quindaro section. To some the site was merely a landfill, but to others the place was an important stop on the Underground Railroad.

A Kansas treat? Go to a party in October in the barn of a friend. Upon arrival, graciously accept your coffee can filled with sand so that one cigarette does not ignite the place. Head for the hay with the person you arrived with, and have a nice cold one. Enjoy the band playing "Cruel Hearted Woman." Sing along. Some hay down the neck is fine. Kansas, though eclipsed on the national scene, still offers some fun on the local level.

Did we forget to mention the largest city in the state?

Wichita, warm in the summer and cold in the winter like the Midlands in general, is a city which is usually an afterthought. When agriculture is discussed, Wichita is not always mentioned. When the joys of the Sunbelt are explained, Wichita, though pretty sunny, is not included.

But all is not lost.

Wichita has 180,000 people who are the down-to-earth working kind, and, believe it or not, the place is somewhat centrally located. If the goal is to get to big-time Kansas City, Missouri, the trip is easy. If the agenda calls for skiing in Colorado, fishing in Arkansas, or watching football in Oklahoma, the task is not difficult.

The story is told that a woman was driving according to the law in downtown Wichita a few years ago, but she was given two tickets by the police. Not the kind of tickets that involve the police and the courts, but the kind that entitle two people to space at Levitt Arena where the Wichita State University Wheat Shockers play basketball. Not a bad idea to make life a little nicer. It is hard to beat Breadbasket values.

Wichita is so much a part of Mainstreet, USA that it has an old five and dime building downtown, erected years ago by S. H. Kress and Co. (never to be confused with Sebastian S. Kresge's stores).

A final stop?

Breadbasket wisdom also obtains along Wyatt Earp Boulevard in Dodge City, although back in 1872 the situation was a little different. Murderers, prostitutes, and others cooled out at the Longbranch Saloon, and Boot Hill was well known to all.

Today Dodge is quiet. The most difficult task in town is to imagine 850,000 buffalo hides being shipped to waiting consumers between the years 1872-1874.

Enjoy Kansas. You may be pleasantly surprised by the people there.

You won't beat them for hospitality and blue skies.

Start your trip in Mudville (in Anderson County) where Mighty Casey struck out.

You'll enjoy Kansas .

Missouri

Bushwackers and Baseball

The divergence that is Missouri is truly remarkable. From Kansas City to St. Louis and from the Bootheel across to St. Joseph there is the feeling that Missouri is a special place.

Here are the reasons: hunting, fishing, hiking, farming, swimming, a gentle pace, sports of all types, friendly people, and two big cities.

Missouri is Dixie and Breadbasket, Southern as well as Midwestern. The North gets in the mix, too. The *Missouri Republican* in 1855 said of St. Louis that "the sugars of the South lay mingled with the cereals of the North." Today look in all four directions before crossing Clark Avenue near the Kiel Center in St. Louis.

Missouri gave us Chuck Berry and Stan Musial and T. S. Eliot.

William Clay, too.

Missouri has small towns and two big cities, gourmet restaurants and greasy-spoon dives, not to mention folksy bars which dispense (for free) profound advice about life in Missouri and elsewhere. Ask about Peculiar.

Gas up the car.

Where better to start in Missouri than with a place along old Route 66?

Joplin (pop. 39,000) has a history of lead and zinc. While having a hot dog in Schifferdecker Park, try to figure out the correct label which describes Joplin. Is it Breadbasket or Dixie? Try to locate the old "Klavern" where the Klan planned their night's work back in 1922. Put a check next to some of things listed above that can be found here.

Ask about the Champagne Cafe on Main Street in Joplin. The food is just as tasty as the fare at the Pig Hip in Broadwell, Illinois, also along old Route 66.

During dessert contemplate the southern roots in Missouri. Those roots are so strong that the term "Little Dixie" will be noticed. Ask for a clarification in Columbia, a part of Boone County.

A Southern "feel" is also obvious in Missouri's Bootheel, six counties in the southeast corner. Name the six counties for homework.

Do not say that Little Dixie and the Bootheel are not in the South. They walk, talk, and work Southern. Some people claim that the areas are in the Midwest. The two regions have very little in common with the Midwest, as any politician or geographer can tell you.

The Midwest is another matter.

Go to Kansas City (population 435,136), the capital of America's Breadbasket, for the Midwest.

Locating Kansas City might be the first task. The city is in western Missouri, near Kansas City, Kansas, which is in eastern Kansas. The Missouri River and the Kansas River are noticed, too.

That was the Missouri, not the Mississippi or the Nile. People who don't do their homework make fools of themselves constantly at luncheons at Crown Center in Kansas City (Missouri!) when they say that they are so happy to be visiting "the plains of Kansas."

Kansas City is known well to football fans who remember the dapper Hank Stram coaching the Chiefs to the Super Bowl trophy in New Orleans in January 1970.

The Chiefs now play their games in gorgeous Arrowhead Stadium (cap. 78,000). The place is a must on a warm October afternoon.

Kansas City has a black community that is studied seriously by whites when music history is the subject matter. Names like Count Basie, Buster Smith, and Bennie Moten should be memorized.

Kansas City serves as a barometer for the weather, too, not

just for racial and musical matters. The National Severe Storms Forecast Center is there. Draw a line from the Texas Panhandle to Lamoni, Iowa to find where the tornados go.

It looks like a tornado has passed over much of Prospect Street in Kansas City. Black jazz club after black jazz club has tried and failed to make it there.

The Midwest/South "mix" can be studied by driving the car east from Kansas City.

The drive east on Interstate 70 toward Columbia and St. Louis will allow a person to see signs for Kemper Military School and College (born 21 years before the Lincoln assassination) in Boonville. The South, remember, is "freely martial." Those at the Missouri Military Academy in Mexico know all about that.

Brochures along Interstate 70 will talk about Branson (south of Springfield). Those in fast-growing Branson can talk about Southern life, too.

Country music in Branson is a big thing. The two sounds you hear in the 1990's are a cement truck pouring a foundation and a sideman warming up.

Kansas Citians meet St. Louisans in Branson.

Brushing up on St. Louis is a must.

St. Louis (390,000 baseball fans in city, 2.4 million in metro area) is a city which reminds some of Cincinnati. Each has factories galore, a love of chili, a major river, Southerners come north, many corporate headquarters, a Jesuit university, and a "working man's" feel to things. Each place has some vestiges of ethnicity, tolerable winters, paddlewheelers, no professional basketball, and thousands who love baseball.

Begin in St. Louis with notes about the 1857 Dred Scott v. Sanford (not Sandford!) case. The phrase "We the people" may take on new meaning.

Move on to 1880. At that time there was the use of German in the public schools. People from St. Louis, mentioned above, can verify that there indeed was bilingual education in the United States many years ago.

St. Louis based its future on the river about 140 years ago, but Chicago turned to the railroads. The difference is big.

Many blacks have come to St. Louis from the South, but the sledding has not been easy in the recent past. In 1966 41.8 percent of the community was below the poverty line in the city. In 1990 the figure was 33.1 percent.

St. Louis is centrally located enough for some people to think that the nation's capital should be there? Sure. The location, the agriculture, the demography, the Mississippi, and the ample work force make some people think that this is a good idea.

Visitors by air to St. Louis may think that the height and the base of the Arch are not equal in length. They are.

Many will equate St. Louis with baseball announcer Harry Carabina (aka Harry Caray). Shouts of "Holy Cow" still echo inside Busch Stadium.

Sipping a Bud or two may make you think of the old days at Kiel Auditorium. One can dream of basketball's Bob Pettit and wrestling's Wladek "Killer" Kowalski. Both were big draws at the old Kiel (dedicated 1934).

A few blocks from the new Kiel Center (dedicated 1994) is Union Station (born 1894) where the modern is preferred over the not-so-modern. Trendy shops dot the territory, similar to a cultural clone 200 miles to the east, Union Station (born 1888) in Indianapolis. The last passenger train pulled out of Union Station in St. Louis on October 31, 1978.

The mention of Budweiser brings the name of August A. Busch, Jr. to mind, but there was another beer baron in St. Louis who received some attention years ago. The name was Christian Frederick Wilhelm Von Der Ahe. He owned a beer hall and the St. Louis Browns baseball team. Apparently the man was a real character ("I am der boss president of der Prowns"). He told his players to hit the ball to places where the other team was not standing. When the other team got a hit, Chris would complain to his men that they were playing out of position! (Do not confuse Von der Ahe with the Von der Horst family from Baltimore. The latter produced Eagle Beer. Another "cultural clone," if you will.)

Some sports venues have been fixed up recently in St. Louis. The joke was that St. Louis people were thinking that a "luxury box" was a 12-pack of Michelob.

One would be wise to keep an eye on both beer and baseball in St. Louis. Those who toe the rubber and belly up to the bar must be careful not to spoil the image. Beer is very important to baseball, and vice versa.

Another note will be about the St. Louis Arena (born 1929). Those who study old buildings will notice the Lamella roof ("a continuous network having the appearance of a fish net and the efficiency of an arch"). That is enough to keep architecture students busy for two Cardinals home stands at Busch Stadium.

Let us not get confused with the label of "Gateway to the West" applied to St. Louis. Some pretty big places like Omaha, Ft. Worth, and even Schenectady have called themselves the same thing, and some smaller places like Independence, Missouri and Dickinson, North Dakota have, too. There are many gateways.

Now hum the "St. Louis Blues" (not really a blues song, and written with the mind on Memphis, not St. Louis).

A Missouri staple is the legendary Paul Harvey, whose voice is gospel to Missouri people and to the Breadbasket in general. Paul Harvey's "closers" are very well known to hardworking farmers ("The lady who used to get sawed in half in the circus has finally retired. She lives in New Orleans ... and Chicago. Paul Harvey. Good Day").

We do not want to forget St. Joseph, the place where the Pony Express started on April 3, 1860 and where Jesse James ended on April 3, 1882. Inquire about Jesse along Edmond Street. Was he a hero or a villain?

In Springfield (140,494 folks) one must know the meaning

of B.A.S.S. (Bass Anglers Sportsman Society). The B.A.S.S. people not long ago had to face the issue of having women in its national tournament.

Sedalia (pop. 140,000) is quiet these days, although once in a while someone studying history will look up the origins of "ragged time" music in 1895. Ragtime, described by some as "white music played black," was played rather well by Arthur Marshall and Scott Joplin. Marshall once used the words "upholstered sewers" to describe the downtown brothels of Sedalia.

Life is poor, if not ragged, in the Bootheel, an area that has a kinship with Memphis more than with St. Louis. In Gobler and Braggadocio there is the distinct feeling that things can only get better in categories such as teenage pregnancy, infant mortality, education, and substandard housing. Study either New Madrid County or Pemiscot County in order to see the effects of 360 cancer deaths per 100,000 people, compared to 212 nation-wide.

It was said at the start of the chapter that Missouri was a mixture of things.

The state truly is.

All aboard for St. Louis.

Oklahoma

Two o'clock, No Sooner

Oklahoma is OK. Schizophrenic perhaps, but okay.

The state is oil patch, cowboy, folksy, friendly, forgetful (to be explained later), and in some places as much a part of the Breadbasket as Kansas or Nebraska.

Oklahoma is young. Oil came to Titusville, Pennsylvania in 1859, but it took until 1901 in Red Fork, Oklahoma. Racial problems surfaced in East St. Louis (1917) and in Omaha (1919) before Tulsa (1921). Oklahoma statehood did not come until 1907.

Let us look at Oklahoma City first.

The good news in Oklahoma City (444,000 in city; 975,000 in metro) is the climate, the friendly people, and the mild pace.

The bad news is that OKC is not taken too seriously by a lot of people. Those who are cowboy-Sunbelt-oil patch know that not being taken seriously is not a big problem.

All is not lost after all.

Oklahoma City, a noticeable part of the Breadbasket, gave the world college basketball coach Abe Lemons at Oklahoma City University (1956-1973). His endless one-liners were a treat. He once remarked that playing in New York City is tough, especially when two eggs and coffee the day after the game can cost a person $14.50.

Oklahoma City people lose their sense of humor when they remember the 1930's. There was the Dust Bowl, of course, as well as the death of the legendary Will Rogers.

Rogers is required reading ("my ancestors didn't come on the Mayflower, but they met the boat"). Trivia fans love to point out that Will was born in Oklahoma in 1879, not a state at the time, and died in Alaska in 1935, not a state at the time. Rogers was one-quarter Cherokee, a fact that is forgotten by many who are not Cherokee.

Perhaps Carl Sandberg said it best when he said that Rogers was "as homely as a mud fence, yet as beautiful as a sunrise over an Oklahoma field of alfalfa."

Do not even dream of visiting Oklahoma without reading about Will Rogers first.

Another happy note about OKC involves Bricktown (never to be confused with Bucktown in Chicago or Indianapolis, or with Buckhead in Atlanta). Folks in Bricktown enjoy a Dos Equis beer near the spot where women years ago took delivery of a spanking new stove.

Not far from Oklahoma City is Norman, synonymous with the University of Oklahoma. OU is a good place to go to school, although its football team is a lot better known than its Board of Trustees. OU football seems to be in the top five on everyone's list since Adam and Eve first ran the wishbone offense.

Before any OU alumni, friends or fans get too pumped up, it is only fair to report that some incredible events were taking place at the OU campus in late 1988 and early 1989. Pay-offs and drugs were part of the scene. At one point the FBI was called in. Some students found it hard to study as they watched a new Nissan 300 ZX being delivered to the star quarterback.

At OU people are really enthusiastic about football. The fans are behind the coach and the team win or tie.

All OU athletes would be wise to use the OU library which has many excellent works about life in Oklahoma and life in the entire Southwest. Whether the interest be trappers in New Mexico, "forgotten frontiers," or Apache Indians, the OU library does a nice job.

Doings in Norman are reported in the *Norman Transcript*, a bit of irony not lost on rival football coaches.

Of all the quotes featured in this book perhaps none is more laughable than this one given to the world by Oklahoma University's George Lynn Cross many years ago. He said, "I would like to build a university of which the football team can be proud." (Will the day ever come when college football undoes itself from television contracts, sweetheart deals for gym shoes, and big crowds watching the games? Robert Maynard Hutchins of the University of Chicago on January 12, 1940 said, "The greatest obstacle to the development of a university in this country is the popular misconception of what a university is. The two most popular of these are that it is a kindergarten and that it is a country club. Football has done as much as any single thing to originate, disseminate and confirm these misconceptions. By getting rid of football, by presenting the spectacle of a university that can be great without football, the University of Chicago may perform a signal service to higher education throughout the land.")

Tulsa (pop. 365,000), a place not easily connected with the Breadbasket, is associated with God. That is, the "g" stands for gas, the "o" for oil, and the "d" for drilling. Such things are *not* similar to life in OKC, he said culturally.

God has seen to it the bills get paid in Tulsa, due in small part to the presence of Oral Roberts. The eyes of the world focused on the city in January 1987 when Oral revealed that the Almighty would take him if $8 million were not received by late March.

Some Tulsans call on the Creator at the Will Rogers Methodist Church on South Yale Avenue.

Tulsa is "the most Northern Southern city." Friends should not let friends use such labels.

For legitimate fun and a rousing good time, see Tulsa University battle their hated rivals from Wichita State University in a game of roundball. Oil versus wheat is the storyline.

Tulsa has the old and the new, the obvious and the obscure. The old is the Union Depot (born 1931) with its art deco motif. The new is the Gilcrease Museum of Art. The obvious is the petroleum. The obscure takes place when the farmers and the drillers talk of their (differing) lifestyles.

North of Tulsa is Bartlesville (pop. 38,000), the chief complaint about which is the lack of something to do. Phillips Petroleum is Bartlesville. Bartlesville is Phillips.

Other books have capably described the plight of Indians in Oklahoma, but only a few books have dealt with black Indians in Oklahoma. Notice the "city" of Boley (founded 1904). A black Choctaw, Abigail Barnett, played a key role there. Visit Pecan Street.

Claremore, already mentioned, is a place some associate with the "Tennessee Waltz" (as recorded by Patti Page on the Mercury label). She was born in Claremore on November 8, 1927. The song sold over 7 million copies. Patti Page (real name: Clara Ann Fowler), who had paid her dues in Tulsa, was a sensation.

In Claremore and throughout Oklahoma avoid the term "Okies," by the way. Only those researching the (now gone) cottages along Reno Street in OKC are allowed to use the term.

Oklahomans (not "Okies") in Cimarron County can provide details about the Dust Bowl, the Depression, and Prohibition. Life was tough.

The Dust Bowl taught Oklahomans about survival, of course.

One must fight for survival today in both wheat farming and oil. The "boom or bust" cycle is a matter of emotion as well as politics, one is told. Memorize that line in order to understand Oklahoma life.

Another important item can be found within a radius of 60 miles of Boise City in Cimarron County. If you draw the radius correctly you'll touch parts of Oklahoma, Colorado, Kansas, Texas, and New Mexico. Those inside that circle must learn about wind erosion and its effects right quick.

The cultural mix that is found in Oklahoma has linguistic ramifications. If you are passing through southeastern Oklahoma you better know a "fireboard" from a "backlog" from a "backstick" near the fireplace.

It may be interesting to note that in recent years many have moved back to Oklahoma from, believe it or not, California. Seems that things like food, insurance, housing, and taxes in one were more costly than in the other. A total of 106,454 people from California moved to Oklahoma between the years of 1975 and 1986. As someone said, "westward, ha!"

On Black Sunday (April 14, 1935) a child of four was running around in northeast Oklahoma, and his name is Mickey Mantle. The Mick slugged a few homers as a young person in places like Spavinaw, Commerce, and Baxter Springs, and later went on to the New York Yankees, of course.

Baseball may mean the Tulsa Drillers to some people, but to veteran researchers there were the Pawhuska Indians and the Marietta Legionnaires, among others. The game goes well under a peaceful Oklahoma sun. For homework look up the history of the old Oklahoma City Natural Gassers.

Some today think of quickie marriages in Oklahoma, not baseball. Many a couple from the Kansas City, Missouri area hiked down Highway 69 to get married in Vinita or Miami, Oklahoma.

Have a nice time in Oklahoma. All one has to do is walk and talk like Will Rogers. He was just "an old country boy trying to get along."

We all should be.

Texas

Urban Giant

Texas can be flat and dry, very large and not too high, and, in the words of some people, an "urban frontier."

A state that is in its youth, Texas may be still feeling its way, at times clumsily. Illegals in Brownsville, adequate housing in Houston, and empty office space in Dallas continue to be problematic.

The state's agenda is a full one. Gas, wheat, water, real estate, computers, and large government contracts are fought over with as much energy as the Dallas Cowboys use to keep the Houston Oilers out of the end zone.

Oil Patch? Yes. Medical Patch, Government Patch, and Natural Gas Patch, too.

Impressive numbers (and concomitant bragging?) are part and parcel of the Texas story. Approximately 39,000 millionaires filed with the IRS a few years ago. Five million baby boomers were uncovered just the other day. A total of 3000 children were missing as this book went to press. A total of 260,000 kids got the paddle in 1988 alone. Fourteen people were executed in Texas from January 1 through Labor Day, 1993. Those figures would make anyone take notice, and there are more numbers to boot.

Texas (pop. 18.4 million people) surpassed New York (pop. 18.2 million people) in late 1994/early 1995, just for the record.

Texas is big (266,807 square miles), so we will start with a big, Texas-size challenge involving a native son, singer Jim Reeves. The challenge, or better the bet, is that no one can be snuggled up on the couch with a significant other for fifteen minutes as Reeves' "Am I that Easy to Forget" is being played on the radio. Most can last three minutes. A few can hold out for five. At last look, there wasn't a human (not even a Texan!) who can reach the required fifteen minutes. Now listen to "Oh, How I Miss You Tonight." The bet is safe. (For those who are asexual, put on "Welcome to My World.")

Stop reading this book now. Have some tamarind-glazed pork chops. Wash things down with a cold Lone Star long neck.

Now that everyone has cooled down, we might as well take a few notes about Jim Reeves, born in Panola County on August 20, 1924. For fifteen bucks he labored with a band or two in Shreveport. He was signed to a baseball contract by the St. Louis Cardinals. He was for years the best kept secret south of Tulsa. Although Reeves died in 1964, his music continues. People in Panola County still speak of him with reverence.

Texas is easily divided. Grab a yellow underliner again and put a large yellow dot over the following cities: Dallas, Houston, Laredo, Austin, San Angelo, El Paso, and Amarillo. Those places can be labeled with these names respectively: North Central, Coastal Plain, Southern Texas-Lower Valley, Hill Country, Edwards Plateau, Trans Pecos, and High Plains. These divisions may make this large state (254 counties) more manageable.

Please be advised that speaking English is highly recommended in Dallas, but speaking Spanish is necessary in Laredo. Speaking intelligently in any language in Austin is necessary, although Anglo lawyers prefer English. Consult your local cultural geographer if there are any questions.

Realize, too, that some Mexican-Americans in Texas feel that the hyphen in the label above can divide or unite. Others may not feel an ethnic "pull" at all. Walk gingerly through this.

For some Texans the history of the state began in 1836 at the Alamo, but for others the history began when April 10, 1962 rolled around. That was the day major league baseball played its first regular season game in domed Houston.

Texas bragging and Texas history take an interesting turn in the words of historian T. R. Fehrenbach. He has written that "the great difference between Texas and every other American state in the 20th century was that Texas had a history. Other American regions merely had records of development."

We will do a zig-zag across the state. Cities will appear in alphabetical order. Such a pattern is no more circuitous than the state's politics. The various Belts (Cotton, Sun, and Bible) are hard to separate anyway.

Abilene does not make the news very much. Our only note is that the atlas on the coffee table shows Abilene as the city that separates East Texas from West Texas. The entire state cannot fit on one page of the atlas, and the line must be drawn somewhere, so Abilene it is for now.

In September 1918 a well was drilled in Amarillo (pop. 188,000 now), and an immense natural gas field was discovered. The story about Amarillo continues if you are into a Panhandle-Bible Belt-old Route 66 city. Many people on Polk Street can tell you about the days when railroad people bragged that the city was conveniently (?) located between Ft. Worth and Denver.

Austin (465,000 souls) thinks that high-tech is the way to go. Oil, cattle, and timber are important to Austin people, but those things may have to do with other parts of Texas, not so much with Austin.

Austin has to do with Christian existentialism, Christian liberalism, and civil rights activism.

On Sixth Street in Austin many segments of the city can have a good time. Wear jewelry. Tell the joke that July and August are the only two bad things about Austin.

A garage sale in Austin in 1969 marked one of the early stages that led to the (Jane) Roe v. (Henry) Wade court case. Proceeds from the sale went to help women who wanted a safe, although at the time illegal, abortion.

Austin has water problems from time to time. Make a big note of that. The lack of water causes people to worry.

A quiet atmosphere exists over in College Station when Texas A&M is not playing football. When Texas A&M is playing Texas (the one in Austin), however, all hell breaks loose, and the losing coach frequently fears for his job. The quiet returns when A&M people file into church to sang the "Aggie Our Father." This is not a joke. (There really is, dadgummit, such a song, just like there is an "Hawaiian Our Father." True.)

Corpus Christi (257,000 people, 9.2 percent unemployed) is known universally for its sun-baked vacations, although the city is known by some today as a battlefield. Abortion opponents and proponents have had some real stemwinders. Ironically, the name of the city means "Body of Christ" in Latin.

We all know that Dallas (1.1 million souls) boasts of big numbers. There are about 3 million people in the metro area. The city alone will have 2.7 million inhabitants by the year 2000. In July 1987 the population of Houston was surpassed by Dallas, much to the chagrin of Houstonians and to the delight of Dallasites.

Amid the shiny buildings and expanding population, however, there are big problems in Dallas. Its very soul is being fought over, since blacks and other minorities feel they have never had a fair shake. Some black leaders label the city a racial time bomb, while some whites believe that it is time "to put J.R. back in the saddle."

Reported on the front page of the *Dallas Morning News* on February 6, 1991 was an item that mentioned that Dallas was 29.5 percent black and 20.9 percent Hispanic. The title was, "Census Shows Minorities Make Up Dallas Majority."

For many people the city is equated only with the football Cowboys and with November 22, 1963. On that day President Kennedy was shot, and the term "book depository" came into the English language.

Dallas was the apple of the eye of the National Football

League in 1960, the same year the Dallas Texans of the old American Football League were starting. The NFL saw big, big dollars in the Texas city. The AFL Texans, more victorious than the Cowboys during a co-existence of three years, moved to Kansas City in 1963. Money spoke.

Money and sports receive large attention and big smiles in Dallas, especially when the talk involves the Cowboys. In 1994 it was revealed that the franchise was worth more, believe it or not, than the New York Yankees.

While in Dallas one might make a note about Waxahatchie, a great name. It is the kind of name a wild and woolly person might come from, so the world of professional wrestling grabbed it. Waxahatchie is the "announced" home of Dirty Dick Murdoch. Also, singer Jerry Lee Lewis, whom some would put in the same book with the villainous Murdoch, was once thrown out of Waxahatchie for playing "My God is Real" boogie-woogie style.

Also within the orbit of Dallas is Hunt County, home years ago to military hero Audie Murphy (1924-1971). A dynamo in World War II, Murphy returned home to suffer through more than a few personal problems. (A great line was delivered by Murphy when he was on his field phone fighting the oncoming Germans. The voice on the phone asked, "how close are the Germans now"? Murphy responded, "wait just a minute and I will let you speak to one." He rests in peace at Arlington National Cemetery.)

The late Roger Miller frequently dropped the name of Ft. Worth (pop. 450,000 in city, 1.3 million in metro area). He epitomized the folksy style of its citizens ("I worked one time at a gas station. A woman came in and asked if she could use the rest room. I thought that she said 'whisk broom,' so I said 'back it up here near the door, and we'll blow it out with a hose.'").

Ft. Worth, the land of the pragmatic, the unpretentious, and the accommodating, is nice, but please do not use "where the

West begins" to describe the city. Instead, put energy into having a steak after a stroll along Exchange Avenue in the Stockyards area. You will be so mellowed out that you will almost hear some longhorns heading for Abilene, Kansas.

Some Ft. Worth buildings have been labeled "Cowtown Moderne" by architecture people.

The part that some brochures leave out is that Ft. Worth and Dallas are different. One is trendy, the other not. One is in the headlines, the other not. One is flashy, the other not. Guess which is which.

Galveston (pop. 59,000) is really something. First, the place was named for Bernardo de Galvez who never took the time to visit. Second, Postoffice Street at one time featured every pleasure known to man or woman. Third, in 1950 a great line came out of Galvez-ton. It was, "A hick town is a town with no place to go that you shouldn't."

Houston is quite another matter.

The city has 3.9 million people in the metro area. The "awl bidness" is important. So is football. So is tourism. So is medicine. Banking and real estate can go well from time to time, too. That is the good news.

The bad news is that the city is stratified pretty badly. The city is 59 percent minority, and some hard feelings are present. Notice the hard living in zip code 77026.

Houston was supposed to be a desirable city ("entopia"?), but has had trouble living up to the billing. Too much growth too soon, they say. Zoning was (and still is?) an inexact science.

See the towering Allen Center. Ask if development downtown has had any plan to it.

Houston is a metaphysician's dream. The ideal and the real clash there. Matter and form are important because in Houston the form matters, not the matter. Drop in at affordable Rice University to sort all of that out.

Form is everything at the immense Texas Medical Center

(55,000 employees). The complex is larger than Central Park. The form of the human heart and the function of dacron grafts are big concerns. Doctors from around the globe stop by.

See if you detect an attitude of "anything goes" in Houston.

Some feel that Houston, now in middle-age crisis, must pay some "social bills." Notice what goes on inside Loop 610 and contrast that with what goes on outside of it.

Notice, too, how pay phones are installed with great speed and precision in certain parts of town (for drug deals?) but not in others. This falls under the "moral geography" of the city of Houston.

Lubbock (pop. 186,000) is Bible Belt, which probably accounts for so little being done in the city about Buddy Holly. The argument is that cotton, corn, and housing developments pay the bills, not souvenirs of Holly. When Holly passed away the *Lubbock Journal* story appeared on page three, with seven short paragraphs. Things were so bad that in 1988 the 11th annual convention of the Buddy Holly Memorial Society gathered in Clovis, New Mexico.

A state of affairs in the Lubbock galaxy that some might find amusing is the presence of the Llano Estacado Winery. Wines are not generally associated with the Lone Star state, but things may be changing. A few skeptics have labeled the products "Chateau Bubba" and "Cactus Blanc."

The presence of George Bush in the White House gave a boost to Lubbock. The city was a bellwether, much like Peoria was to the Nixon administration. Lubbock's racial composition, population, and per-person income seem to give observers an accurate feel for what Americans will or will not tolerate.

Lubbock is part of the area that has been labeled a potential Buffalo Commons by Deborah Epstein Popper and Frank J. Popper. Their point is that the area west of the 98th meridian and east of the Rockies should be, they say, "returned to its original pre-white state." The theory has not been received well by those in Lubbock.

Some counties east of Lubbock that are easy to remember are Hall, Dickens, Briscoe, and Cottle. They are mentioned because they all lost population in the 1980's, a proof that not all of Texas is basking in success.

Oil in Midland is the first priority for the 100,000 people who live there. Those who study the Texas and Pacific Railroad know that Midland and Odessa differ in the number of Yale and Harvard grads in town. Midland has more. Both cities were elated when the price of oil increased 800 percent between 1973 and 1981.

Odessa, part of the Old South and the Wild West, features good oil in the Permian Basin, not to mention good high school football at Ratliff Stadium. Those who "mojo" over to a game will learn that football is almost a religion with the Permian High Panthers.

Odessa is one of those places where change comes very slowly. Blacks, whites, and Hispanics at times do not share the time of day. Ask about the history of Ector High. Notice who attends and who does not attend the Watermelon Feed.

The Odessa Chamber of Commerce outdid itself not long ago when it was telling prospects that the city was "ideally located between three coasts." Find out which three for homework.

In the 54 to 58 counties of the Permian Basin in Texas (and over into New Mexico) the lexicon is rather easy: pumpjack, plunger lift technology, trends, and bioremediation. The oil business, dressed in Toni Lama lizard boots, is the name of the game in the Basin. "Suits and boots" is an important term.

Let us mosey out to El Paso. Let us also forget the alphabetical order. Much of Texas is out of order anyway.

Out in the west Texas town of El Paso there are only two questions. The first has to do with the definition of an illegal alien. The second has to do with the date of the first

Thanksgiving. The answer to the first is tough, since Ciudad Juarez is the sister city to El Paso. The second item about Thanksgiving is not easy, either. It seems that on April 30, 1598 Spanish colonists feasted on geese, ducks, and fish along the south bank of the Rio Grande. Later the river changed its course, meaning that the banquet was on United States soil.

Study the chapter on Mexamerica in Joel Garreau's *Nine Nations* book before making a major move, since El Paso for many is an unknown quantity.

Impress your friends by telling them that El Paso and Ciudad Juarez are one large Anglo-Hispano binational metropolis.

To the east of El Paso is large Hudspeth County, one of several places along the border where drug shipments, illegal aliens (what a term!), and much monkey business are found. The county's border (120 miles long) is tough to cover. Local officials have a hard time getting a good pair of night-vision binoculars, never mind doing the paper work to put someone in jail.

El Paso's Hispanic flavor today makes a person forget that six non-Hispanics had considerable impact on the place back around 1850. Hugh Stephenson, T. Frank White, Benjamin F. Coons, James Wiley Magoffin, Simeon Hart, and Parker H. French are the names for those who wish to do research about early El Paso. Or should we say the cities of "Franklin" or "Smithville"? Historians recognize both names used along the Rio Grande.

Going from West Texas to South Texas is easy enough. El Paso to Eagle Pass is only 480 miles. Make a note about two types of houses (dugout and box-and-strip) along the way.

South Texas contains something that is a veritable Texas institution – quail hunting. In Jim Hogg County (not called Jim Bob Hogg, as some Northerners might think) a great time can be had with a prized shotgun, some well-trained dogs, and some Lone Star beer. A real man can make it through the waist-high grass. Women are not really invited or welcome.

In South Texas voices from XERF (AM 1570) in Ciudad Acuna, Coahuila, Mexico can be heard. Much history is found at the station, including the career of Robert Smith (aka Wolfman Jack). Raise your hand if you remember XERF selling sexual products, baby chicks, rat killer, and an autographed portrait of God. The station was heard "from border to border, and coast to coast." It has been years since anyone heard the Wolfman say, "Rock 'n' roll wid da Wolfman. Lay yo' hand on da radio right now 'n' feel me"!

Be aware that Texas can be "southern" in places that are not equated easily with South Texas. Like East Texas, for example.

Cotton mules have been spotted in East Texas. So has red clay in Rusk County. Make a note, since more than a few Southerners come from East Texas.

We should include some "poor white folk" from Harrison County, too, in our notes. The lack of land, calories, education, medical care, worldly goods, and security should be noted. The people have been called "Dixie's forgotten people."

How Southern is East Texas?

Southern enough to have had baseball teams in the mid-1930's using the term West Dixie League (with teams in Henderson, Paris, Longview, and Palestine in Texas and in Shreveport in Louisiana). That's Southern. Would Piney Woods League have sounded bad?

East Texas parts company with Louisiana when college football is on television. Texas will get the game involving the University of Texas, while Louisiana will get Kentucky versus Florida, for example. Otherwise, the border is blurry.

A different culture exists in San Antonio, a city said to be on the "front burner" culturally and otherwise in the United States.

How Mexican is San Antonio? A lot. In fact, San Antonio

(935,900 people) may be a good place to study the regional nature of bilingual education.

Our thoughts about heroes and villains find a ready home at the Alamo in San Antonio, no doubt because so much there needs to be demythologized. Who outnumbered whom? What ethnic group was on which side? What is a "Texican"? Do some people really maintain that there was "moral superiority" on the part of Anglos and a "degeneracy" among Mexicans? The heroes and villains are not easily identified. Read the history carefully.

San Antonio is so Hispanic, by the way, that the President's picture is on the desk of many people there. Not President Clinton. President Zedillo.

Impress your friends by asking about the industrial city three times the size of Dallas, 45 times closer to South Texas than Taiwan, and within 145 miles of the Texas-Mexico border. The answer is not Corpus Christi. Nor is the answer Brownsville. Do not say Brownsville-Harlingen, either. The answer is Monterrey (pop. 3 million), Nuevo Leon, Mexico. The question is not trivial to business people. They fly between Dallas and Monterrey daily.

Texas looks to Mexico constantly for jobs. By the late 1980's over 200 corporations in the United States had already discovered the city of Monterrey. (Of no small importance is that Monterrey in the 1950's became the first team to win consecutive Little League World Series!)

An item that catches the attention of many Texans is that the median age of the citizenry in South Texas is quite low. In the late 1980's Brownsville-Harlingen ranked seventh (25.7 years) in the country, Laredo third (24.8), and McAllen Edinburgh fourth (25.3). If it is young people you want, look no further. The South Texas figures make even Provo-Orem (21.5) and Salt Lake City-Ogden (25.5) take notice.

The areas in Texas mentioned in the previous paragraph are also poor. Laredo and Brownsville-Harlingen both have a very low per capita income. (Interestingly, the Provo-Orem in Utah area followed suit with a low per capita income. Being poor and being young can and do go together in certain places.) Laredo is the home of Martin High School where the legendary Alma Pierce once taught Spanish. That statement is not too earth-shaking, except that Alma was supposedly a relative of none other than President Franklin Pierce and, secondly, she used to ask the little kids about the name of the lake in South America that everyone has heard about, Lake Titicaca. Since "caca" in Spanish means s**t, Alma would quietly ask "Lake Titiwhat"?

A much more serious mood dominated all in Laredo on June 3, 1954 when the Rio Grande was up to about 62 feet.

Heroes and villains?

A native of Beaumont who is remembered with affection is Babe Didrickson Zaharias (1914-1956). The woman was a one-person sports Hall of Fame, since she excelled in running, swimming, diving, high jumping, baseball, basketball, the javelin throw, golf, billiards, and wrestling. Well, maybe not wrestling, although she did marry pro wrestler George Zaharias, "the cryin' Greek from Cripple Creek, Colorado." Babe was a sports legend and, imagine, she made all of her own golf clothes, grew several varieties of roses, caused heads to turn on the dance floor, and played a decent harmonica! Her death of rectal cancer in 1956 ended an amazing success story. Beaumont folks (361,000 in metro area) should be proud of her.

Beaumont and baseball have a long history together, and the names of the teams tell something about the area. There have been the Blues, Millionaires, Orphans, Oilers, Exporters, Navigators, Roughnecks, and Golden Gators.

Enjoy Texas.

Y'all come back soon now.

The West

Lots of Hydrocarbons

Ah, the West. Land of cliffs and mountains, deserts, basins, and canyons. The Cascades, the Rockies, and the Platte River.

Yes, the West. The area which gives us a President every so often.

Alas, the West. Home to too few people or too many people, depending on where you are standing. Santa Clara County in California grew from a population of 290,547 in 1950 to 1,300,000 in 1980. Loving County in Texas did not grow at all.

The Delta Center, the Rocky Mountain News, the Grand Canyon, the Space Needle, Los Alamos, Mount St. Helens,

KOA radio (AM 850) in Denver, Bryce Canyon, Shamu and the football 49ers. A little something for everyone.

This chapter will feature about "twentysome" statements which will toss around a few ideas about what the West is about. Feel free to pick and choose. That's the American (and the Western) way.

The West is the land of Indians, whites, blacks, Hispanics, and Asians.

The West is arid in Nevada, wide open in many places, high in western Colorado, wet in southwestern Oregon, dry in Los Angeles, poorly populated in eastern Utah, and "chock full" of immense distances.

The West is the area west of the 98th meridian. Fly into Kansas City, and head west on I-70 for a few hours. Notice how time moves more slowly when and where the population thins out.

The West is Marlboro Country. Notice the "feral" horses in the ads.

The West is not really Alaska and Hawaii. The two should not be put together on the same page by the Rand McNally people in the *Road Atlas*.

The West is the sum total of the federal lands west of Fargo, North Dakota. Be prepared for "mile upon mile, and not a tree, a bird, or a river," in the words of Robert Louis Stevenson more than a hundred years ago.

The West is the place from which Coors beer was smuggled East for so long.

The West is where Hondas and Subarus are popular, not Fords and Chevrolets.

The West is the free-trade heart of the United States.

The West begins, some say, where tallgrass prairie gives way to mixed-grass prairie.

The West is that part of the world labeled "Pacific Rim."

The West is comprised of places where there were gunfights and murders when county seats were moved (for economic reasons naturally).

The West is not a colony of the East. Not a "plundered province," either.

The West is the land of frontier wars, pioneering, and conquest. Conquest should get four stars in the notes.

The West is home to 20 percent of the American people, but it is growing twice as fast as the country as a whole. The region will grow 26 percent between 1990 and 2010.

The West is both Salt Lake City and Las Vegas, two places on opposite sides of things.

The West is where the train whistles of the Union Pacific and the Southern Pacific signaled prosperity for years.

The West is the area where the deadliest highways in the country wait for the careless driver. Sections of I-84 in Cassia County, Idaho and I-25 in San Miguel County, New Mexico are two easy examples.

The West is the region where people do not know the Pork Congress from the Dairy Expo.

The West is indeed wild, at times because some people wish to preserve the language and the culture of their past, while refusing to embrace the language and the culture of their future.

The West is the place where you can study the Civil War. Look up Glorieta, New Mexico.

The West is the area where there is always a growth in personal income according to the daily paper (unlike New England and the Breadbasket).

The West is the land of the squatter, the rustler, the desperado, the gambler, and the lumber thief. Main themes are a) protection versus exploitation, b) the availability of water, c) the cycle of conservation versus waste, d) depletion as opposed to pollution as opposed to high consumption, and e) self-determination as opposed to integration as opposed to separation.

That about covers it.

Or does it?

Not a word was said about the excellent schools in the West (e.g. Stanford).

And, imagine, there was nothing said concerning the nuclear power that is housed in the waters of Puget Sound.

Here we go again.

Here are three items for consideration for those who wish to learn more about the West.

One either protects the environment or builds subdivisions. The folks from Portland with their "urban growth boundaries" can argue against those from Orange County, California all day on this one.

Putting nuclear rubble in the West always seems like a good idea.

One must weigh carefully the numbers quoted about the West. Colorado says it has about 490,000 Catholics, but 900 miles east the Catholic Diocese of "small" Joliet, Illinois alone has more than that.

Well, that should do it. About everything that should be included was included.

Humor?

Consider Tom Lehrer, who once wrote of the Atomic Energy Commission:

> *Down the trail you'll find me lopin'*
> *Where the spaces are wide open,*
> *In the land of the old AEC.*
> *Where the scenery's attractive*
> *And the air is radioactive,*
> *Oh, the Wild West is where I wanna be!*

Where better to get a final picture about the West than in Green River, Wyoming?

Where?

Green River, Wyoming.

The place was reached by rail in October 1868, and has

been the scene of more than a few boom and bust cycles. Note, too, Wyoming's first brewery (built 1872), long before Green River built its first school. Today the hauling of soda ash is important.

Would Green River be "typically Western"?

It is hard to say.

Where do we go from here?

Simply pick three places to study. Like Los Angeles. Seattle, and Denver. You will come away with three different ideas about the West.

Or pick Green River, Rapid City, and Tucson. You will have three more (different) impressions.

Three more that fit under the same title, West, but are not real similar? How about Phoenix, San Francisco, and Spokane?

The quintessential Westerner? Bill Cody.

He was born in Iowa. He lived in Nebraska for many years. Wyoming was his Utopia. His resting place is Colorado.

Finally, realize that much of the West is a mindscape as well as a landscape. A crescent moon at twilight in Arizona's Marble Canyon can make a person see everything differently. A person trained in music could write a book about how the West is a vast soundscape, too. The possibilities seem endless.

Enjoy the West as it is and was, not as our imaginations today may have it. That difference is large, too.

Happy trails.

Colorado

Cowboys, Water, and Broncos

Colorado must be watched carefully. A "bellweather state," according to John Naisbitt, Colorado is a state which many people watch in order to find out what is happening in the country. Newsmakers include ranchers, farmers, politicians, skiers, miners, cowboys, and hippies.

There are only four divisions to think about. They are Central Mountains, Front Range, Western Slope, and Eastern Plains.

Understanding Colorado is not difficult if a line is drawn connecting Trinidad in the south to Cheyenne, Wyoming up north.

History books show that the area west of that line was a "disputed area" 150 years ago. There were at that time "independent peoples," too.

The dispute and the independence are natural since two cultures, farming and mining, come together at the line. One sees high ground as opposed to low, watered land as opposed to non-watered, and federal land as opposed to private land. It is imperative to know about these two sides. Farmers (on the east side) and miners (on west) agree on that.

History books since 1840 have shown that Colorado has come a long way.

In 1871 the Ute Indians were sent packing from Colorado to Utah, receiving for their troubles some lands that others did not want. Gas street lighting arrived in Denver in 1871 (only 55 years after the city of Baltimore). The population of Denver was only 106,713.

Statehood came in 1876.

In 1890 things were progressing. Mining was the big story in Telluride, as well as the 1889 bank robbery by Butch Cassidy. The railroad had been in Denver since 1870, and the gold rush of 1858 has made Denver more than a wide spot in the road. The famous Strater Hotel in Durango, at 7th and Main, was only three years old. There were 412,198 people in all of Colorado. There were between 322 and 478 saloons in Denver (depending on the figure you want to use). Coloradans looking East saw the World Series being played by the Brooklyn Bridegrooms (featuring Thomas "Oyster" Burns!) and the Louisville Cyclones (with William Van Winkle Wolf!).

In 1892 the Brown Palace Hotel in Denver was born.

That was then.

Denver and Colorado now seem to be on the move, although not without a struggle.

Let us go to Denver now.

Denver (2.1 million in the metro area) is a major league city. Thousands and thousands love the football Broncos. Businesspersons along 17th Street cut million dollar deals involving gold and chromium. The recreational areas nearby (Aspen, Vail, Arapahoe Basin, Purgatory) flourish. Farmers, not great pals with the gold and chromium folks, labor amid "amber waves of grain."

Denver people like to support winners, not unknowns, by the way. On August 26, 1964 the Beatles did not sell out Red Rocks Amphitheater.

Major league baseball is in Denver now, and baseballs flying out of the park (into the "purple mountain's majesty"?) can be explained at the Center for Atmospheric Research. Curveballs bend about 25 percent less. A batted ball will travel 9 percent farther in Denver than at sea level. Outfielders will be able to throw a ball 9 percent farther.

Things scientific find a home in Denver more easily than things artistic. Satellites were used in 1992 to install home plate at Coors Field. Engineers used some trigonometry to find a known point (or "monument") and, voila, there was the installation of the pentangular object known as home.

Coors beer is consumed at Coors Field, of course. The beer

is brewed with "pure Rocky Mountain well water." The part about "springs" is a little shaky. Ask a geologist to verify.

It is easy to verify that 4,483,350 people attended Rockies games in 1993, their first year. That is a record.

Much of Denver's future is tied to the new airport, and here is where some of the struggling, mentioned above, comes in. At last look a total of $4.9 billion was needed to pay for the thing. Baggage sat. Blame was tossed about. Confusion reigned. DIA ("Doesn't Include Airplanes"?) is twice the size of the city of San Francisco and twice the size of Manhattan.

Denver's location is important. Same-day business phone calls can be made to both Western Europe and Eastern Asia. You cannot do that from Pensacola.

Denver also gives a person one-bounce satellite communications between the continents. Ask an MCI rep to explain.

Denver mixes the old and the new near the Mayan Theater on Broadway. The theater was dedicated in November 1930 with Indians carrying flaming spears, but now the area has a shop or two that advertise "20 percent off all leather harnesses."

The homeless in Denver live where the river meets the old railroad yards near Delgany Street. On the way out of the Coors ballpark ask for directions.

For some people life in Colorado will always be connected to events in Boulder, home of the liberal University of Colorado, not so much by what goes on in Denver.

Life in Boulder (83,200 people) is nice, although the place has been a hotbed for some racism over the years. Things got so bad at one point that an Indian, George Blue Horse, was called in to do a hogan blessing so that people of differing colors could get along a little better.

A more pleasant side to Boulder is its scenery, of course. Those cutting through use their cameras daily. The name of the local paper is the *Daily Camera*, required reading as you go. The pretty scenery is costly. Just try buying a home along

Snowberry Court.

Problems of race and ethnicity can be addressed in Boulder at the Center for Studies of Ethnicity and Race in America. Some find that the "vanilla" flavor of the people in Boulder makes the area less than ideal for racial and ethnic study. Folks in San Francisco can fill in details. So can those from Hell's Kitchen in New York City.

Some Boulder students attend New High School. A "nontraditional" education is offered.

Colorado Springs, a burg of about 290,000 people, is scenic, too. Movie fans know that the city was the birthplace of Lon Chaney. Few realize that his maternal grandparents were instrumental in helping deaf and blind Coloradans many years ago.

Chaney would be proud of the old City Auditorium downtown. The sturdy old girl is really something.

It will be interesting to see if Colorado Springs can keep the peace amid the "natives" and those representing the many religious groups who have moved in (17 groups from January 1989 until November 1992). The military, some microchips, and the religious types should make for interesting (violent?) times.

A good fight can be seen when it comes to the use of water from the Colorado River.

Humans need water to cover the big distances between Colorado places. Get some now.

Southwest of Denver is Hinsdale County, home to very few, but once the residence of the infamous Alferd (not Alfred) E. Packer. Packer ate, drank, and was merry in Hinsdale County, and the trouble was the eating. He supposedly ate five gold prospectors in the winter of 1873-1874! The judge working on the case was Melville B. Gerry, a Democrat, who was heard to say to Packer, "they was siven Dimmycrats in Hinsdale County but you ... yah eat five of them"!

As this book went to press there was some arguing about this case of cannibalism (aka "anthropophagy"). Stay tuned for more details about hungry Alferd.

South of Colorado Springs is quiet Pueblo (pop. 98,000), where entertainers and others flying between Chicago and Los Angeles gas up.

The Arkansas River flooded badly on June 3, 1921 in Pueblo. The flood may be a good reminder that water in the West is absolutely vital.

In Pueblo study the Goodnight-Loving Trail in the year 1866.

Imaginations do not exactly run wild in sun-drenched Pueblo, although a few cowboys and cowgirls have enjoyed themselves along Union Avenue near the old train depot. The area will remind some of Court Avenue in downtown Des Moines or 11th and Howard in Omaha.

The railroad first arrived in Pueblo in 1872. Some would say that not much has arrived in Pueblo since.

Drink more water and head north.

While looking for the ski boots in Pitkin or Summit counties, realize that you are in areas known for divorces and high education levels. Not too many years ago 23 percent of Pitkin County residents were divorced, yet had 15.63 median school years completed. In Summit County, where *Rolling Stone* magazine clearly outsells *Reader's Digest*, the figures were 16.47 percent and 14.89 for the respective categories. Aspen, the county seat of Pitkin, features a lifestyle that is very attractive to both the divorced and the intelligent.

Do not be surprised by the way if the high school football in Aspen (7900 feet up) is not good. Real estate is so expensive that few people can afford both a house and some children. Do not blame the coaches. Knowledgeable football fans in Colorado follow both the Brush High Beetdiggers and the Alamosa High Mean Moose.

Real estate executives in Aspen were fearing for their lives in late 1992. It seems that Hollywood people were thinking that gays were not exactly being catered to in Colorado. Such a stand was unacceptable to those who pay huge dollars to ski and to socialize.

Aspen is a resort, not a community, mind you. Servants are welcomed, not neighbors. Understand these things before entering. The organic cider is optional.

Durango (elev. 6,523) is not as high as Silverton (elev. 9,032), but that is no problem. Bike riders going from the former to the latter can peddle to their heart's delight each Memorial Day weekend. Bikers must climb over two 10,000-foot passes along the way. Hundreds per year find Durango to be heaven for bicyclists.

Glenwood Springs, one pretty place among many in the Roaring Fork Valley, is friendly, casual, and quiet. Visitors and locals enjoy the therapeutic vapor caves and hot spring mineral pools. Unfortunately, sections of downtown have become a geological hazard due to the presence of "very active earth flows." Some homeowners have faced the problem (east of Grand Avenue) of having to shore up foundations that have moved 19 inches. Those in Rock Springs, Wyoming know the scene perfectly.

In western Colorado there is Grand Junction, one of many places that know about boom and bust. When times are good, names like Gulf and Tenneco are thrown about freely, but in bad times there is child abuse and suicide. On May 2, 1982 Exxon said it was not interested in crude oil, and the effects were felt in Mesa County and beyond.

One very disturbing feature in the West is that in several of the mountain states (Wyoming, Arizona, Montana, and Colorado) the suicide rates can be frightening. Divorce, alcoholism, and drugs are found, too, which can be distressing for those who have moved in from the East in order to avoid those things.

To learn about high-sitting Leadville, just pick up a copy of the *Herald Democrat* of July 6, 1900. The issue describes drilling contests, wherein a few of the boys tried to pound steel into granite. A boulder (of Gunnison granite) weighing

20 tons provided such great opposition that big betting made everyone on Harrison Avenue take notice.

Leadville, supposedly the highest incorporated city in the nation, has not been in the news much since. The city's unsinkable Molly Tobin Brown (1867-1932) was one of 706 survivors of the Titanic in 1912. Molly commandeered one of the lifeboats, and with the help of a Colt .45 bellowed, "Keep rowing, you sons of bitches, or I'll toss you all overboard."

In southwest Colorado there is San Juan County, known as the "Switzerland of America," never to be confused with Monroe County, Ohio, known as the "Switzerland of Ohio." San Juan County can be breathtaking.

Something must be said concerning the Eastern Plains of the state, a place very different culturally and economically from the Western Slope. The Plains are filled with places like Lamar, Sterling, and Kit Carson. The boys eat lunch with their hats on. Agricultural talk invariably mentions Kansas City, not Denver. Mining is thought to be an activity done by savages.

It has been said that Eastern Colorado should be used for the building of prisons in the future, and it has been mentioned contrariwise that the area between the two panhandles (Nebraska on the top side, Oklahoma on the bottom) should in no way be used for prisons. Head for Morgan County and decide for yourself. Learn swine management first.

We might end with a mention of Katharine Lee Bates, a visitor to the Pikes Peak area in 1893. She gave us the words to "America the Beautiful." Aggressive Coloradans should remember Bates' original words ("Oh beautiful for halcyon skies").

Colorado is not halcyon.

One county commissioner recently said, "diversity is perversity."

Hang on tight in Colorado.

Wyoming

High Altitude, Low Multitudes

This state, in the top ten for land area and in the bottom five for population, is perhaps best studied from the air.

Whether sailing over "big places" like Cheyenne and Laramie or smaller areas like Riverton and Lander, one's eyes will have to work overtime.

The eyes will notice that Wyoming is for use, not for show. That much is our first perception.

Wyoming can be rough, too. History books tell us that twenty-eight Chinese were murdered in 1885 at a massacre in Rock Springs.

Wyoming is huge, and there is much to observe, including the unreachable stars above. Although Montana uses the title "Big Sky Country," Wyoming does not do a bad job at it, either.

A flight starting Laramie or Cheyenne, for example, will allow a person to start some note-taking over Crazy Woman (CZI on the low altitude enroute charts, 117.3 on the radio dial) in northern Johnson County, a speck southeast of Sheridan. The notes will not show much.

Sail on.

Notice Interstate 25, the "nuclear highway" between Las Cruces, New Mexico and Buffalo, Wyoming. Ask about plutonium. Ask about possible dangers, too.

The open spaces of Wyoming will allow time for thought about some things, including about how the radio is to aviation what the telegraph was to railroading. (The equipment makes the vehicle operational while at the same time changing space and time!)

Take that concept to "big city" Cheyenne (pop. 47,000). There we can learn about Wyoming history, visit the capital, and see the train depot where so much in Cheyenne took place years ago.

Visitors to Cheyenne are asked to draw precisely what writer Perry Duis has labeled the "moral geography" of a given place, in this case Cheyenne. The term has to do with lines which separate the legal from the illegal. Look for the location of saloons through the years. Then move on to gambling houses. Ask about people's ideas of privacy. Inquire, too, about bathouses. (Who said there is nothing to do in Wyoming?)

Cheyenne and Casper (pop. 51,000) are Wyoming's best efforts at being "urban centers," although Laramie (pop. 26,000) may take exception. It has the state university, where athletes huff and puff at an elevation of 7100 feet.

The *Farmer's Almanac* tells us that three climates come together in southeast Wyoming. Check out the weather before taking off again.

Few meteorologists know about places like Horse Haven (west of Jasper) and Cherokee Peak, although a telecommunications expert may be able to find them. Tie Siding, Curt Gowdy State Park, Crowheart, and Lightning Flat may be located instead.

Locating Lightning Flat is easier than predicting the next tornado in Laramie County. Between 4pm and 6pm during May the going can be pretty tough. Heavy winds not visiting Laramie County have been known to visit Weld County, Colorado.

Wyoming people know that cars are dangerous in tornado weather, but that does not scare people from using their cars. In Casper there were 729 cars per 1,000 people a couple of years ago. Other Western addresses (Reno, Ft. Collins, and Billings) were high on the list, too.

It seems that now more than ever the cars in Wyoming have women in them. Could it be that the West was becoming a place for women? (Several women remember December 10, 1869 when women in the Territory got the vote. The men were heard to say, "Here's to our wimmin'. The good Lord knows they're our superiors, but damned if they don't wanna be our equals.")

The presence of women in particular and people in general are reminders that this part of the West may be a great place to hide someone. If a major basketball school wants a kid to polish his athletic skills and at the same time beef up a mediocre report card, why not have him do his apprenticeship at Casper Junior College in Casper?

The open spaces of Wyoming may mask a problem not visible from the air. The 1990 Bureau of the Census found 196 homeless in the entire state. Home is the range in Wyoming, and some do not have a home.

Additional talk about Wyoming people must reveal that the people can be tough, having to survive cold winters, big distances, occasional job loss, and isolation. A macho spirit is necessary. The term "agararian barbarians" might describe certain Wyoming people.

Drugs on worksites and alcoholism at home are not uncommon. Newspapers in the last ten years have well documented the social problems of Wyoming.

A journey to Rawlins, the jewel of Carbon County, may be informative. The north end is well off. The south end is not. Plusses in town are coal, oil, gas, and hard-working Mormons. Minuses include a significant Mexican population which thinks its voice is not heard. The scene is not unlike much of the West, he said sweepingly.

Required reading in these parts is Mark Aaron Robinson's 1987 classic *One Hundred Grams of Uranium Equal 290 Tons of Coal*. Reading that book will make us all familiar with many things on Wyoming's agenda.

The desire to dig up the earth turns off some people, but others feel turned on by tourists in Teton County. Teton is home to about 2 percent of Wyoming's residents, but bustles with visitors.

Airplane passengers (looking down) and tourists may wish

to study the Oregon Trail, but one has to be careful. The research can involve a "sanitized" Oregon Trail (made for Hollywood) or a dirty, rat-infested history that will turn off some people. Let the researcher beware.

Let us end this chapter in an unconventional way as our small plane is landing.

Here is the recipe for a real Western delicacy, "sonofabitch stew":

2 pounds lean beef	1 set brains
Half a calf heart	1 set marrow gut
1-1/2 pounds calf liver	salt, pepper
1 set sweetbreads	Louisiana hot sauce

Kill off a young steer. Cut up beef, liver and heart into 1-inch cubes; slice the marrow gut into small rings. Place in a Dutch oven or deep casserole. Cover meat with water and simmer for 2 to 3 hours. Add salt, pepper and hot sauce to taste. Take sweetbreads and brains and cut in small pieces. Add to stew. Simmer another hour, never boiling.

Enjoy Wyoming, one and all.

Montana

No Indoor Sports

Most observers of Montana, the treasure state, will probably mention a few "buts" about the place at the very beginning.

Montana is today the fourth largest state in square miles, but its largest city, Billings, is smaller than Utica, New York.

Glacier National Park can be breathtaking, but Butte and Anaconda, well known to the mining companies, are not.

The "buts," frequently mentioned by outsiders, are not necessary. Montanans, and Westerners in general, are tired of them.

Montana should be examined on its own merits.

What has happened elsewhere, especially "back East," may not be a big help.

In 1882 the arrival of the Northern Pacific Railroad to the Yellowstone Valley was significant to the people living there at the time. Period.

The region had its hands full with the platting of Great Falls in 1883. The completion of the Brooklyn Bridge and the debut of baseball player Billy Sunday in the same year were of little import to Montanans. Period again.

Busy Montana hands in 1890 were concerned about some roads that were "wholly unclassable, almost impassable, and scarcely jackassable." Period. Period. Period.

The blackboard is now clean. There will be no more "buts."

A yellow underliner will divide the state into six regions. They are Glacier Country (Kalispell-Missoula), Charlie Russell Country (Great Falls), Missouri River Country (Wolf Point), Gold West Country (Butte-Helena), Yellowstone Country (Bozeman), and Custer Country (Billings). Those who love the outdoors will now be salivating. Salivating on old clothes, of course.

Going to Yaak in the northwest corner of the state may be a good way to see Montana culture. The nearest big city is

Spokane, 150 miles away. Yaak is so remote that only hippies and movie stars go there, no doubt because both can enjoy the very popular housing in the area – the log cabin. Water and electricity are luxuries. The menu calls for turkey gizzards and Olympia beer. On second thought, forget about Yaak. The going may be too tough.

Divide Montana by saying that things are either west of the Divide or east of the Divide.

Montana is not divided when it comes to wonderful poetry. The immense spaces, lovely vistas, timeless valleys, mountains and plains make both the heart and the pen flutter. People sensitive to space and landscapes report that things which appear far away can be taken into the human heart quickly in Montana.

Montana is a state of about nine (9!) climate zones, the most interesting name of which may be "Northwest Chinook." See Cut Bank on the map. Visit in December with caution.

A city?

Great Falls (pop. 55,000) is understood well if just a few items are committed to memory. First, there are some who love to gamble, and that explains the signs that say "Welcome, Canadians." Second, schools mentioned in the daily newspaper reveal much about Great Falls and about Montana. The schools are Big Timber, Roundup, Box Elder, Rocky Boy, Blue Sky, and Deer Lodge.

To look good in Great Falls just adopt a style described as "Montana Broke." Broken-in jeans and boots plus some huckleberry jam and syrup can impress. In the future look for sun-dried cow chips for barbecue buffs, pickup trucks, bottled clean air, pulverized elk horns, and "a week's stay with a grizzly bear," courtesy of the 708,000 people who inhabit Montana. The possibilities are endless.

The joy is endless in Great Falls when Great Falls High School and C. M. Russell play high school football against each other. Fasten the seat belts.

Great Falls people can discuss the rodeo, of course. The bumper stickers say it best, "rodeo is the most fun you can have with your boots on." No comment is necessary.

Those in Butte (pop. 35,000) know about the rodeo, and they also know about rough winters and a slow economy.

The map of Butte shows Aluminum Street, Kaw Avenue, Platinum Street, Iron Street, Copper Street, Granite Street, Mercury Street, and Steel Street. Notice the old brothel on Mercury.

The mention of copper and iron may remind some people that the Chinese have a history in Montana's mines. Read Tibbitts v. Ah Tong (1883) to understand this (delicate) situation.

Through the streets of Butte in 1900 walked many Irish. The city was paradise for the Irish then. A large number came from County Cork.

Butte, by the way, had about 70,000 souls in it in 1915, and the city boasted that it was the biggest between Minneapolis and Seattle!

Do not hold your excitement at a baseball game played by the minor league Butte Copper Kings. The name is on the lips of many travel-weary scouts who journey to Butte in the summer.

There is a small Jewish community in Butte, believe it or not. Ask for Congregation B'nai Israel. The city's first mayor was Jewish (Henry Jacobs in 1879). Jews say that these days it is tough to be Jewish in Butte since so much of the culture is gone.

Up the road from Butte on the way to big-city Helena is Boulder, which made headlines in November 1986 when the parents of "Dallas" star Patrick Duffy were killed. The Duffys ran a tavern on Main Street. The phone book in Boulder has two pages.

The city of Bozeman (born 1864) is long on guns, fishing

rods, waders, and barbed wire. The city may be one of those proverbial "good places to jump off from."

Some have "jumped off" to great things in Billings (pop. 81,000) because there is serious livestock business to be done there. Notice that Billings was at one time supposed to be "the second Denver."

Take Highway 212, the Beartooth Highway, out of Billings for a lovely drive. Head for Red Lodge. Notice the switchbacks and the soaring eagles.

Helena (24,600 souls) is the place where big issues are tackled in government offices. Here are some topics to consider now and in the future: the lack of water in Petroleum County, wolves who want to roam all over the place, the needs of the Blackfeet Indians, out of control buffalos, hungry elk in Gardiner, bears doing their own thing in Libby, environmental troubles in Butte, and oil derricks in Glacier National Park. That is a pretty hefty list of things to think about.

In Helena try to find a barroom nude. For years one could sit in Anaconda or Nevada City and drink demon rum while gazing at a beautiful goddess. Critics claimed that women and liquor should not go to a man's head. Opponents argued that in the West, which is called "man's country," a beautiful nude gazing into space never hurt anyone. Regardless, the nudes are fading away.

North-central Montana is great fossil country. It seems that maps on the subject are deliberately kept out of the way, so that hundreds of crazies do not head into Billings and go north, thereby possibly destroying what some experts feel is a special reserve for serious study.

North-central is now home to bighorn sheep, cougar, elk, and grizzly bears. Dinosaurs, too. Not too many years ago the find of a Tyrannosaurus rex had those at the Museum of the Rockies in Bozeman jumping out of their chairs. Life in Hell Creek was, pardon the expression, heavenly.

For the record there are 23 types of dinosaurs accounted for in Montana (25 in Wyoming, 17 in Colorado). The work of Jack Horner is fascinating.

All the wonderful research about dinosaurs in Montana will not erase the hard feelings connected with Little Big Horn on June 25, 1876. It is old news that in the minds of some people Custer was massacred, but in the minds of others he was simply defeated. In 1992 the confusion was so great that efforts to re-enact the details were infuriating both Crow Indians and some members of the Seventh Cavalry. Even the name of the battlefield brings a battle.

One word to summarize life in Montana?

How about "raw"?

See if that word does not apply after a tough day lumbering. Or after a day farming. And we still have copper to go.

The word "raw" may do it.

Enjoy Montana.

Wear old clothes.

Idaho

Betwixt and Between

All those who have been in the state of Idaho will now raise their hands, please.

All those who have met someone from Idaho will now raise their hands. That was predictable.

Finally, and you get the point by now, all those who can name someone famous or semi-famous from Idaho should raise both hands and waive them.

That is right. Idaho is not a big deal to too many people, although some have had wonderful vacations there.

Right from the start let us all remember that Idaho is large. Idaho County can hold Massachusetts. Owyhee County can hold New Jersey. Custer County could do the same to Connecticut. Just try to drive from Twin Falls in the south to Sandpoint in the north. You will be so tired you will not care to know that the name Owyhee came from the name of a few fur-trapping Hawaiians who got lost in 1820.

Realize that Idaho has many, many mountains. In fact, the joke is that if Idaho were flattened out it would be as big as Texas. That is an exaggeration.

Idaho is the least metropolitan state. Only 20 percent of the people live in a metropolitan area.

Only 945,000 people live in Idaho.

Since it is the custom to divide a state into regions for travel and study purposes, here are some in Idaho to think about. There is Big Water Mountain Land (Pend Oreille, Coeur d'Alene, and Priest Lakes, for example). There is Lewis and Clark Country (a five-county area that includes Nez Perce Indians, the University of Idaho in Moscow, and Hell's Canyon). There is Treasureland (featuring Boise and the Seven Devils Mountains). Let us not forget Magicland (Sun Valley, the Oregon Trail, and Shoshone Falls). There must be a mention of Pioneer Country (bottom right, with Lava Hot

Springs and Idaho State University). Lastly there is Mountain River Country (The Snake River, Craters of the Moon, and the city of Idaho Falls). Picks and shovels are not optional in some of those places.

Such divisions take us to a mention of some cities.

Pocatello (pop. 46,000) is a drive of three hours from Salt Lake City, which may not be big news, except that the Mormon people in Pocatello think the short drive is important.

Established in 1863 during the siege of Vicksburg, the city of Boise (pop. 125,500) is big by Idaho standards. The city has decent restaurants, much history, and some Basques who should be studied.

Western features in Boise include the ever-present Union Pacific Railroad, a mania for gold and silver, and a meal (buffalo roasts) that tickles the stomachs of all Boise people.

Small enough to be enjoyable and large enough to occupy tourists for a few days, Boise also has Pioneer Cemetery, where Joseph Misseld rests. He was a brewer who drowned in his own well when he proved too fat to be rescued.

Those into ethnic studies will enjoy the Basque people. Try to locate Catholic worship sites which Basques used in 1920. Include in your answer names like Arregui, Azcuenaga, and Etulain. The Basques work hard. Dedication and persistence are valued as much as or more than skills. A need to assimilate is not obvious.

A good price for a home in Boise is obvious to some people. Californians know peace and quiet as well as a good economy when they see them.

Idaho Falls (pop. 44,000)? Go there for research about the history of Mormons in the West.

Smaller Lewiston (pop. 28,000) is home to a real Western treat, the rodeo. The *Lewiston Tribune* remarked on May 21, 1914 that "there wasn't a vacant spot in any stable or yard and the feed barns did a rousing business as hacks and buggies filled the area. The parade was led by the Culdesac band, followed by the Nez Perce Indians in full regalia. Cowboys and cowgirls, 600 in number, rode behind in twos. The spectacle brought cheers ..."

Sun Valley, in growing Blaine County, is home to some rich and famous who can take or leave the rodeo. Skiing goes well there. It is "in" to talk of Ernest Hemingway while waiting to ski on Mount Baldy. It is "out" to tell locals that Phoenix people would just love to see pretty Ketchum.

Wallets for men and purses for women are not optional in Sun Valley. Read between the lines. Notice the Californians again.

All is not sweetness and snow in Idaho, however.

Some turmoil took place in Coeur d'Alene (pop. 24,500) not long ago. Members of the Aryan Nations Church voiced a desire for white supremacy, and pretty soon there were bombings, name-calling, and hatred all over this silver-rich area. Emotions ran wild, with a demand for "more white children in the Northwest." Jews should realize that only 55 Jews were counted in Kootenai County a few years ago.

There is a good side to Coeur d'Alene and North Idaho. Coeur d'Alene is easily accessible from Spokane's airport, and Coeur d'Alene is an area of mountains, lovely lakes, blue skies, no smokestacks, and peace and quiet in abundance.

Make a note, too, that from the northern panhandle of Idaho to Rochester, New York is a terrific distance, although in a way they are not that far apart. The northern part of Idaho has the so-called Silver Valley (e.g. around Kellogg, to keep it simple), and Kodak people in Rochester keep their eyes on it constantly. To make film you have to have silver.

Truckers of Idaho products, like potatoes, are aware that along certain stretches the driving can be very dangerous. Interstate 84 through Cassia County was labeled the most deadly highway in the country not long ago after a study by the National Highway Traffic Safety Administration and the Federal Highway Administration. Dust and high winds can arrive in a flash when you exit Utah and enter Idaho.

Big distances in Idaho provide an opportunity for music. Roger Miller composed "King of the Road" in a motel in Boise.

The cowboy hats seen in Nashville are the same ones being sold in Boise. Between lonely trips in Idaho find out where the line between Nashville and the West is.

Moving around, in, and through Idaho may require a few extra biscuits for breakfast due to distances. Meriwether Lewis and William Clark warned us of such things when Lewis wrote of the need to "esswage the pangs of a keen appetite."

Notes about the northern panhandle should mention that people from that area relate more to Spokane than to Boise, but people in Idaho from the southeast part of the state relate to Salt Lake City. That item is a must to understand.

There is a point in Idaho, not easy to locate, where the Pacific Northwest tag gives way to a consciousness about the Rockies. Ask before speaking.

Asking questions is especially relevant when Idaho's Snake River is mentioned as a way to help water-hungry Californians. The gist is that the Snake River and the Columbia are seen by some as a solution to a problem. If you hear Idahoans complaining to Oregonians about sending water hundreds of miles south, you will know the background to the complaining. Complaining is not really a strong enough word.

Enjoy Idaho. If the opportunity presents itself, stop by the rodeo.

Pass the salmon, too.

UTAH

A Large Agenda

Many people reading this book will probably have a difficult time naming a famous person from Utah. Utah and its people are not that well known.

Perhaps that is the case because many Americans, especially those who live in the East, tend to disregard what happens in Utah.

The disregard is not a problem.

Was it the state's fault that the first post office in Salt Lake City was not established until 1849?

Was it not newsworthy that the *Salt Lake Daily Herald* announced "Cattle Coming" in 1871 (to the chagrin of the people living quietly there)?

Was there not legitimate euphoria at the Lehi Sugar Factory in Lehi when the cornerstone was laid in 1890, the same year that Ft. Wayne, Indiana was moving from grain and lumber to iron and steam?

Where was each of us when the last streetcar operated in Salt Lake City in May 1941?

What was the problem of having the Japanese "relocated" in Topaz in September 1942?

Utah has been moving right along, the writing of history notwithstanding.

Many people in the Beehive State today do not care about Irish politics in Boston, Chicago-style pizza, ingots in Cleveland, or aerobic workouts from Los Angeles. Salmon in Seattle and beer in Milwaukee are not important, either.

Let us look at some things that "flesh out" what Utah is like these days, with the firm promise to study the state when the first opportunity arises. The study must be done without the contamination of Eastern prejudice and bias, of course.

First, figures concerning abortions and live births should be examined closely. Abortion in Utah is a big subject.

Second, the counties of Davis, Salt Lake, Tooelle, and Weber grew 32 percent in population from 1970 to 1980. Population increases since 1980 have not been unusual, either.

Third, the Overthrust Belt cuts through the area, putting it in the forefront in the race to harness minerals necessary for the upcoming century.

Fourth, a person can expect to have a long life in Utah. Add for Utahns approximately one year to the national figure (75.8?).

Fifth, perhaps contrary to popular belief, there is much to do in Utah. The skiing (e.g. Little Cottonwood Canyon) is very good, especially when compared to what some Californians have ("Sierra cement," to quote the complainers there).

There is a "Bionic Valley" in Utah where high tech does its thing.

There was Frisco, Utah, a very tough town in the 1880's when silver mining attracted thousands.

There are also hoodoos, odd-shaped rock formations left standing by erosion.

And there is Randolph, a place so cold that the locals tease about the cold weather "causing" the birth of many, many children in Rich County.

So there.

Utah has much to offer. Neglected above were the Lincoln Highway (U.S. 30), some Civil War history, and the Pony Express.

Those things should get our notes going. The notes must go to Salt Lake City.

In Salt Lake research about the Church of Jesus Christ of Latter-day Saints is essential.

One will find that Mormons are not loud, obnoxious people. They approached the federal district land office in Salt Lake in 1869 to do their business with respect, and they presume others lead their lives that way, too. Read the March 24, 1869 *Salt Lake Deseret News* for more details.

Homework will reveal that Mormons see themselves as a persecuted minority.

They see, too, that in their history there is an emphasis on "a communal utopia under a theocratic government."

Genealogists will have a field day when they study Mormon history. Ann Eliza Webb was the 19th wife of Brigham Young when they married in 1869, the record shows.

While in Salt Lake these days realize that 660,000 people live in the area. Or is it 1.1 million? Can it be that only 160,000 people live in the city itself? It seems that the figures change person to person and book to book.

Do not be surprised if you cannot count Mormon heads on every street corner in Salt Lake. Provo has a greater percentage of Mormons in it than does Salt Lake. (Provo has the Lord's University, by the way. That is Brigham Young University.)

In Salt Lake City a Jew is a Gentile, at least according to columnist Paul Greenberg.

Some books have mentioned that the Mormon people have a weakness for ice cream. Would that all of us could be so afflicted!

Despite Salt Lake City's efficiency and a sense of what indeed makes sense, there is one item that seems odd, and that is the name of the pro basketball team in town. The name is Utah Jazz. It is difficult today to imagine Oscar Peterson playing jazz in a smoke-filled room in Salt Lake City.

The word "jazz" is difficult for many Mormons. The term has a sexual side to it that some find offensive. The term also has to do with the spontaneous and the raucous. That may be a problem, too.

Duke Ellington has said that jazz can be located "anywhere and everywhere". For Mormons, however, place is no doubt a much more specific concept, regardless of which stake a Mormon comes from.

The smell of cigar smoke and hops in a jazz-filled room

may not smell any worse than the Great Salt Lake today.

A more positive note is the visual range of 120-130 miles from Salt Lake City. Not so in places in like Colorado or Kansas (55-80 miles). On a clear day in Salt Lake you can see the Basque people living in Winnemucca, Nevada. Not really. (Do not even ask what the visual range is for those standing at Meridian and Washington Streets in Indianapolis.)

Through clear air Mormon leaders can dialogue with Catholic hierarchy both in Salt Lake City and beyond concerning the "full and equal" treatment of women in their flocks. The ordination of women to the priesthood is a difficult subject.

Now one needs a new notepad. (What happended to Utah being quiet and out-of-the-way? Turn the page.)

The number of women in the Utah legislature is a sore subject for some, too.

So is "Mormon feminism."

A final touchy subject is that in June 1978 Spencer W. Kimball announced that he had received a revelation which said, "all worthy male members of the Church may be ordained to the priesthood without regard for race or color." Some claim that the revelation was not a revelation at all, while others had the feeling that the Church would be in big trouble if black men were ordained. (Did not Brigham Young say in 1852 that blacks were better off slaves, since they could not rule themselves? Did not Elder Bruce R. McConkie say in 1958, "Cain, Ham, and the whole Negro race have been cursed with a black skin"?)

Perhaps some strides have been made. Notice the monument at Main and South Temple in Salt Lake City. The names of Green Flake, Hark Lay, and Oscar Crosby appear. They were slaves.

The lives of blacks and whites in Utah are discussed daily in Salt Lake schools. Some of the schools are private and other schools are public. Write two paragraphs about how the public schools in town are really private because of the Mormon presence, and then explain how a Catholic school (St. Ambrose?) can end up being a public school because of the Mormon presence.

Such heavy subjects can make a person head for the hills, but in those hills our notes will receive no rest.

Not in Topaz where some Japanese people were "concentrated" during World War II.

Nor in Ogden. At the half of a Weber State University football game study the Immigration Act of 1924. At that game there may be some children of the "slap happy Japs" who once lived in Topaz.

There may be some Indians there, too, and no understanding of Utah can be gained without a mention of the Indian peoples (Ute, Paiute, and Shoshone) who pre-dated the arrival of certain others (Joseph Smith, Miles Goodyear, Etienne Provost, and Peter Skene Ogden). The concerns of the Indians still are mentioned today, of course, but the agenda for the state is predominantly that of "The Church."

Members of "The Church" know that much of Utah's future is tied to vanadium, chromium, aluminum, and uranium, but there have been some problems therein.

An exposure to uranium has caused the death of several "virtual uninhabitants" in the Four Corners area. Places like Shiprock, New Mexico and Mexican Hat, Utah have residents who know all about radiation. That word, incidentally, does not exist in the language of the Navajo people.

Could it be that some "far away" places like Mexican Hat may get gambling some day?

Some people wish not.

Some Mormons have a tough time with gaming in Utah, although some seem not to mind if the gaming is not in Utah. The joke is that Catholics do not recognize birth control, Jews do not recognize Jesus Christ, and Mormons do not recognize each other in Nevada.

Mormons prefer to recognize hard work and family commitments. Not even vermiculite, talc, rozelite, limonite, gilsonite, oolitic sand, aragonite, hallyosite, and rhenium can change those Mormon priorities.

Hard work is placed next to Joseph Smith's talk of a "kinder, gentler nation." That's right. The phrase was taken from the pages of Mormon history.

Read up.

Get ready for that big agenda.

Nevada

A House Divided

Nevada is the place to go for those who wish to get away from it all. The Chambers of Commerce in Reno, Carson City, and Las Vegas may not want to hear such things but, for some, the truth is always problematic.

Getting away from things is so important in Nevada that 60 percent of the phone numbers in Las Vegas are not listed.

Getting away is easy. Nevada is large.

Years ago the state was a place of silver lodes, gunfights, and railroads, but now Nevada is synonymous with glitzy casinos, fistfights, card counters, water shortages, swimming pools, and nuclear bombs, not to mention that there are only three cities, cited above, that deserve the name.

Nevada is most easily understood if we just cut it in half, into northern and southern, and be done with it.

Reno is in the north, Las Vegas in the south, and that about does it.

At least that is the way Chicago Cubs baseball scouts used to do it. Their scout living in Livermore, California looked after Northern Nevada, and another one living in Cucamonga, California looked after Southern Nevada. That way work can be done without having to live in Nevada, and without having to conquer great distances.

Any discussion about the state must take into account not only the immense open spaces, but also that there is so much federal land, thereby making for outside control. Outsiders (Phoenicians, Angelenos, and New Yorkers, for example) create a political, cultural, and economic menu that is hard to read and even harder to do anything about.

What do Nevadans do with their time?

Natives in Elko (pop. 10,000) enjoy seeing a train passing through now and again, as well as cowboy poetry ("A room of fancy ladies/and gents with drinks in hand/lengthy in discussion/ preserving the coyote of our land").

People in Gerlach (pop. 350) think that discussing land speed records is a nice afternoon's entertainment. Such things do not seem typical along Euclid Avenue in downtown Cleveland.

And imagine the problems that take place on the Mustang Ranch if the jacuzzi is not working.

Most visitors head to the gambling (better "gaming") tables, of course.

Gaming pays the bills, and probability is the name of the game.

It is probable that after one hour of play at baccarat there is a 46 percent chance that the player will be ahead, but after 70 hours of play the number dips to 15 percent.

It is probable that gamblers do not see the psychological trouble with gambling. The psychology has to do with aggressive people who have an unconscious wish to lose. Losing, all but guaranteed by the arithmetic, becomes frequent. Losing becomes the penalty for the aggression. A winning wager will restore power and control. Or so a gambler thinks. So it goes, to the tune of millions and millions of dollars per year.

It is probable that some will picture a hot streak ("the enumeration of favorable circumstances" according to math experts) to be only a moment away.

It is probable that few see the irony of having Las Vegas and Salt Lake City in the same part of the country.

It is probable that many Americans find Las Vegas (pop. 258,000) to be a pleasant place to visit for a while.

Gaming is such a big part of Las Vegas that Guardian Angel Cathedral accepts poker chips as well as green paper in the collection basket. The odds are 3 to 1 that you will not be hassled by an usher if you contribute that way.

A constant theme in Las Vegas is that things must make a buck, even if lopping off heads is necessary. For years musicians have been replaced by canned music. Robert Goulet has said that the corporate moguls want even the men's room to show a profit.

The money with which Las Vegas deals is formidable. Vegas makes Atlantic City look small, of course.

A curious twist takes place when drinks and other things are "complimentary" in Las Vegas. The money for the items stays in the pocket just long enough for a person to get to the nearest slot machine or table. At those places nothing is complimentary.

The rise of Las Vegas and the casino economy has not exactly helped the black community through the years. The record shows that blacks in the 1930's were barred from the gaming tables along Fremont Street.

Your rent-a-car map today may not show areas where black people live.

Jewish gangsters will not be mentioned, either. Abner "Longy" Zwillman, Arthur "Dutch Schultz" Flegenheimer, and Jake "Greasy Thumb" Guzik are alive, however, in the history books at the University of Nevada at Las Vegas.

Not talked about much is the feeling years ago that Las Vegas would not survive financially. In November 1946 the group running the Flamingo had to borrow money to keep going. Benny Binion was a nervous wreck.

So was Meyer Lansky, but for different reasons. He thought the weather in Vegas would scare off everyone. He once commented upon visiting, "it was so hot that the wires in the car would melt."

Times have changed.

Las Vegas is in such good shape that family entertainment and gaming are mentioned in the same breath.

Several cowgirls and cowboys can be found at the National Finals Rodeo, a Las Vegas possession since the mid-1980's. The NFR left Oklahoma City for Las Vegas a few years back. The $14,000 prize money in 1937 would be pocket change for some of today's cowpokes.

Visitors will love to study the Old West in romantic places like Armagosa, Bullfrog, Beatty, Gold Center, and Rhyolite. Wear your old clothes. Such apparel is necessary when miners, drillers, and geologists do their thing.

Save your good clothes for a show in Las Vegas, Reno, or Sparks. In Nevada being seen is much more important than seeing.

Wear good clothes in Las Vegas to the Thomas and Mack Center (cap. 19,000) for a basketball game hosted by the University of Nevada at Las Vegas Runnin' Rebels. The game will be fun, although many people will label the players "bad actors." The label fits the image that the school has in the minds of some opposing schools.

Please keep in mind the location of Nevada. California is the next state going west. Realize that the fertile fields of California are downwind from the nuclear testing in Nevada. Many feel that a gamble is being made about how often America will eat per day (three times? twice?) if the testing goes on.

It is a gamble to travel America's loneliest road, Highway 50. Get on at Ely, not too terribly far from the Utah line, and head west for Carson City. The state's Commission on Tourism will assist you with its *Survival Guide Book*, just in case you tire of reading how Highway 50 roughly parallels the Pony Express Trail. Native Nevadans can tell us all about survival.

Politics?

In September 1986 a curious set of circumstances raised a few eyebrows and produced a few chuckles in Nevada. It seems that "none of the above" was declared the winner in the Democratic race for treasurer after getting 24 percent of the vote! Runner-up Patrick M. Fitzpatrick got 22 percent. Such things are not uncommon in Nevada, a state where politics can be confusing, and at times funny.

Let us now look at some items which will summarize some

things about Nevada.

First, the lack of water will shape people's lives in every phase.

Second, the presence of a fast buck in gaming will make for a society that is unreal by almost anyone's definition.

Third, the lay of the land will be attractive for nuclear testing.

Fourth, elderly America surely will not find a home in Nevada. They may find a place in which to live, but that place will probably not be home in a psychogeographical sense. Teens who are pregnant may have the same experience.

Fifth, domination by outsiders will continue.

Sixth, although the state talks of five regions to visit (Reno/Tahoe, Covered Wagon, Pioneer, Pony Express, and Las Vegas), few will care about what Nevada looks like beyond the gaming tables.

Seventh, the "outdoor museums" in the state (e.g. the Toiyabe Range) will provide a fascinating laboratory for research for those who have an interest in such things.

Eighth, an attitude of detachment or escape ("let's visit for a few days and return home") will dominate life in Nevada from now until the end of time. Mark Twain fabricated stories about Virginia City and its wild living when he thought that people needed to read something interesting.

Ninth, the state will be big on mining and drilling. Exxon and friends will keep a close watch on things.

Tenth and last, sagebrush and alkaline lakes throughout the state will be a large "workbench" for the government (which will do pretty much whatever it wants).

Let's go up to Reno, home to 133,800.

When going through Reno to do a little gambling, have a good time, but do not look for much that explains the history of the city. Just try to do research about the Mormon-Carson Emigrant Trail or about U.S. 40. Those who mix gaming with study may be disappointed.

Could it be true that Reno is west of Los Angeles? Look at a map between trips to the slots, uh, family entertainment.

A nice side to Reno is an afternoon spent at the rodeo sponsored by the PRCA (Professional Rodeo Cowboys Association). The action is fast and dusty. Saddle up the horses.

Now we should put up our tray tables and seat backs. The fun is just starting.

Or is it?

New Mexico

Enchantment and Encampment

Let us start our mention of New Mexico with a little quiz. No cheating. Match the two columns.

1. Los Alamos   A. location of New Mexico State University
2. Santa Fe   B. a stop on old Route 66
3. Lordsburg   C. an "atomic town" (like Aiken, South Carolina)
4. Las Cruces   D. a location visited by Charles Lindbergh in 1927
5. Tucumcari   E. the state capital

Now that you, the reader, are frustrated, it may be necessary to say that the average person would not do too well with the quiz above. To millions of Americans New Mexico is not well known. Only a precious few will remember reading about the July 1947 UFO incident in Roswell.

The answers to the quiz are 1-C, 2-E, 3-D, 4-A, and 5-B. Don't feel bad if you didn't get them all correct. The state is not a major factor in American politics, economy, etc.

It might be good now to state five things about New Mexico that should be kept in mind at all times.

Memorize the following.

First, the dreamy days of both summer and winter in the state are gorgeous, although the lava beds east of Grants are not so gorgeous.

Second, it is easy and fun to connect with the past in New Mexico. Coronado visited in 1541.

Third, there is a fascinating mix of cultures in the state.

Fourth, the red man for decades has been seen as nothing but a barrier to progress in New Mexico.

Fifth, four items (aridity, the Indian cultures, Hispanic institutions, and poverty) should be studied thoroughly by all who intend to understand the state.

It might be good to remember, too, that New Mexico and Florida, not Virginia and Massachusetts, boast about the oldest Christian churches in the United States. American history books tend to forget such things.

The history of New Mexico is interesting, in part because the record seems to reveal some differing points of view over the years. Many years ago Catholic bishops from France (like Jean Baptiste Lamy, born 1814) labored among Mexican people who, to be kind, probably had a differing theology from the Frenchmen. Names like Gallegos and Martinez conflicted with a name like Jansen. (Lamy came to the Territory in 1851 to discuss business with Jose Antonio Laureano Lopez de Zubiria y Escalante, bishop of Durango in Mexico. The Mexican bishop probably saw the newcomer as a challenge, he said euphemistically.)

The big fish in the New Mexican pond, or the big cactus in the New Mexican desert, is Albuquerque (385,000 souls).

A sleepy place before World War II, the city is now the economic, demographic, and political heart of New Mexico.

Albuquerque was ranked 84th by *Money* magazine for livability a few years ago. The city is nice to visit, and is also a jumping-off point for other attractions in the state.

Waiting at the Albuquerque airport may be as good a time as any to read about bilingual affairs. Some readers will need help in order to understand the difference between one bilingual community and two monolingual ones, while others will be confused by arguments about self-esteem that overlap with arguments about a desire to learn a new language. Hold on tight.

A more calm atmosphere exists about 50 miles outside of Albuquerque where everyone enjoys gazing at the stars. In the words of one observer in Belen, there is "a black cloth with a lot of diamonds dropped on it."

Taos (4,500 in city, 22,500 in county) is one pretty place. Synonymous with the Pueblo Indians for centuries, Taos is very nice, but faces the danger of being overrun by those who find it so gorgeous. Perhaps the best thing this book can do is to pass over Taos quickly.

Santa Fe (pop. 56,500) is "a thin, wavering adobe town," we have been told. The same rules apply to Santa Fe as to Taos ("visit, but please do not stay.").

Santa Fe contains visiting photographers who are fascinated by the beautiful terrain. During lunch listen to the photographer (from Los Angeles?) describing how the desert and the ocean(s) are similar from a photographer's point of view.

Santa Fe also can be called "Santa Fake." Some trinkets are not real. Distinguish the chic from the charm.

One problem for Santa Feans is that many whites have moved in and displaced many Hispanics recently. This issue is a sensitive one.

In Santa Fe in 1989 a symposium entitled "Trails: Toward a New Western History" took place, and Western History has not been the same since. One is told that process is more important than place, that the frontier is nationalistic and often racist, and that progress and improvement are not acceptable categories. This is delicate material, too.

Upon leaving Santa Fe one should pursue that item mentioned above about studying both the desert and the ocean(s). Did the photographer say something about "openness"?

The sense of "openness" can be a problem at least in the desert. Drug dealers can verify that the rickety fences that separate the United States from Mexico can indeed be "open" for some drug trafficking through southern New Mexico.

People who fly from Dallas to Tucson through the blue skies of New Mexico are told by the pilot that the plane is flying over Columbus, New Mexico where Pancho Villa made headlines in 1916. He found the land "open."

The pilot will not talk of drugs brought into New Mexico.

Another negative is the dangerous driving on the roads of New Mexico. It seems that more than a few people have lost their lives along I-25 east of Santa Fe in San Miguel County. Proceed with caution on interstates in the windy and winding West.

Unattractive is Gallup (pop. 19,100). Coal is about the only "language" spoken, and Navajo Indians are trying to eke out a living. The place was named after David Leeds Gallup, former employee of the Atlantic and Pacific Railroad. In the more recent times some remember the old Thunderbird Lodge along old Route 66.

Heading north out of Gallup will be a chore. Places like Gamerco, Mexican Springs, Tohatchi, Naschitti, Toadlena, and Sanosti will be waiting. Gas stations and other signs of life are not plentiful.

Heading from Gallup for the very northwest corner of New Mexico will get you into San Juan County, a place that not even the well-organized Seventh Day Adventists can label correctly. The county is part of the Adventists' Mid-America Union Conference, not the Southwestern Union Conference. Certain parts are too dang tough to classify easily.

Perspective in San Juan County is difficult in more ways than one. The geological wonders at Shiprock look one way from the ground, but another way from the air. American Airlines pilots will fill in all details.

In the southwest corner of the state there is the Bootheel, complete with the smallest port of entry gate between the United States and Mexico at Antelope Wells. Piñon pine and juniper are more obvious than cars. The Bootheel lives a lonely life.

To the west of Las Cruces there is Deming, a small place on the Interstate leading cars to Arizona and beyond. Deming enjoys telling stories about Billy the Kid, but the place has a more valuable role. It has clean air.

The air in Deming is also good for an aerostat balloon that is perched (tethered really) above Deming so that a "radar fence" can be set up along the border with other similar aerostat balloons. The hope is to intercept incoming planes that cart drugs to waiting merchants.

The quintessential town in New Mexico?

Let's try Las Vegas (pop. 14,800). The place has busy Douglas Avenue. Who could forget Murphey's Drug Store? Divisions between the haves and the have-nots are sharp. The different sides of town do not get along. Read the *Las Vegas Optic* for more details.

Baseball in New Mexico?

There was the Panhandle-Pecos Valley League back about 1923. Teams were then located in Roswell and Clovis in New Mexico and in Lubbock and Amarillo in Texas.

Today ask for the Albuquerque Dukes, a Dodgers farm team.

Ask, too, for more information about New Mexico. A lovely place awaits.

Arizona

Copper, Cotton, and Crooks

Arizona, large and late-arriving, contains many things that everyone knows about already: natural beauty, immense open spaces, cacti, lovely sunsets, peace and quiet, many cowboys and approximately 160,000 Indians.

Those items are probably familiar to most of us.

This chapter will try, however, to put some "spin" on Arizona that may not be so familiar to everyone.

First, though, there must be a dividing of the state. There are five easy-to-identify areas. They are Northland-Canyon Country (ask for the Grand Canyon as well as ponderosa pine), Indian Country (the land of the Hopi and Navajo), Mountain Country (to the right of center, including the Mogollon Rim), Desert Sun-Border Country (Phoenix, Tucson, Douglas, Bisbee), and Colorado River-Gem Country (Hoover Dam down to Mexico).

Pick one or two areas for vacation or study, but proceed carefully. A few cautions are necessary.

Here comes the "spin."

Studying Arizona may be done best by delving into some philosophy, or at least by citing the words of philosopher Alfred Korzybski. He has said, "a map is not the territory." His point, at least in part, is that a map gives some information, but a map cannot possibly be perfect. A map provides a "similar structure" (his words). What is "covered" by a map, in other words, is not always the only thing "there."

Applying this small bit of philosophy to Arizona is not difficult. Be aware that languages, behaviors, and attitudes do not appear on a map. Exact and precise distances do not, either.

The point is clear.

In Arizona (and in the large states like it) a map alone will not tell the whole story.

The more ambitious in the group may want to begin by studying Arizona as a Promised Land. (For practice it may be good to research the meanings of compromise in Alaska and survival in Oklahoma, just to get this process started. A map alone will not do for those jobs, either.)

Be ready for several psychogeographic "spins" in Arizona. One cannot understand the people or the places otherwise.

Now let us proceed.

An issue in Arizona that must be isolated at the very start is the availability of water. A prominent politician once said, "Today we see cracks in the earth because our underground water supplies are being used faster than they are being replenished. With the completion of the Central Arizona Project, the Colorado River will deliver about all the water it comfortably can. Oregon and Washington will not likely come to our aid." Everything from basketball practice at McKale Center in Tucson to attracting tourists to mining in Jerome is shaped by water.

The problem of water in Arizona "intersects" with other notes about the state. Notice that there are ghost towns, rodeos, mandatory air conditioning, five climate zones, two metropolitan areas, six micropolitan areas, optional air conditioning, rapid population increases, tardy child support, snow birds, boom and bust local economies, Apache Indians, molybdenum, and Yaqui Indians.

Those items on our checklist, plus the "spin" explained above, enable us to move to some cities in Arizona.

First, there is Tucson, "the old pueblo." Put the name of Tucson next to the category "snow birds" found in the list above.

The Civil War was fought only about 40 miles northwest of Tucson. That may surprise some people.

Tucson was a quiet place from 1867 until 1878 when it was the capital of the Arizona Territory. The "city" had to hold off booming Prescott for such honors.

In the early 1900's the people of Tucson seemed to get along pretty well with each other. The record shows that L. H. Manning, entrepreneur, and Federico Ronstadt, carriage maker, were friends.

Tucson for a long time was slow-moving. Some remember that Speedway Boulevard was not paved until after World War II. (Locals cringe if you use the word "sleepy" today.)

If the 1950's in Tucson were slow, the 1970's were not. Drugs from Nogales (a quick drive south) made the news. So did the local Catholic high school (Salpointe) when it labeled its religion courses "Christian Culture" (so that no one would be offended?).

In 1993 the oath of citizenship was administered in Spanish, not English, to Hispanics in Tucson. Some celebrated the day, although others countered that the use of Spanish would not empower the newly-arrived at all. Still others remarked that the activity was merely an exercise of (multiple) choice.

Around the pool today in Tucson all are well advised to study racial and ethnic history in the United States. The words of Francis Parkman ("the Sioux are thorough savages") and Meriweather Lewis (certain people were "the vilest miscreants of the savage race") will be put next to "the only good Indian is a dead Indian" (General Philip Sheridan?). Realize over whose heads the border of Arizona was drawn in 1912.

Many hope that Tucson and Arizona are not returning to the days when political allegiance and racial ancestry were a problem like they were in 1942. Recall that the Japanese were living in places like Poston due to Franklin D. Roosevelt's Executive Order 9066. Western addresses like Poston in Arizona and Heart Mountain in Wyoming seemed to be good places to store people.

Where might Tucson (pop. 440,000) be going? The way of its larger relative, Phoenix? The way of Los Angeles (with smog, insufficient water, increasing in-migration, etc.)? The way of El Paso, a city reminiscent of Tucson, but practically forgotten in its own state? The way of Albuquerque, a cultural clone? Who knows?

A second city on the notepad is Phoenix (306 days of sunshine per year). In 1940 the census counted 65,414 souls there. In 1980 the number was 1.5 million in the metro area! Today there is little reverence for the "l word" ("limits") in Phoenix (983,000 souls). There is expansion on many fronts. That much is business as usual.

Some feel that the business in Phoenix looks a lot like the business in Los Angeles (smog, traffic, and too little water).

Jews in Phoenix can compare notes with Jews in LA about the lack of a Jewish identity. The "old home" of Jews in the West is not Lodz or Lemberg, but New York and Philadelphia. (William Zuckerman has spoken of Jews who are "Americans by birth and instinct, not by nationality and gratitude." There's that "spin" again.)

There is not much flavor to Phoenix. The state capital of Kansas (Topeka) has about as much a western feel to it as Phoenix does.

Major league baseball is coming to Phoenix soon. Was the weather the only reason it was not there sooner? Answer that before another lap in the pool.

We all know of the troubles in Phoenix associated with the Martin Luther King Holiday a few years ago. The Super Bowl bypassed Phoenix. Race is no small issue in Phoenix, he wrote editorially.

A third "city" to examine might be Tombstone, home to *The Tombstone Epitaph*. The grave of George Johnson reads that he was "hanged by mistake."

Notice Toughnut Street in Tombstone. See the Bird Cage Theatre, too.

Tombstone is the place where a total of five people lost their lives in the famous gunfight. (Killings today make the Wild West look tame. The number of Chicago gangland slayings in the decade of the 1920's [522 total] is large, but by the standards of the 1990's even that number looks small.)

Bisbee (aka "Rubble Without a Cause") is not much these days, either, but at one time years ago there were 68 saloons in town. Only about 8,000 souls live in Bisbee now, and prostitutes like Crazy Horse Lil, Red Jean, and Kate Elder are not among them. Examine this history at Main and Brewery.

Prostitutes (aka "soiled doves"!) have not been a problem in a long time over at the Gadsden Hotel in Douglas (pop. 13,000). The Gadsden is famous. Eleanor Roosevelt, Tom Mix, and Pancho Villa have been noticed in the lobby. Let your imagination go wild in romantic Douglas.

At the other end of the state there is quite a different story in Yuma (pop. 55,000). The city is located near Mexico, close to California, and an easy drive from Phoenix. Yuma is about 185 miles from San Diego.

Yuma is "sun-punished," to use the words of John Steinbeck.

The sun is also a factor in trendy Sedona, a place that is fast becoming the "New Age" jazz capital. Add some wine to a little music by Acoustic Alchemy or Kenny G(orelick). Have a star party at night looking for the Swift-Tuttle comet. Add significant others. Discuss light pollution. Do not discuss people who are job-rich but housing-poor. Subtract traffic. Add turquoise. That's Sedona.

Then there is Flagstaff (pop. 46,000), close to the Grand Canyon. "Flag" is certainly not your typical sit-by-the-pool Arizona location. In fact, the city can be quite cool at night. Those who like the mountains will have a ball. Lumberjacks, too.

Many "Flag" people love or hate Phoenix, approximately 140 miles to the south. "Flag" folks brag of a white Christmas 50 percent of the time. That beats Phoenix (0 percent of the time). Opposites at times do not attract.

The Babbitt Building in "Flag" is familiar turf for the city's

Basques. There are Chinese in town, too.

The Grand Canyon (4.8 to 5.0 million visitors a year) deserves much space by itself, of course. This book could not even scratch the surface of just the geological information necessary to talk seriously of the Canyon.

A hero in Arizona?

How about Cochise?

He lived in southeast Arizona before statehood, of course, and was perceived by Anglos to be a peace-loving, hard-working person. He first encountered Anglos in the fall of 1858, and the record shows that he did not disturb the Butterfield Overland Mail Route. The path ran from Mesilla in New Mexico to Tucson. One can almost see Cochise heading east after a day's work gathering wood and hay.

Get on the old clothes.

Get a good map, too.

CALIFORNIA

A Shining Colossus

Where does one begin to talk of this megastate in order to give it a fair shake? With the bars in Bakersfield where rednecks talk of despising Mexicans? With a thought received on top of Mt. Shasta? With the parties hosted by the late Irving Paul "Swifty" Lazar before the Oscars? It is mindblowing (a hippy term?) to contemplate how much there is in the Golden State.

One way to go about trying to understand the Pacific Republic of California might be to divide the state into twelve categories which those in tourism would understand.

The twelve areas are North Coast (Crescent City to Sonoma), Shasta-Cascade (see Dunsmuir), Gold Country (Nevada City to Mariposa), Central Valley (Sacramento and friends), High Sierra (north of Lake Tahoe to Kernville), the San Francisco Bay area (self-explanatory), the Central Coast (Salinas to Ventura), Greater Los Angeles, Orange County (Anaheim, for example), Sun Diego County (San Diego gets a lot of sun), the Inland Empire (as in Ontario), and the Deserts (Barstow, of course).

A simpler picture involves the three "nations" of author Joel Garreau: MexAmerica, Ecotopia, and the Empty Quarter. The first centers around Los Angeles, the second around the San Francisco Bay Area, and the third around the area west of Las Vegas, Nevada up to the northeast corner of California where mining, drilling, and copper picks meet with sparse populations, a lack of water, and numbing work schedules.

Choose the regions of anyone you wish, but keep in mind always that the state is an immense social laboratory. Frisbees were laughed at years ago, but are now assimilated into American life. Granola was thought to be a hippie joke, but is now a part of American life. The same goes for the salad bar. Fads come and go, but trends do not, and California deals with both on a daily basis.

This atmosphere has consequences. Keep in mind that California is shaped like a couch belonging to a psychiatrist.

We will start in the San Diego area, and then we will proceed to the top of the state along the Pacific Ocean. Then we will descend from the Shasta-Cascade section to the three areas near the center of the state (Gold Country, Central Valley, and High Sierra). Then in a clockwise motion we will cover the two remaining areas (Deserts and Inland Empire). Then we will be tired. Then we may wish to read about Stowe, Vermont to give ourselves a break.

The break may allow us to ponder some general comments about California.

One such comment involves the cost of a house in California. The median home price a few years ago stood at $217,708 in Los Angeles, $229,999 in Santa Barbara, $247,397 in Orange County, and a cool $267,634 in the Bay Area. Those figures would scare most of the world to death, but they are pretty much par for the course. A bargain might be found in a house in the High Sierra region ($92,500) and/or in Gold Country ($106,270). In northern California (e.g. Shasta-Cascade and upper North Coast sections) $79,038 can get you a house.

We should not be too surprised about the high prices floating around in California. Historians tell us that the state is named after Queen Calafia, a mythical figure, who knew her rags from her riches.

California may turn out to be the ultimate contradiction. In the 1920's Mexicans were pushed out of downtown Los Angeles so that a theme park promoting the region's Spanish architecture could be built. Today some Californians gladly attend a benefit for a rain forest (El Yunque in Puerto Rico?) while grudgingly paying their Korean maid a wage that is an embarrassment.

An item of importance is that California has between 9 and

17 climate zones, depending on whose terminology one wants to use. Check your local newspapers. A good idea is to use a NOAA weather radio (as in 162.4 megahertz). California is not always and everywhere 85 in the sun.

In fact, few Californians understand the weather. In Marin County, for example, there can be about 1.5 inches of rain over 5 months and then, to everyone's surprise, there will be 50 inches of rain.

California's benign climate is deceiving. Most regions are either wet or dry, but rarely both. Many are not extremely dry and, suddenly, so wet. The eucalyptus trees erupt. California, after all, is supposed to burn, given the climate, the trees, the water, the winds, and so forth.

SAN DIEGO COUNTY

San Diego is a city which tries to be quiet and peaceful, but there are many signs that the opposite is happening. There are thousands who love the place, but thousands also who hate the increasing traffic and huge in-migration. The city has 1.1 million inhabitants. The county contains 2.6 million.

San Diego does play an important role. The city gives us the San Diego Chicken/Famous Chicken and Water Dispersant 40!

Del Mar is popular. One is told that in Del Mar the surf meets the turf, and, if not on guard, the tourist meets the jurist.

How could one forget the missions? They can put a person in a religious mood. Such a mood may be very helpful since there are so many religious groups for a person to choose from in these parts.

Few associate San Diego with baseball's Ted Williams, and fewer still realize that his childhood was not all that happy. Ted's lifetime batting average (.344) was a marked improvement over his San Diego upbringing.

San Diego may not wish to be called part of Southern California, an obvious attempt at avoiding the "friendship" with Los Angeles that many think has existed since the Franciscans set foot on Balboa Park.

The book on San Diego has been that the city's geography was a problem. To the west there is the ocean. To the east there is the desert. To the south Mexico. To the north big Los Angeles. For being "boxed in" (?) San Diego seems to be prospering.

The city will be prospering to the tune, some say, of 5 million people in the Tijuana-San Diego "metroplex" by the year 2000.

Do not be surprised if you find in San Diego some people from the "religious right." Colorado Springs people know the feeling, too.

Easier to deal with may be the incoming people from Oaxaca, a part of Mexico, and the Indochinese. They come looking for work.

Could San Diego be facing some of the same unpleasant things that Los Angeles has? Did not many people hope to avoid unpleasant things by moving to San Diego?

A sign that directs the crowds at the San Diego Zoo was seen a while ago. It said, "please do not annoy, torment, pester, plague, molest, worry, badger, harry, harass, heckle, persecute, irk, bullyrag, vex, disquiet, grate, beset, bother, tease, nettle, tantalize, or ruffle the animals." The request mirrors what many sense about human relationships in these parts.

Stressed-out San Diegans can find relief by listening to the "San Diego Stomp," a must in everyone's "New Age" or "smooth jazz" discography (Warner Brothers CD 26939-2). The song is not really a stomp, but it is mellow. Not unlike many San Diegans, he said descriptively.

A final note about San Diego is that the city has been trying to care for its destitute. Ask for the Baltic Inn, named for the inexpensive property on a Monopoly board.

ORANGE COUNTY

Orange County (as in Anaheim, Costa Mesa, and Santa Ana)

is a curious place.

Many of the inhabitants are described as "to the right of Attila the Hun."

Main stops in the county are Disneyland, the California Angels baseball park, Knott's Berry Farm, and the Crystal Cathedral.

The Crystal Cathedral espouses what some feel is a "crossless Christianity." The idea is that good times are just around the corner, suffering is not essential, and Jesus makes us all "brand new." Many feel that this item is fine for those who are in the majority and are upwardly mobile, but God help those in the minority who see life as a valley of tears.

Tears were noticed in abundance in 1994 when Orange County (12th highest retail revenue total in country) was seeking bankruptcy court protection.

A good study could be done about what exactly drives the movers and shakers over at Disney and at Disneyland (born 1955). Money? Power? Magic?

In Orange County there is the John Wayne (American!) Airport. That name, fictitious but carrying a message nonetheless, reveals a lot about where the folks are at.

Orange County plays a game called "Name the Neighbors," in which everybody tries to identify the locals. The late Harriet Nelson, Bette Midler, and the commissioner of baseball were correct answers not long ago.

Laguna Beach in Orange County is the kind of place that has terrible social problems. That is because the young girls in Laguna Beach wear their bikinis not only at the beach but also in areas away from the beach.

Spending some time in Laguna years ago was Jack Norworth. He wrote a tune that America sings frequently, "Take Me Out to the Ball Game." He did not see his first game until 1942, however, when a friend asked him to go to Ebbets Field in Brooklyn. Norworth moved to Laguna Beach in 1952. He died in 1959.

GREATER LOS ANGELES

Los Angeles (3.4 million in city, 14.5 million in five-county area) is an incredibly vast mix of many peoples, myriad dreams, and increasing fears.

The people can be Vietnamese, Anglo or Mexican. Or the people can be Filipino. Or Japanese. Or Iranian. Indeed, the Iranian presence has prompted the use of the term "Teherangeles." Think about all of this while visiting Koreatown/Mid-City.

Think, too, about college registration forms involving LA kids. Many are "other." Imagine what that term will mean in a few years.

Designating what year something took place can be iffy in LA. The year 1988 was either the Year of the Dragon or the year the Dodgers won the World Series.

Getting away from all of that can be done in Hollywood, the land of call sheets and grip carts, where there are many heroes and many villains. There are arguments aplenty both pro and con, and the list is endless.

One must keep an eye, too, on how Hollywood portrays non-white males in its films. As brutes? As buffoons? The portrayal has ramifications involving perceptions about race, gender, class, and sexuality.

Who gets what in Hollywood is another matter. Tom Selleck instead of Harrison Ford in "Indiana Jones"? Burt Reynolds instead of Jack Nicholson in "Terms of Endearment"? Hollywood's first choices through the years are interesting.

Hollywood lives in the present, of course. It is the only time the citizens understand.

For the present have some ice cream at C. C. Brown's (born 1906).

Hollywood is a place where some end their time. The H in the Hollywood sign is the most common letter for those attempting suicide. Adventureland and Tomorrowland, two Southern California landmarks a short drive away, apparently are not the Promised Land.

Some dream of LA becoming a world-class city. Others dream that it will be a place of endless confusion, consternation, and fear.

The fear has to do with what happens when people of different ethnic and racial backgrounds do not get along. Some feel the city could blow up any day. In 1992 the "civil unrest" in South Central Los Angeles was ample proof of this.

All of the above takes place in a basin where ozone, gridlock, lack of water, and the credit card come together, to the disgust of those who like life clean, simple, and in cash.

Keeping an eye on LA is required reading for anyone who studies the American experience. The place produces new behaviors and differing lifestyles all the time. Some observers feel that all the differences (languages, attitudes, values) may produce a city that is ungovernable.

The United States will become the "Disunited States," to hear some tell it. The phrase is that there is too much "pluribus" and not enough "unum."

Life in Southern California can be, like, piglike to the max. For sure. Totally awesome is the speech of, you know, certain young ladies and their babes. Wear Spandex and do not look gross. The scene may make some people hurl.

A more serious sample of life in LA might be the discussion at a school board meeting about why Tuan can't read and why Maria can read so easily, and why Ralph's parents have to attend such an evening to start with. Realize that LA is, in the words of Richard Rodriguez, "a city of separateness."

Jewish LA knows about the city's sociology. Some Jews who graduated from North Hollywood High years ago socialized with Jews only. The "whole world" was Jewish, or so it seemed. A trip east boggled the mind, and a whole new world was unveiled. Keep the sociology book open in LA these days.

Los Angeles will tell you that it is a city wishing to be first in many categories. Those with a discriminating eye will tell you that Los Angeles hosted on January 15, 1967 the first World Championship Game between football's Green Bay Packers and Kansas City Chiefs. The annual tilt is now known as the Super Bowl, and it is not played in California every year.

Relaxing can be done at a Dodgers game, but you must realize that you are part of an immense success story. The Dodgers came from Brooklyn in 1958, after having counted 5,459,359 fans through the turnstiles in the final five years before the move. In the first five in Los Angeles a total of 10,729,922 fans attended (without having to dodge Brooklyn trolley cars). And in the next five years the club counted 11,602,321 fans in attendance. Pretty profitable stuff.

Did you take the Century Freeway (cost: $2.2 billion) to get to Dodger Stadium? It was an expensive 17.3 miles.

Santa Monica may be the West Coast capital for the homeless. A compelling reason for this is the attractive "room temperature" found outdoors.

The "up" side of things may be some rejuvenation at the next Whole Life Expo in Pasadena. Go to the workshop called "Cosmic Orgasm Through Crystals, a Fun Way to Transcend Flesh Sexuality for Any Reason."

An institution in Southern California is Francis Dayle "Chick" Hearn, radio voice of the Los Angeles Lakers pro basketball club. He has been at the mike for more than a quarter of a century, and, if he has his way, will be there until he dies. Hearn has had a hand in elevating basketball to the popularity it enjoys today in Southern California. Hearn, a former pharmaceuticals salesman, is known to millions.

The Forum where Hearn works will always be remembered as the place where Magic Johnson revealed in November 1991 that he was carrying the H.I.V. virus. The announcement may be remembered as much as any of the Lakers victories in the title-filled 1980s.

It is time to mention a contribution of Angelenos: PFBFers. Such people are "People Who are Famous for Being Famous." Examples are George Hamilton, Charo, and the Zsa Zsa Gabor. They all look good and fill in whenever needed. Hollywood always can use PFBFers, and their presence always initiates a conversation about tummy-tucks and suntans. Zsa Zsa in 1980 was the goodwill ambassador for the Montgomery Ward Auto Club.

This book would not be complete without mentioning that Southern California may some day get "the big one," referring to an earthquake as powerful as the one that hit San Francisco in 1906 (8.3 on Charles F. Richter's scale) or Kern County in 1952 (7.7). Some think that "the bigger one" could be caused not by the legendary San Andreas fault, but by the one labeled Newport-Inglewood. "Quake talk" is part of the California landscape, pardon the expression.

Champagne wishes and caviar dreams are part and parcel of Beverly Hills, especially along famous Rodeo Drive. Porsches are visible everywhere. Oldtimers claim that the place has gone from rustic to the fast lane too quickly, thereby making life too congested in America's richest zip code (90210). Johnny Carson once joked that youngsters at Halloween approach a home and say, "trick or Gucci."

Starry, starry nights in Los Angeles are vanishing little by little. In 1985 the skies were six times brighter than they were in 1920. Gazing at the stars in Hollywood may be easier than trying to see the real stars overhead.

Central Coast

Beautiful Carmel is a picturesque seaside tourist town. Carmelites like Clint Eastwood very much, although the newspaper, the *Pine Cone*, tries to soften his occasional troubles. Tread lightly when visiting, and do not throw an empty pack of cigarettes on the ground. You may get jailed.

Santa Barbara (85,000) is nice, although the homeless there have made local people anxious. Paradise should not have to deal with such issues, the thinking goes. Santa Barbarans can talk with Santa Monicans about the homeless.

Monterey County is really something. It has lush meadows, wild flowers, white sand beaches, enormous jacuzzis, and great wines. The weather is great for growing chardonnays and rieslings, cabernets and zinfandels. Enjoy.

Realize, too, that Monterey County always keeps an eye on the Napa and Sonoma areas. The wine business is very competitive.

Years ago entertainment was competitive, too, at least in the eyes of Joe Malcewicz, wrestling promoter. The facts are that he figured he could really earn a few bucks if Filipino people attended his matches (due to their thinness). This is not fiction. The truth was that Filipinos, Mexicans, and Japanese picked lettuce day and night, and the Filipinos jammed the place for the matches.

Some Japanese used to take their rears over to the baseball games played by the Salinas Spurs. The irony was that some Japanese people were interned in Salinas years ago, yet in 1991 there were Japanese people high up in the Spurs management. Hideyuki Mifune was the talk of the town.

A speck north of Oxnard is Bates Beach where swimmers at times do their thing sans swimsuits. The bodies can be seen from Amtrak's "Coast Starlight" train which connects Los Angeles and Seattle.

Any number of important topics is discussed daily in Oxnard, and one of them involves dinks, sets, and sideouts. That is volleyball talk, and some pretty good players are found in Oxnard. Players roll their eyes when told of the location of their sport's Hall of Fame (Holyoke, Massachusetts). The number of volleyball players in California may soon exceed the total population of the city of Holyoke (pop. 43,700).

SAN FRANCISCO BAY AREA

The history books show that San Francisco was really something years ago. The city even had a large fair (complete with electricity!) in 1915, following the lead of cities like Buffalo (1901) and St. Louis (1904), also on the cutting edge at the time with their fairs.

That was then.

Now an important dimension in and around the San Francisco Bay Area is the ethnic diversity of the people(s) there. San Francisco, San Mateo, Alameda, and Santa Clara counties house Hispanics, blacks, Asians, and "ethnically varied" whites, more so than any other area in the country.

For the record there are 723,960 people in San Francisco, but 6.1 million in the Bay Area that encompasses nine counties.

It is important to note that diversity is a way of life in these parts. In sexual preference, for example. In recreation habits, too.

Notice how the weather, the terrain, the politics, the jobs, and the food can differ from one place to another. Only a free-thinking, Ecotopian, cause-oriented humanoid can exist in such an environment.

Some in the Bay Area spend time trying to understand how the various people(s) mingle best. One theory has it that people are either monochronic (time is fixed) or polychronic (time is flexible), and that people prefer either low context (explicit information is important) or high context (status and timing are important) situations. Many Anglo people can be labeled low context/monochronic. "Gay time" exists, too. Figure all of this out after lunch in Milpitas.

Figure out, too, how gays were once part of the counterculture, but are now part of the mainstream.

Notice the thick and sturdy windows at certain gay bars.

Notice the guy in the corner talking of the X chromosome possibly causing gayness.

See the woman discussing transgender protection.

A quick story may best explain the diverse lifestyles in the area.

Three scenes are taking place on the beach. A man is eating an orange and reading a magazine. A woman is sunning herself topless. Two men are kissing each other passionately. Which party gets run off the beach? The man with the orange, since he is leaving the peels on the beach! Doing one's own thing is gospel in these parts, but impacting anyone else's world negatively is not.

Additional homework about San Francisco will be to study the historical connection between North Beach, Haight, and the Castro. Include beats, hippies, and gays in that order in your research.

Do not be shocked about the prospect of two men kissing each other in the Castro. It takes place daily. Halloween 1990 will forever be remembered by those viewing the persons who dressed as Mount Rushmore. The four presidents wore eye shadow.

Just about everyone knows that San Francisco General Hospital knows a few things about AIDS. The hospital has an excellent reputation that way.

It is good to be both knowledgeable and ahead of your time in San Francisco. The Social Justice Commission of the Catholic Archdiocese of San Francisco in January 1974 called on the United States House of Representatives to "initiate the impeachment process in relation to President Nixon."

That item leads to a mention of Berkeley (aka "Berserkly"), a place of many ideologies. In fact, ideas tossed about in Berkeley (how to do more with less, how not to pollute, how to recycle, how to blend and understand cultures) may be a key to understanding the future. Everything from sexual intercourse to harnessing the wind is debated, and solutions that look bizarre may end up mainstream in the future.

Where better than Berkeley to learn about dealing with your mother's Iranian doctor, Mexican landscaper, Irish priest, Jewish lawyer, and Polish banker? Politically correct Berkeley labeled October 12 "Indigenous Peoples Day" in 1992.

Some Berkeley people years ago failed to fulfill their wellness potential due to drugs.

Other Berkeley people spend their time looking at "naked stars" 30,000 light years away from the earth through powerful telescopes. The activity seems in perfect keeping with the Berkeley agenda.

Still others in Berkeley are involved in co-housing, a concept that is unknown in Sioux Falls and Amarillo.

History (or "herstory") is important in Berkeley, too. Both men and "womyn" should do their homework about Berkeley and its past.

Study computers in large San Jose (pop. 821,000), a city with more people than San Francisco. The *San Jose Mercury News* features a Sunday section on computers. Ride your carbon-fiber bike to get to the nearest computer.

In computer country there is also an awareness of domestic partner benefits for those of the same sex.

One's personal welfare is an important subject in the Silicon Valley, and the place can be dangerous. In 1981, a year associated with discussing a "gay pneumonia" among white males, some trichloroethane (TCA) was found in the Valley. To this day some feel uneasy when there are semiconductor companies around.

Those with a real interest in the Bay Area are well advised to study the Chinese, those non-Christian, non-Western immigrants who were taken ("shanghaied"?) from dirty job to dirty job in the West years ago.

Such treatment neglected to acknowledge the intelligence of the Chinese. They knew that Canton to San Francisco (a voyage of 60 days by sea) was faster than the Missouri River to San Francisco (six months by wagon train) many, many years ago.

The Chinese Exclusion Act of 1882 (officially entitled "An Act to Execute Certain Treaty Stipulations Relating to Chinese") is required reading.

Notice how and why Chinatown in San Francisco in 1887 was "a concentration of crime, vice, filth, lechery, disease, and slavery."

Then explain how Chinatown was labeled "mysterious and sinister" in 1962. Ask about those labels along Grant Street.

Read about Lau v. Nichols (1974), too. The reference is to Kinney Kinmon Lau and Kam Wai Lau, two participants in bilingual affairs.

Oakland (pop. 372,000) is big. Brush up on economics. The city is trying to catch up.

Oakland might be a good place to study CPT ("Colored People's Time"). "Standard time" is future-directed, but CPT is present-directed. Chance plays a larger role in one than the other.

Black Oakland is a good place to study how certain rumors and innuendo run through the black community, but not the white one. Contaminated water, the spread of AIDS, and the quality of the food at KFC are three themes among many. "Kooks, corporations, and cults" are to blame, say the rumors.

In black Oakland one is reminded of the need for black entrepreneurs in the community. A spirit of "ujamaa" ("cooperative economics") would not hurt, either.

Our final stop will have us come to rest in Berkeley where we can forget about the faults nearby (San Andreas, Calaveras, Hayward, and Rodgers Creek). Shop along Telegraph Avenue or Solano Avenue. The visit may remind some of life 25 years ago with all the beads and the incense.

North Coast

Over in the Napa and the Sonoma areas there are some things that are the same, and some things that are different.

Huh?

Both are long on enologists (those who study wine).

Both are ripe (pardon the expression) for beautiful strolling, and in both one will find jeroboams, methuselahs, and nebuchadnezzars. Wine went metric, by the way, on January 1, 1979.

Sonoma, however, seems to emphasize cheese more than Napa. With that gastronomic advice one is equipped to tour both places.

Lastly, both areas are a little sensitive about being compared to Monterey and its wine orientation. Include Napa, Sonoma, amd Monterey in one sentence at your own peril.

To be approached with much care are meetings in San Rafael which have to do with channeling. Do not laugh. This is serious business for those who live in and around Marin County. Locals gather to raise their Kundalini energy and to determine the color of their auras. In 1989 some psychics could not determine exactly where the psychic "convention" was to be held. One could ask how they could be stumped if indeed they were really psychic!

Do you remember "Fur Amnesty Week" in San Rafael not long ago?

Things are a little more down to earth in Petaluma which has been the site of both movies and commercials on Brown Court. Listerine and Toyota, two real slices of Americana, have been two among many who have strung wires and erected port-o-lets along pretty Brown Court.

Life is very nice in Eureka, too, the jewel of Humboldt County. History can be studied concerning the doings "north of Fourth" Street years ago. Three notable people in the area "north of Fourth" in 1873 were Jasper Arbuckle, Jesse

Walker, and Peter Honck. Their names are almost as interesting as the details surrounding their not so wicked deeds.

Be ready for some heavy fog in these parts. It comes with the territory.

Eureka was ranked at the top of the list for heartburn in 1990. The burn was due to food. Some feel the heartburn can be blamed on population growth.

Shasta-Cascade

The Shasta-Cascade area is the one with volcanoes, glaciers, waterfalls, dense forests, and (surprise!) less than half a million people. Mt. Shasta (14,162 feet) and Mt. Lassen (10,457) are worth a trip or two themselves. From Corning in the south to the Oregon border in the north, and from east of Arcata to the Nevada border, this section features boiling lakes, not many people, bighorn sheep, a few people, alpine lakes, some people, and rugged canyons.

How does one get there from here? Just go to San Jose or San Francisco by air, and then fly to Redding. Once in Redding you can go in any of the four directions and you will have a lovely stay.

Jackets and long-sleeve shirts are imperative. An air conditioner runs only about 450 to 550 average compressor hours per year. In the Deserts the figure is 1750.

Come to this area knowing that it is not LA.

Gold Country

Fly into Sacramento in order to visit Gold Country, comprised of Sierra, Nevada, Placer, Amador, El Dorado, Calaveras, Tuolumne, Mariposa, and Madera counties. Pretty places include picturesque Nevada City, the Placer County courthouse in Auburn, Placerville itself, and Mariposa.

Although not many people see this section of California, it must be said nevertheless that the area is nice to visit, especially in old clothes. Many still look for gold. For those who love the Old West this area may be the favorite.

It is only fitting that Highway 49 (as in 1849) connects places in Gold Country like Placerville, Angels Camp, and Chinese Camp, for example. With a little imagination one can see a Wells Fargo agent picking up a day's haul.

Realize again that this is not the place, either, for glitzy movie stars and two-martini lunches.

CENTRAL VALLEY

As you sit inside Arco Arena in Sacramento (pop. 370,000), think about how the city has come a long way recently. It has more than enough people. Not long ago Arco Arena did not exist. The Pony Express was getting more ink than some of the governors of the state.

Now things are "big time."

In fact, everything is fine in "sack o' tomato" (aka Sacramento).

Sacramento has areas like Fair Oaks, Greenhaven, Land Park, and Grass Valley nearby. They are nice, although the citizens complain that the nice living does not include the services that former residences had elsewhere. Why people left old homes for a new one remains a mystery.

When doing the tour of the Capital, make sure in the elevator that your coffee cup has a lid on it. There is an Ecotopian spirit alive and well in Sacramento.

Some complain that Sacramento is not really California, but that depends on where one is standing.

The label "Ecotopia" is richly deserved in Sacramento because a constant local topic is the condition of the Sacramento and the American Rivers as they meet at Discovery Park. A certain paper mill about 130 miles north of Sacramento has been dumping dioxin in the Sacramento River for years.

Major league baseball in Sacramento? It is possible, although some feel that California has too many teams already, while certain other spots (Washington D.C. and Tampa) languish. Avid Sacramento Solons fans of the 1930's will remember the late Johnny Vergez with fondness.

In Sacramento more homework about the Chinese should be done so that no one improperly "kowtows" to anyone else. The word has to do with kneeling and touching the ground with the forehead. Look for 10th and F in Sacramento to learn more.

The Chinese used to call Sacramento "the city of second chance" at one time, believe it or not.

Not far from Sacramento is Lodi, as in the song "Stuck in Lodi" recorded years ago. Few who read this book will ever end up visiting Lodi, although most of us have tasted something that started in Lodi long, long, ago. That is A & W rootbeer. Back in 1919 Ray Allen operated a roadside stand hawking rootbeer. The following year Frank Wright (The "W" of A & W) worked with Allen. The rest is (delicious) history.

Dusty Bakersfield does not make the news much these days, but it did in 1939 when Leo Hart was elected Superintendent of Schools for Kern County. He had the task of trying to educate kids from the Plains states who came west to avoid the Dust Bowl. Hart was successful, proving that torn and tattered youngsters can be dealt with despite incredible odds. Arvin Federal Emergency School was the site of this success story.

HIGH SIERRA

If you are flying into Sacramento, and if Gold Country is not your cup of tea, there is always the High Sierra region to explore.

This strip starts at the north fork of the Feather River in the north and heads down to Lake Tahoe, then to Yosemite, then to Sequoia National Park, and on into Kernville in the south.

This part of "the Californias" may be the best at distracting one from thinking about the trials and tribulations found in Los Angeles, San Francisco, Oakland, and even Fresno, simply because one's eyes are filled with mountain peaks, beautiful lakes, gorgeous trees, and pretty skies. Spending a day around Mono Lake can lead to the feeling that one's whole life should be spent in such a beautiful area.

It is difficult to understand how one could pollute this High Sierra area.

As lovely and as breathtaking as this High Sierra region can be, there are nevertheless some problems. Like television reception. Sharing antennas and a fuzzy Super Bowl in late January can be part of the price one pays for living in this pretty area. There is that lack of services "theme" again.

Another "theme" is that people prefer that the area not be visited by additional humans.

Members of the Donner party who died in the snows of 1846-1847 can be studied some more. Start with the words, "Even the wind seemed to hold its breath as the suggestion was made that were one to die the others should live."

THE DESERTS

If you are into miles and miles of desolation, but also tennis, golf, and a good facial, then the Deserts are for you. Some major stops in the region are the Mojave Desert, Death Valley, the Imperial Valley, Barstow (the butt of many in-the-middle-of-nowhere jokes), Palm Springs, Needles, and Calexico. The official language in those parts is English, except in Calexico, of course.

The coming and the going in this area can be boring and even sleep-inducing, but there are many items that all Americans are familiar with: Zabriskie Point, 20 Mule Team Borax, Cher, Rancho Mirage (for golfers!), record-setting heat, and several ghost towns.

For those into golf, a sport that receives too little attention in this book, there is the wonderful experience of being in Palm Springs and seeing a tee shot climb and climb against the beauty of the mountains nearby.

For those into tennis there is the wonderful experience of having a cold one after a day of going to the net, followed by a dip in the pool and another cold one.

Palm Springs features hotels and resorts that cater to gays and lesbians. Ask along Warm Springs Drive.

The role of the Colorado River must be thought about. People into environmental things say that the river should be given more attention, and that less attention should be given to the outrageous cost of suntan lotion along I-10 (Palm Springs, Cathedral City, Rancho Mirage, Palm Desert, Indian Wells).

The very harsh existence in the desert is perhaps best seen by focusing on the areas between Barstow and Needles. Interstate 40 connects them, and going by car between the two is no big problem.

But let us picture this trip on a freight train.

You leave Barstow at noon, say. You go through "places" called Daggett, Hector, Pisgah, Lavic, Ash Hill, Klondike, Siberia, Trojan (no jokes, please), and Bagdad.

Your impression so far is, "why am I doing this"?

You are now near the Amboy Crater, and you begin to notice from here on in that some weird alphabetical order is in place: Amboy, Saltus, Bolo, Cadiz, Siam, Danby, Arimo, Essex, Fenner, Goffs, Homer, Ibis, Jama, Hartoum, and on into Needles.

The trip is finished.

You almost froze to death at Goffs, and you thought you were going to broil to death at Amboy. You have wanted water throughout.

You have also wandered why you didn't quit at Cadiz and hop into a rent-a-car so you could get to Phoenix for some air conditioning.

The trip has been lonely.

Several mountain ranges have been within a stone's throw.

This story has been told in order to show that California is not only Los Angeles, San Francisco, San Diego, or Disneyland. Visit the desert(s) with caution.

In Death Valley another side of life can be seen. First, there are people in Furnace Creek who can share interesting information concerning the local geology. Second, the Shoshone Indians have been in the Valley for a few years now, so there are stories to share there, too. Third, stargazers will be delighted. Halley's Comet came by in April 1986, but one does not have to wait until its next trip to admire the heavens over Death Valley.

Just pray July 15, 1972 does not return too soon. It was 201 degrees at Furnace Creek that day.

Inland Empire

Similar to the Deserts, the Empire is comprised of both Riverside and San Bernadino counties. The city most often mentioned in Riverside County is the city of Riverside, and the city most often mentioned in San Bernadino County is the city of San Bernadino. That should be easy to remember.

Interstate 10 pretty much cuts the area in two, with San Bernadino sitting to the north of Interstate 10, and the other place to its south.

The city of San Bernadino was the site of a drive-in restaurant opened in 1940 by Richard and Maurice McDonald at 14th and E Streets. How many remember that McDonald's restaurants used the stainless steel lazy susan, invented by Richard McDonald?

Some aboard the Amtrak train, the "Desert Wind" appropriately enough, may know, as they go through San Bernadino.

By 1895 the city of Riverside had 20,000 acres of navel

orange trees and had become the wealthiest city per capita in the nation.

By 1989 the county of San Bernadino had increased in population 44.4 percent (since 1980) to 1.3 million souls. Nothing to sneeze at.

Why not end this chapter with some talk about dividing up California?

We should draw a line from Santa Cruz over to the eastern end of the state. Anything below the line is Central and Southern California, and anything above it is Northern California. Maybe that could be a starting point.

Or perhaps the 11.3 million people in the North could raise their hands, and the 18.5 million who do not raise their hands will be labeled true Southern Californians.

Is money the main issue here?

Is water the issue?

The San Andreas Fault?

Lifestyles?

Regardless, do not look for the split soon. The idea may make too much sense. Those who live in the District of Columbia and those in Michigan's Upper Peninsula can tell us all day about New Columbia and Superior, and we may not be moved.

Use a big notepad in California.

OREGON

Ecostate and Enjoying It

In the writing of this book Oregon was almost the final chapter completed. That was not because the state is not interesting or important. Nor was it because Oregon's location in "the back of the mind" of millions of Americans mattered that much.

Perhaps it was because Oregon (pronounced "ORE-uh-gun") is not in the headlines every day.

No problem.

Oregon does well nevertheless.

The first item on the agenda is to locate the state for the novice. The state's western edge is on the Pacific Ocean. The eastern edge touches Idaho. To the north is the state of Washington. To the south are California and Nevada.

The second item is to realize that one can drive to Oregon, fly to Oregon, or walk to Oregon, although the walking is not recommended. It is a long distance from Ontario (on the Idaho border) to Portland (in the northwest corner). It is 374 miles in fact. Hikers know that it is only 378 miles from Klamath Falls to Pendleton. Oregon is very large.

The third item on the list is to remind everyone that in Oregon issues are a big, big deal. A tree farm is not a forest, for example. Just about everyone from Oregon knows what that means. Those not from Oregon should find out. Soon.

Indeed, the notes about Oregon must show that issues differ in Ecotopia and in the Empty Quarter, two different "nations" in the Pacific Northwest. Joel Garreau's *Nine Nations* describes them well.

It is not difficult to figure out how the two sides operate.

There is the ecology/economy debate. Hydroelectric projects oppose lovely rapids, too. To protect the rivers or not is another heated debate. (Think of these contrasting styles as you leaf through *River Runner* magazine.)

One side talks of the availability of water, while the other talks of wheat, cattle, and an occasional gold rush.

In Ecotopia there are conversations about lowering the standard of living in order to increase quality of life. Inhabiting a yurt gets some attention, too.

In the Empty Quarter work schedules and what to do with crazy hippies are discussed with great energy. Holistic medicine does not get much of a hearing. Nor does the labeling of bioregions.

And on and on it goes.

Be sure that the quality of one's death is very important in Ecotopia. Notice that the Hemlock Society is headquartered in Eugene. "Good Life, Good Death" and other such phrases are tossed about freely. The thinking about death is in perfect keeping with the Ecotopian agenda. Self-deliverance (as opposed to assisted suicide) must be studied thoroughly, too.

Making a note or two about aging, death, and dying might include a brief tour of Pioneer Cemetery in Salem as well as Lone Oak Cemetery in Stayton. In Lone Oak find the grave of Dennis Christensen. One reads, "where there walks a logger, there walks a man." For both Oregon pioneers and emigrants those words are important. Decide for yourself if Salem and Stayton are part of Ecotopia.

Eternal rest (eternal life?) may be an important idea to some Oregonians, but perhaps not to too many. Some in religious work say that religion does not make much of a dent in certain parts of the Northwest, although one is told, too, that the ones who are involved are "significantly committed."

Those not committed to a marriage will run the risk of upsetting their Ecotopian brothers and sisters. Divorce brings about an increase in households and an increase in solid waste. Such increases are frowned upon, of course, by Ecotopians.

All Oregonians realize that sooner or later those from California have to be talked to, and why not do so when a profit can be made? Such an opportunity exists in the wine business.

In Oregon there are rough and ready souls who labor daily in Washington County and Yamhill County, silently admitting a relationship with their brothers and sisters from California.

Oregonians may not care for those in the Southeast United States. It seems that the forests of the Northwest are being challenged by those of the Southeast. Portland opposes Atlanta. Old-growth trees are matched against relative newcomers. Douglas fir takes on loblolly pine.

The Northwest brags it has the American Plywood Association in Tacoma, but the Southeast counters with the presence of Georgia Pacific.

Is Oregon the winner?

It is difficult to say, since a few regions have played the role of leader over the years. (In 1890 Chippewa Falls, Wisconsin had a population of 8,670, at least three sawmills and a planing mill, four logging companies, three banks, and two hotels! But, unfortunately, the Chippewa Lumber and Boom Company closed in 1911.)

Status, dollars, jobs, and image are all at stake in the "wood-products wars."

Logging is big in Oregon, or maybe it is better to say that logging is at least as big as the nearest spotted owl. The debate is familiar by now.

A break from that debate can involve a quiet day in Naughty Girl Meadow in the southeast corner of the state. Better make that Whorehouse Meadow. It seems that in the 1960's a man was camping with his daughters and was asked the name of the place by a passerby. He responded "Naughty Girl," but locals still say "Whorehouse." The area is quiet.

Some of the fields and quiet highways of Oregon are so attractive that almost anyone can find the way to places like Antelope or Madras, in counties like Wasco and Jefferson in central Oregon. We all know by now about the Bhagwan Shree Rajneesh in the early 1980's. Those in Fossil and Horse Heaven will explain.

Confusion vanishes in Bend (pop. 20,400), a place "in the middle of nowhere." That is how a politician described Bend not long ago. Trouble followed the remark.

Malheur County, Harney County, and Lake County make up Oregon's High Desert. The area is the land of failed homesteads, aborted settlement schemes, and Indian wars. Things were at one time so bad that a 1902 mining engineer labeled the area "so isolated, so non-communicative ... that its topography, its mineral wealth and its scientific wonders are comparatively unknown." The warning is free, but the road map is extra.

Cities?

Those in Grants Pass (pop. 17,500) must keep an eye on things in Gary, Indiana. Gary provides the steel necessary to fight off termites who harm lumber and the prices paid for it. Build a home in Grants Pass with one eye on ponderosa pine and the other on steel. Read *Random Lengths*, a lumber industry newsletter, for more details.

In order to contemplate the history and the beauty of Portland (pop. 458,000), go to Waterfront Park. Eat an apple on the grass. Do not throw the core away on the grass because ecology is very important.

Consider how far Portland has come in a short time.

Front Avenue was only Front Street until 1931.

The mighty Trailblazers won the NBA title in 1977 with Bill Walton and Maurice Lucas. The team was practically in its infancy then.

Today cars from Japan, not Detroit, are mentioned with great seriousness in Portland.The Portland/Ecotopian mind watches the Pacific Rim daily. Ideas and products from Detroit are not liked at all, come to think of it.

Many people come to Portland by road every year to see the city, and those who drive trucks are always glad to see a landmark on I-5 at exit 307: the Jubitz truck stop. Many a Freightliner and many a Kenworth have visited.

Those flying into or out of Portland may remember that the city is listed with Sacramento, Raleigh, Seattle-Tacoma, and Jacksonville for fogginess. The National Weather Service says that about 10 days a year the Portland airport is tough to get into and out of.

The youthfulness of Portland may give the impression that the city has not "been around" long enough, but the feeling must be interpreted a bit. In 1928 Portland did not have an electric chair like Joliet, Illinois did, although Portlanders were able to erect a Paramount movie palace (designed by Rapp & Rapp), just like Brooklyn and Toledo. Do not judge the West with an eye on the East.

An unpleasant side to Portland is the way the national pastime is treated. Remember the old Portland Beavers at Civic Stadium? The great Mickey Cochrane played in Portland, but there does not seem to be much interest there in the game these days.

Interest in gaming was generated in 1989 with the announcement that come September 10 there would be legalized gambling on NFL games in order to support university athletics in Oregon. Some eyebrows were raised because many observers thought Oregon would not stoop so low. Oregon is now the land of the over/under. (We might want to blame Charles K. McNeil of the University of Chicago who set down the formulas for codifying point spreads in 1931.)

For intellectual life go to Corvallis (pop. 44,700), home of the Oregon State University Beavers. Corvallis was ranked second in an *American Demographics* survey of good and bad micropolitan areas in 1990.

For more intellectual life go to Eugene (pop. 112,700), home of the University of Oregon Ducks. Waddle over to a basketball game. The Ducks love to defeat teams from California. All the Californians do is squander electric power anyway.

That comment brings us back to the front of this chapter.

Get ready for a debate in Oregon.

Choose your side of things carefully.

Washington

Both Sides Now

Washington.
What does that name bring to mind? Clear air? Cleanliness? Small populations? Isolation from the East and Midwest? The apple business?
Washington state.
What do those words signify? Do the words refer to pollution-free neighborhoods and ordered lives? Do the words refer to vinyl siding replacing cedar siding in Seattle after the city gets its 39 inches of rain a year? Or does the lumber business come to mind?
Several of the things listed above may come to mind.
Does the word "evergreen" get in the mix? Those in Olympia at Evergreen State University (nickname: Geoducks) will think so.
This chapter will be geared to those who are strangers to Washington state. That way some of the items just mentioned might be clarified.
First, a stranger needs to know that some in Washington do indeed like things lean and clean. "High tech but eco soft" is the phrase. Those along the Chile-like strip on the western edge of the state are that way. Ecotopia is the name for the place.
Second, a different "nation" awaits in places like Adams County and Klickitat County. Empty Quarter is Joel Garreau's term. Digging up the ground, not popular in Ecotopia, is one example of an item done easily in eastern Washington, but not so much in western (read Ecotopia) Washington.
The difference can be remembered easily if you can keep the word "garbage" in your mind. Ask about the activities of Waste Management. The waste of Seattle should not be stashed in eastern Washington, eastern Washingtonians say. They say it loudly. Seattle folks respond by saying that clean

Seattle would be even more beautiful if the garbage were lodged in eastern Washington, in the so-called Empty Quarter. The debate (war?) goes on and on.

One is wise, by the way, to study the state of Washington with British Columbia in Canada and Oregon in one package. Inquire about how some use the term "Cascadia." For starters head for Vancouver (aka "Hongcouver" to hear some people talk about those from Hong Kong).

This chapter will try to bridge both sides of the "slender line of glistening light" that runs north/south in Washington.

Let us start with a clean (what else?) notepad.

All sides of Washington were made aware of a place called Mt. St. Helens in May 1980. The eruption blew ashes into parts of eastern Washington, Idaho, and Montana. Quiet since 1857, Mt. St. Helens caused damages that totalled more than $1.8 billion in property and crops. Today scientists report that some people in Cowlitz County and environs are not really convinced that there are dangers associated with living near the big girl. Large books say otherwise.

Let's move to Seattle, as many do anyway, to sort out a few thoughts.

Seattle (population increasing) is easy to understand. It is yuppie, plaid shirt, and hiking boots. It is also cloudy 227 days a year.

True Seattleites love the "l word" (i.e. limit, as in "let's limit growth in the area"). False Seattleites are those who come in from somewhere else (especially California) and try to build condos and create traffic jams.

In Washington's most populated city three "r words" are redesign, redefine, and refine. (Or are they reduce, reuse, and recycle?)

Seattle is Boeing in the minds of many people. On May 15, 1954 Bill Boeing was enthused about a prototype of the 707 jetliner, a mere 124 times the weight of his first plane in 1916. (Others at that time were more concerned with the result of

Brown v. Board of Education of Topeka two days later.)

Seattle now has poetry "slams" in lower Queen Anne Hill, where aspiring poets do their thing. Truck drivers are welcome.

So are those who listen to Yanni (Chryssomallis) and other "New Age" musicians.

Seattle always wishes to be on the cutting edge. Contact the Mariners baseball club at http://www.mariners.org.

Logic may demand a question about Seattle and its people. If the area is so gung-ho about cleanliness and ecology (and being on the cutting edge), then why is it that King and Kitsap Counties are so concerned about blowing the world away with the use of nuclear power? Part of the answer is that Seattleites think that powerful weaponry is much cleaner than the smokestacks of Buffalo, the chicken coops of Eastern Maryland, the drugs of New Orleans, and the piles of manure in Sioux City. Cleaner and more pleasant to work with. Simple as that. Life goes on in King and Kitsap.

Catholic Archbishop Raymond Hunthausen once referred to the area as "the Auschwitz of Puget Sound" a few years ago. That got everyone's attention.

In Seattle ask along Yesler Way about loggers who once skidded timber down to waiting ships. Hence, the term "Skid Row" (born "Skid Road"). Social problems followed the skidding, the history books tell us.

Find Seattle's Garlic Gulch, a great vernacular name. It brings to mind the wild West, but the area is not too wild now. It gave the world Ronald Santo, who toiled for years for the Chicago National League Baseball Club, Inc. Santo fielded hundreds of grounders as a youth in Garlic Gulch.

Another "g word" is grunge. The grunge subculture includes fuzz (heavy wool sweaters), cob nobblers (losers), and plats (platform shoes).

A more mainstream activity is Mariners baseball at the Kingdome. Big crowds are not common. One explanation is that the weather in Seattle, where it does not rain much but rains often, does not lend itself to indoor baseball on a carpet.

Seattle people wish to do indoor things when it is nasty out, but not baseball.

Outdoor activities are popular when the weather is good, especially when Mt. Rainier "is out." Caught in this dilemma are the Mariners.

The troubles of baseball in Seattle became worse when Hiroshi Yamauchi of Kyoto, Japan wanted to buy the Mariners not long ago. "Non-North American ownership" and "majority local control" were major factors in the negotiations. Few realize that Gyo Obata of the architectural firm of Hellmuth Obata & Kassabaum is a Japanese man who went to Missouri years ago to avoid the internment camps. The company (HOK) has worked on several sports venues.

Heroes and villains, someone asked?

We have to look only at Chief Seattle, about whom there is much confusion, but here are some facts. He was born in 1786. The name "See-ahth" is about as close as we can come to the name of the man. He was a Suquamish, one of the Coastal Salish tribes in the Puget Sound region. He died in 1866, one year after the city named for him passed a law making it illegal for Indians to live in Seattle.

The four sentences that follow are nonsense, we know.

Chief Seattle sent a letter to President Franklin Pierce and wrote in the letter that it is good to protect the environment. Seattle was a gifted orator and a visionary. He spoke of the tragedy of killing the bison. Seattle felt bad that wild horses would be tamed right before his very eyes. Nonsense, he wrote historically.

Words (like "See-ahth") that do not seem to be everyday English are not uncommon in Seattle, especially if you are aware of what a tsunami could do. The item refers to a giant sea wave that is part of a geological triple threat that could make Seattle rock and roll in the future. Volcanic eruptions and earthquakes are the other two dangers. The American Institute of Physics can explain the Juan de Fuca plate, the Seattle Fault, and so forth.

Seattle and the Pacific Northwest do not live and die with things scientific, by the way, as much as other places do. True artists, the theory goes, are not overly concerned with mud slides and shifting land levels.

Those in Tacoma (pop. 177,000) at the American Plywood Association have their eyes on Florida from time to time. Not when the Seattle Seahawks play the Miami Dophins, but when a hurricane blasts Florida. Some nails (4 instead of 33?) were put into some wood when Hurricane Andrew visited a few years ago. The difference was significant for those in Tacoma.

Life on the other side of the Cascades in Spokane (home to 177,000 folks) is nice. Quiet, however. Ask about wheat, fruit, and cattle. Ask about the 1857 gold rush, too.

Notice the amount of rainfall in Spokane compared to Seattle.

Do not bristle at the criticism of Seattle by Spokane people. The talk comes with the territory.

Speak to those in Yakima to settle things.

Now have a gold delicious.

Alaska

A Life Apart

It may be best to read this chapter in August in North Platte, Nebraska. That way the summer heat will probably have a person perspiring, and perhaps everyone can realize that Alaska, a long drive from North Platte, may not be equated with the cold and the dark every single day.

We all have heard little gems about Alaskans having (Eskimo) words for new snow, drifting snow, snow in the air, and so forth.

We tend to think that Alaska is totally different from any other state.

Relating to Alaska is not impossible, however.

Lines can be drawn in Alaska just like they were in Tennessee and Texas. Alaska has the Arctic, the Bering Sea Coast, the Interior, the Alaska Peninsula and Aleutians, Southcentral/Gulf Coast, and the Southeast. Easy.

Alaska (pop. 535,000) can be lovely, warm, sunny, and comfortable. Qiviut, the wool of the musk ox, is not necessary every single day.

One must remember to adjust and re-adjust the mind about practical matters a little bit, however. The Bells might be replaced by Arctic Slope Telephone, for example. Try calling from Deadhorse to Atqasuk, or from Point Lay to Point Hope. The names alone seem to be from another world.

Alaska does pay its citizens dividends instead of taxing them, come to think of it. That sure makes the state different.

Earthquakes in Alaska do not get fair treatment, either. Southern California, not Alaska or South Carolina, gets the ink. Adjust the mind again.

Alaska (0.7 people per square mile) may not be out of the mainstream that much. Consult the Gayellow Pages for more information.

Memorizing the words of Alfred Korzybski may help, too.

He has told the world that "a map is not the territory." To study Alaska from afar ("the map") is one thing, but to know "the territory" is quite another. Ask a physicist how at times the model is a poor map of the system. Same point phrased differently.

Similar warnings about perception were included in the Arizona chapter because frontiers, borders, conquests, Gardens of Eden, and Paradise itself have to be studied and re-studied after a map is set aside. The land, what is on it, how we perceive it, and how we perceive ourselves will change after we realize that certainly "a map is not the territory" in Alaska.

One's concept of "home" will change. Many Alaskans are really Iowans and Texans in the heart.

Author Robert H. Wiebe has said that geography was a dependent variable in the 18th century in the lower 48, and we might be well advised to think that it is so these days in Alaska, too. The location of one's feet probably finishes second to the location of one's heart in Alaska today. Inquire of an Alaskan if family ties and friendships are more important than a need to protect turf, neighborhoods, and city limits. They probably are.

Less theoretical is the question about the person who arrived at the North Pole first. Was it Robert E. Perry or Frederick A. Cook? In April 1909 or in April 1908? The vote here goes to Cook in 1908.

Easier, too, may be the argument about where the state capital should be. The complaint is that Juneau (28,000 souls) is two time zones away from where things happen in the state. Some suggest Wasilla (see Anchorage area) for the state capital.

No one complains that Mount McKinley (aka Denali, "the High One") is in the wrong place.

In fact, McKinley inspires much respect and fear. The fear has to do with the possibility of the loss of life. A total of 28 people have died there between 1986 and the middle of 1992.

Do not get a member of the rescue squad started about how it feels to watch climbers fall to their deaths one by one — as the squad watches from a helicopter.

Most who head into Alaska do so through Anchorage (pop. 226,000). The city is pretty, warmer than Fairbanks or Barrow certainly, and is the main port of entry into the state.

Many airplanes use the Anchorage airport. Planes, not just cars, play a large role in Alaskan day to day living.

Anchorage for some will bring the word Iditarod to mind, since Anchorage to Nome is the Iditarod trail, 1,100 miles through such places as Knik, Nikolai, Nulato, and Shaktoolik. If you want names that sound differently, the trail goes thru Big Lake, Rohn Roadhouse, McGrath, Ruby, and Safety.

In Anchorage the Permanent Fund can be discussed at length. Know the oil business beforehand. Permafrost is something else.

Eskimos wanting a say and having a say about that Fund may be an important item for non-Eskimos to understand, by the way.

Know, too, that "Anchorage is 25 minutes from Alaska." Some feel that time can be spent in Anchorage without having to know the first thing about Alaska.

One of the first things to know about the 49th state is that the welcome mat is out for those in Japan. Fishing in Alaska is a big attraction. The flight takes less than seven hours. Japanese who arrive in the middle of the night cannot wait to fish.

Night and day can be studied in Anchorage, especially since Anchorage days at certain times of the year are filling up fast. Colonizing the night in Anchorage differs from doing the same in Tokyo or Honolulu. Behaviors like watching NFL football or going to a convenience store can appear different in Alaska. Seasonal affective disorders (SAD) enter the picture, too. Adjust the mind again.

Know that in Anchorage the business crowd is talking about oil in one of two ways — drilled or spilled.

The mind may function best in Alaska in small(er) places, so here are a few.

Barrow? It is at the top of the world. It is cold. You will be advised, "No roads lead to Barrow and water traffic is limited to a few brief summer weeks when ice conditions on the Arctic Ocean permit passage." Barrow has "close proximity to Siberia," the brochures tell us.

Barrow also is a good place to discuss how (not if) Eskimos should share in the oil business and its profits.

Fairbanks? Ask about quartz. Notice 30,800 people. Head to 9th Avenue and Cushman for some socializing. Ask the locals why the newspaper back home will not have Fairbanks in its list of median home prices.

Juneau, mentioned above, is a place where one often hears, "That was done by those jerks in Washington." Getting and sending mail may be a big problem, too, if you want to complain about those people.

For many people the streets of Juneau mark the happy start of Alaska in 1898. The search for "precious dust" in Alaska in 1898 was a newsmaker.

Ketchikan (pop. 8,200)? Important items there include salmon, fjords, totems, and Creek Street. Ketchikan is a good place to study the similarities the city has with Seattle to the south. Find out after lunch if Ketchikan is in Ecotopia or in the Empty Quarter of the United States. Two different agendas, he said once again.

Nome has gold, Anvil Creek, and Front Street. One is told, "no road leads to Nome." Enough said. Travel arrangements to Russia can be made easily from Nome.

Palmer, the jewel of the Matanuska Valley? Go to the Bluegrass Festival. Notice the bluegrass fans from Telluride, Colorado.

Petersburg? Drive down Nordic Drive. Ask for the canneries. Enjoy berries, ferries, and sightseeing.

Sitka (8,500 people)? Go to St. Michael's Cathedral for

starters. Ask about the Russian explorers who came by in 1741. Look for Victorian houses, and then compare them with houses on Russian Hill in San Francisco. Some consider Sitka a great secret for vacationers to visit. Notice the pulp mill and the Russian cemetery.

Skagway once boasted of settlers who "have grown up with the place" after a residence of three months! Precious dust did that. Just try to get a job today in Skagway.

Valdez? The place used to be called Tetaluk ("windy place"). Copper and gold once drew many people. The city was rocked to its foundations on Good Friday, 1964 by an earthquake. Those remarks alone should be good for about a month's research.

Does that about do it for Alaska? No. In no way.

Alaska is a treasure.

Put down the maps. Go.

Study to your heart's content.

HAWAII

Last Stop

A story connected with comedian Milton Berle may make the going a little easier in this particular chapter.

It turned out that Berle was visiting a nursing home years ago, and the people there were wild with laughter at his jokes. Heading for the door after about an hour's work, Berle asked an elderly woman in a wheelchair, "Do you know who I am"? The woman replied in the negative, but added that someone at the front desk may be able to help Berle with his question.

Identity is a large item in life, and identity is also big in places like New England and the South. We should add Hawaii to the list for reasons to be explained in a moment.

What is identity like in Hawaii? What is Hawaii like? How does one identify real Hawaiians? The answers are not easy.

Does fifty percent native blood make a person Hawaiian?

Does it help to have ancestors in Hawaii before Captain James Cook arrived in 1778?

Does the use of the Hawaiian language, with an occasional apostrophe turned backwards, mean much?

For starters a look at skin color may not help. Some people in Hawaii are white ("haoles"), while others are Chinese. Some are Filipino. Others are Japanese. Samoans are noticed, too.

Hawaii may be identified by some as the place which houses the washing and crushing bins at Oahu Sugar, but that perception is unfortunate.

Traditions, characterized by "continual self-modification" one is told, may not help much since traditions can cover both what is long past as well as what one's mother did. Lomi salmon and the slack-key guitar method, for example, are not traditional, but some people say that they are. Grass skirts came from Micronesia.

Do politics and economy tell us anything? The line is that

the Japanese have the politics, the Chinese have the money, the haoles have the land, and the Hawaiians, in the words of a song, "get plenty not too much of nutting."

What to do? Look around.

Some of the people of Keanae (on the island of Maui) claim that they are Chinese-Hawaiian, with occasional other admixtures. Villagers call almost anyone with part-Hawaiian ancestry "Hawaiian" if they are friends or kin or if they "act Hawaiian."

Does that help us? Maybe. For most people Hawaii "means" Asian. Pure and simple. End of story for some.

Questions about identity are not the only things hard to pin down in Hawaii ...

There is a psychogeography, too. Going "outside" is going to a world dominated by white people (the hot, dry world of canefields and tourist hotels), while going "inside" involves friends and family (a cool, wet region where Hawaiians are still predominant).

Our notes may pick up speed once we realize that "different" is the name in Hawaii. With the word "different" in mind, the paragraphs that follow should be sifted through one by one. Slowly.

Hawaii may not be home to too many people, although some people (tourists?) may think that the state belongs to everyone. Of course, what belongs to everyone belongs to no one. Hawaii simply is not home.

Some will like the word play that 29 percent of the homes in Hawaii are condos. Most homes are not condos in Tulsa and Buffalo.

For the elderly homes can be a problem. The Honolulu phone book has a bigger listing under "Nuts-edible" than "Nursing Homes."

Many native Hawaiians are frequently homeless, not well educated, and jobless. This is material that the travel literature does not mention, of course.

Hawaiian sovereignty is not mentioned much, either. Self-rule has something to do with land use, and land use is complicated. Using land to bury a loved one can be an ordeal.

Tourists (6 million a year?) can see a few complications in Hawaii if they want to.

Some of the tourists express surprise that Hawaiians talk about same-sex marriages. Catholic and Mormon leaders have been spotted in Hawaii talking together about their respective positions on the subject, while leaders from the two groups on the mainland (read Salt Lake City) have their hands full talking about the ordination of women.

Other newcomers find that distances can be confusing, too. It is not far from Hilo to Honolulu (217 miles), but it is a terrific distance from the mainland to Hawaii (the state, the group of islands, and the individual island). Distances may prevent the best theories concocted in Los Angeles and New York from making it to Hawaii.

Distances were no problem, however, when Isoroku Yamamoto collaborated with submarine officer Takayasa Arima in the attack on Pearl Harbor. Before December 7, 1941 Arima had been observed covering a few miles while studying at Johns Hopkins and at Yale. Yamamoto, furthermore, studied English at Harvard in the 1920's.

In Hawaii some distances are covered by cars that cost a ton to insure. This is not travel brochure material, either.

Some people go to Hawaii for an abortion. This is at least the third item in this chapter that the brochures will not mention.

A few may see irony in calling Hawaii "the health state" by a few insurance companies. (For what it is worth, the city of Durham, North Carolina features a history of tobacco but is called the "City of Medicine." Sort all this out as you head for Haleakala Crater on Maui.)

There are those, too, in the "Health State" who choose to end their lives in Hawaii. Suicide is common.

Apparently very little is taboo (or "kapu") in Hawaii, to use a word that some Hawaiians can relate to.

One's health can be challenged by a "tsunami," Japanese for "harbor wave." Those from Japan and Chile know the word well, too.

All is not lost, however.

Financial health can be guaranteed by knowing that the time difference between Honolulu and the closing of the New York Stock Exchange as well as between Honolulu and the opening of the Tokyo Stock Exchange are not big problems on Bishop Street in Honolulu.

The Japanese enjoy both pleasure and business opportunities in Hawaii since New York, California, and Hawaii are invested in by the Japanese daily. In fact, some Japanese people fly 3859 miles to Hawaii to play golf. That is 45 miles farther than Hawaii to Houston. A few "honchos," a word certain Japanese-Hawaiians can relate to, can be found golfing. The 18 holes were costing about $69.00 on the average recently.

Many people think that Hawaii relies too much on tourism, of course, although the golfers may disagree. Tremendous energy is given to fixing airport runways and to importing flowers, but little attention is given to marine sciences and volcanology.

Moving easily between the issues are Mormons who have been known to keep an eye on football players from Kahuku High and Punahou High in Honolulu. That way winning teams on the college level can be guaranteed at "Y" (Brigham Young University) in Provo, Utah.

Hawaii is certainly not the boondocks for the Mormon people. They know that the word "boondocks" ("bundok" in Tagalog, spoken by Filipinos) means "mountain." At last look there were more than a few mountains in Hawaii, and there were a few in Utah, too. Watch your English in Hawaii.

Watch your Japanese, too. One might be well advised to study Japanese people seriously before doing anything in

Hawaii. Family, friends, and social relations among the Japanese are first on the list. It is not uncommon to see Japanese taxi drivers and lawyers playing tennis together. In Los Angeles or New York such things may be rare.

Watch your Portuguese. It is possible that the person strumming the ukulele ("jumping flea" in Hawaiian) is Portuguese. The year 1878 marked the start of large-scale Portuguese immigration into the present state of Hawaii, then the Kingdom of Hawaii. The Portuguese should compare and contrast Our Lady of Good Voyage in Gloucester, Massachusetts with Our Lady of Perpetual Help in Ewa Beach.

Baseball in Hawaii involves a mention of the old Hawaii Islanders. A great story has it that a player for the Islanders was called up years ago to the majors, but refused to go. The best laid plans of the parent club went "amok," as the Malaysian people would say. Baseball in Paradise may be nicer than baseball in Baltimore or New York.

How to end this chapter?

With the words "ike pono." Memorize them. The words mean "be prepared."

Nothing less will do in changing, independent Hawaii.

REFERENCES

Alexander, Thomas G. "Toward A Synthetic Interpretation of the Mountain West: Diversity, Isolation, and Cooperation." *Utah Historical Quarterly* 39, no. 3 (Summer 1971): 202-206.

Athearn, Robert G. *The Mythic West in Twentieth-Century America.* Lawrence: University Press of Kansas, 1986.

Bailey, Thomas A. "The Mythmakers of American History." *Journal of American History* 55, no. 1 (Summer 1968): 5-21.

Bawer, Bruce. *A Place at the Table: the Gay Individual in American Society.* New York: Poseidon Press, 1993.

Bayer, Ronald. *Private Acts and Social Consequences: AIDS and the Politics of Public Health.* New York: Free Press, 1989.

Bell, Derrick. *Faces at the Bottom of the Well: The Permanence of Racism.* New York: BasicBooks, 1992.

Berry, Brewton. *Almost White.* New York: Macmillan Company, 1963.

Blau, Joel. *The Visible Poor: Homelessness in the United States.* New York: Oxford University Press, 1992.

Bradshaw, Michael. *Regions and Regionalism in the United States.* Jackson: University Press of Mississippi, 1988.

Brinkley, Alan. "Writing the History of Contemporary America: Dilemmas and Challenges." *Daedalus* 113, no. 3 (Summer 1984):121-141.

Brownell, Joseph W. "The Cultural Midwest." *Journal of Geography* 59 (February 1960): 81-85.

Bukowczyk, John J. *And My Children Did Not Know Me: A History of the Polish-Americans.* Bloomington: Indiana University Press, 1987.

Carver, Craig M. *American Regional Dialects: A Word Geography.* Ann Arbor: University of Michigan Press, 1989.

Caudill, Harry M. *Night Comes to the Cumberlands.* Boston: Little, Brown, 1963.

Clay, Grady. *Closeup: How to Read the American City.* Chicago: University of Chicago Press, 1980.

Clifford, James. *Writing Culture: The Poetics and Politics of Ethnography.* Berkeley: University of California Press, 1986.

Cockcroft, James D. *Outlaws in the Promised Land: Mexican Immigrant Workers and America's Future.* New York: Grove Press, Inc., 1986.

Cohen, George. *The Jews in the Making of America*. Boston: The Stratford Co., 1924.
Coleman, Terry. *Going To America*. New York: Pantheon Books, 1972.
Cox, Oliver C. *Caste, Class and Race: A Study in Social Dynamics*. Garden City, New York: Doubleday & Co., 1948.
Cromie, Alice Hamilton. *A Tour Guide to the Civil War.* 3rd ed. rev. Nashville: Rutledge Hill Press, 1990.
Davidson, Osha Gray. *Broken Heartland: The Rise of America's Rural Ghetto*. New York: The Free Press, 1990.
Davis, Fred. *Yearning for Yesterday: A Sociology of Nostalgia*. New York: The Free Press, 1979.
Deetz, James. *In Small Things Forgotten: The Archaeology of Early American Life*. New York: Doubleday, 1977.
de Graaf, Lawrence B. "Recognition, Racism, and Reflections onWestern Black History." *Pacific Historical Review* 44 (February 1975): 22-51.
D'Emilio, John and Estelle Freedman. *Intimate Matters: A History of Sexuality in America*. New York: Harper & Row, 1988
Dippie, Brian W. *The Vanishing American: White Attitudes and U.S. Indian Policy.* Lawrence: University Press of Kansas, 1982.
_____. "The Winning of the West Reconsidered." *Wilson Quarterly* 14, no. 3 (Summer 1990): 70-85.
Downs, Roger M. and David Stea. *Maps in Minds: Reflections on Cognitive Mapping*. New York: Harper & Row, 1977.
Duneier, Mitchell. *Slim's Table: Race, Respectibility, and Masculinity.* Chicago: University of Chicago Press, 1992.
Edwards, Harry. *The Sociology of Sport*. Homewood, IL: Dorsey Press,1973.
Eisler, Benita. *Class Act: America's Last Dirty Secret*. New York: Franklin Watts, 1983.
Evans, Sara M. *Born for Liberty: A History of Women in America*. New York: Free Press, 1989.
FitzGerald, Frances. *Cities on a Hill: A Journey Through Contemporary American Cultures*. New York: Simon and Schuster, Inc., 1986.
Ford, Larry and Ernest Griffin. "The Ghettoization of Paradise." *The Geographical Review* 69, no. 2 (April 1979): 140-158.
Francaviglia, Richard V. "The Cemetery as an Evolving Cultural Landscape." *Annals of the Association of American Geographers* 61, no. 3 (September 1971): 501-509.

Fredrickson, George M. *The Black Image in the White Mind: The Debate on Afro-American Character and Destiny, 1817-1914.* New York: Harper & Row, 1971.

Fuchs, Lawrence H. *The American Kaleidoscope: Race, Ethnicity, and the Civic Culture.* Middletown, CT: Wesleyan University Press, 1990.

Furnas, J. C. *The Americans: A Social History of the United States, 1587-1914.* New York: G. P. Putnam's Sons, 1969.

Fussell, Betty. *The Story of Corn.* New York: Alfred A. Knopf, 1992.

Garreau, Joel. *The Nine Nations of North America.* Boston: Houghton Mifflin Company, 1981.

_____. *Edge City: Life on the New Frontier.* New York: Doubleday, 1991.

Garrett, Roland. "The Metaphysics of Baseball." *Philosophy Today* (Fall 1976): 209-226.

Gastil, Raymond D. *Cultural Regions of the United States.* Seattle: University of Washington Press, 1975.

Goldfield, David R. *Black, White, and Southern: Race Relations and Southern Culture, 1940 to Present.* Baton Rouge: Louisiana State University Press, 1990.

Gordon, Milton M. *Assimilation in American Life: The Role of Race, Religion, and National Origins.* New York: Oxford University Press, 1964.

Gould, Peter and Rodney White. *Mental Maps.* Baltimore: Penguin Books, 1974.

Grant, Madison. *The Passing of the Great Race; or, The Racial Basis of European History.* New York: C. Scribner's sons, 1916.

Greeley, Andrew M. *The Irish Americans: The Rise to Money and Power.* New York: Harper & Row, 1981.

Hague, John A., ed. *American Character and Culture in a Changing World: Some Twentieth-Century Perspectives.* Westport, CT: Greenwood Press, 1979.

Hakuta, Kenji. *Mirror of Language: The Debate on Bilingualism.* New York: Basic Books, 1986.

Hale, Ruth Feser. *A Map of Vernacular Regions in America.* Ph.D. dissertation: University of Minnesota, 1971.

Harrington, Michael. *The Other America: Poverty in the United States.* New York: Penguin Books, 1962.

Harris, Marvin. "Caste, Class, and Minority." *Social Forces* 37, no.3 (March 1959): 248-254.

Hart, John Fraser. "The Middle West." *Annals of the Association of American Geographers* 62, no. 2 (June 1972): 258-282.

Hawke, David Freeman. *Everyday Life in Early America.* New York: Harper & Row, 1988.

Hsu, Francis L.K. *The Challenge of the American Dream: The Chinese in the United States.* Belmont, CA: Wadsworth Publishing Co., 1971.

Hughes, Robert. *The Culture of Complaint: The Fraying of America.* Cambridge: Oxford University Press, 1993.

Jackson, John B. *Discovering the Vernacular Landscape.* New Haven: Yale University Press, 1986.

Jackson, Kenneth T. *Crabgrass Frontier: The Suburbanization of the United States.* New York: Oxford University Press, 1985.

Jones, Reginald L., ed. *Black Psychology.* New York: Harper & Row, 1972.

Kanfer, Stefan. "The Greatest Game." *Time* 101 (April 30 1973): 82.

Katz, William Loren. *Black Indians: A Hidden Heritage.* New York: Atheneum, 1986.

Kivisto, Peter, ed. *The Ethnic Enigma.* Philadelphia: The Balch Institute Press, 1989.

Klapp, Orrin E. *Heroes, Villains, and Fools: The Changing American Character.* Englewood Cliffs, NJ: Prentice-Hall, Inc., 1962.

Kolodny, Annette. *The Lay of the Land: Metaphor as Experience and History in American Life and Letters.* Chapel Hill: University of North Carolina Press, 1975.

Korzybski, Alfred. *Science and Sanity: An Introduction to non-Aristotelian Systems and General Semantics.* 2nd ed. New York: The International Non-Aristotelian Library Publishing Company, 1941.

Kunstler, James Howard. *The Geography of Nowhere: The Rise and Decline of America's Man-made Landscape.* New York: Simon & Schuster, 1993.

Ladner, Joyce A., ed. *The Death of White Sociology.* New York: Random House, 1973.

Leighton, Isabel, ed. *The Aspirin Age, 1919-1941.* New York: Simon and Schuster, 1949.

Lieberson, Stanley. "Unhyphenated Whites in the United States." *Ethnic and Racial Studies* 8, no. 1 (January 1985): 159-180.

Limerick, Patricia Nelson. *The Legacy of Conquest: The Unbroken Past of the American West.* New York: W.W. Norton and Company, 1987.

Lopez, Barry. *Arctic Dreams: Imagination and Desire in a Northern Landscape.* New York: Bantam Books, 1986.

Lowenthal, David and Martyn J. Bowden, editors. *Geographies of the Mind: Essays in Historical Geosophy in Honor of John Kirtland Wright.* New York: Oxford University Press, 1976.

Lynch, Kevin. *What Time is This Place?* Cambridge: MIT Press, 1972.

Lyson, Thomas A. *Two Sides to the Sunbelt: The Growing Division Between the Rural and Urban South.* New York: Praeger, 1989.

Machor, James L. *Pastoral Cities: Urban Ideals and the Symbolic Landscape of America.* Madison: University of Wisconsin Press, 1987.

Madison, James H., ed. *Heartland: Comparative Histories of the Midwestern States.* Bloomington: Indiana University Press, 1988.

Mann, Arthur. *The One and the Many.* Chicago: University of Chicago Press, 1969.

Martin, Calvin. *The American Indian and the Problem of History.* New York: Oxford University Press, 1987.

McAvoy, Thomas T. *The Midwest: Myth or Reality?* Notre Dame, IN: University of Notre Dame Press, 1961.

Mecklin, John M. *The Ku Klux Klan: A Study of the American Mind.* New York: Russell & Russell Inc., 1963.

Meinig, D. W., ed. *The Interpretation of Ordinary Landscapes: Geographical Essays.* New York: Oxford University Press, 1979.

_____. *The Shaping of America: A Geographical Perspective on 500 Years of History.* vol. II. New Haven: Yale University Press, 1986.

Melbin, Murray. *Night As Frontier: Colonizing the World After Dark.* New York: The Free Press, 1987.

Meyer, Richard E., ed. *Cemeteries and Gravemarkers: Voices of American Culture.* Ann Arbor: UMI Research Press, 1989.

Muller, Thomas. *Immigrants and the American City.* New York: New York University Press, 1993.

Mumford, Lewis. *The Culture of Cities.* New York: Harcourt, Brace and World, 1938.

Naylor, David. *American Picture Palaces: The Architecture of Fantasy.* New York: Van Nostrand Reinhold Co., 1981.

Oakley, Giles. *The Devil's Music: A History of the Blues.* New York: Taplinger Publishing Co., 1976.

Orfalea, Gregory. *Before the Flames: A Quest for the History of Arab Americans.* Austin: University of Texas Press, 1988.

Parish, Peter J. *Slavery: History and Historians.* New York: Harper & Row, 1989.
Patton, Phil. *Open Road: A Celebration of the American Highway.* New York: Simon and Schuster, Inc., 1986.
Pearce, Roy Harvey. *The Savages of America: A Study of the Indian and the Idea of Civilization.* Revised. Baltimore: The Johns Hopkins Press, 1965.
Popper, Deborah Epstein and Frank J. Popper. "The Great Plains: From Dust to Dust." *Planning* 53, no. 12 (December 1987):12-18.
Porter, Rosalie Pedalino. *Forked Tongue: The Politics of Bilingual Education.* New York: Basic Books, 1990.
Reischauer, Edwin O. *The Japanese Today: Change and Continuity.* Cambridge: Belknap Press, 1988.
Roland, Charles P. "The Ever-Vanishing South." *Journal of Southern History* 48, no. 1 (February 1982): 3-20.
Rose, Peter. *Mainstream and Margins: Jews, Blacks and Other Americans.* New Brunswick, NJ: Transaction Books, 1983.
Rosenthal, Rob. *Homeless in Paradise: A Map of the Terrain.* Philadelphia: Temple University Press, 1994.
Rubenstein, Carin. "Regional States of Mind." *Psychology Today* 16, no. 2 (February 1982): 22-30.
Schafer, R. Murray. *The Tuning of the World.* New York: Knopf, 1977.
Schlesinger, Arthur M., Jr. *The Disuniting of America: Reflections on a Multicultural Society.* Knoxville: Whittle Direct Books, 1991.
Seller, Maxine. *To Seek America: A History of Ethnic Life in the United States.* Englewood, NJ: J. S. Ozer, 1977.
Skocpol, Theda. "Social History and Historical Sociology: Contrasts and Complementarities." *Social Science History* 11 (1987): 17-30.
Smith, Henry Nash. *Virgin Land: The American West as Symbol and Myth.* Cambridge: Harvard University Press, 1950.
Sollors, Werner. *Beyond Ethnicity: Consent and Descent in American Culture.* New York: Oxford University Press, 1986.
Sowell, Thomas. *Race and Culture: A World View.* New York: Basic Books, 1994.
Steinberg, Stephen. *The Ethnic Myth: Race, Ethnicity, and Class in America.* New York: Atheneum, 1981.
Stewart, George. *Names on the Land.* New York: Random House, 1945.
Susman, Warren. *Culture as History: The Transformation of*

American Society in the Twentieth Century. New York: Pantheon Books, 1984.

Takaki, Ronald T. *A Different Mirror: A History of Multicultural America.* Boston: Little, Brown & Co., 1993.

Tuan, Yi-Fu. *Space and Place: The Perspective of Experience.* Minneapolis: University of Minnesota Press, 1977.

Turner, Frederick. *Beyond Geography: The Western Spirit Against the Wilderness.* New York: Viking Press, 1980.

Turner, Patricia A. *I Heard It Through the Grapevine: Rumor in African-American Culture.* Berkeley: University of California Press, 1993.

Veysey, Lawrence R. "Myth and Reality in Approaching American Regionalism." *American Quarterly* 12 (Spring 1960): 31-43.

Wade, Richard C. *The Urban Frontier: The Rise of Western Cities, 1790-1830.* Cambridge: Harvard University Press, 1959.

Weber, David J. *Myth and the History of the Hispanic Southwest.* Albuquerque: University of New Mexico Press, 1988.

White, Deborah Gray. *Ar'n't I a Woman? : Female Slaves in the Plantation South.* New York: Norton, 1985.

Wiebe, Robert H. *The Segmented Society: An Introduction to the Meaning of America.* New York: Oxford University Press, 1975.

Wilson, William Julius. *The Declining Significance of Race: Blacks and Changing American Institutions.* Chicago: University of Chicago Press, 1978.

Wright, J. Leitch, Jr. *The Only Land They Knew: The Tragic Story of the American Indians in the Old South.* New York: Free Press, 1981.

Zelinsky, Wilbur. *The Cultural Geography of the United States.* Englewood Cliffs: Prentice-Hall, 1973.

_____. "Selfward Bound? Personal Preference Patterns and the Changing Map of American Society." *Economic Geography* 50 (April 1974): 144-179.

Zerubavel, Eviatar. *Terra Cognita: The Mental Discovery of America.* New Brunswick, NJ: Rutgers University Press, 1992.

Zinn, Howard. *The Southern Mystique.* New York: Alfred A. Knopf, 1964.

_____. *A People's History of the United States.* New York: Harper and Row, 1980.

ABOUT THE AUTHOR

Edward R. Ward was born in Chicago, Illinois.

He received a B.A. in Philosophy from Marquette University (1969). He also has received an M.A. in Spanish from the Catholic University of America (1974) and an M.A. in Theology from the Washington (D.C.) Theological Union (1974).

He is a member of the Carmelite Order.

He lives in Bogota, New Jersey.